Hitler
and the
Nazi Leaders
A Unique Insight Into Evil

Hitler
and the
Nazi Leaders

A Unique Insight Into Evil

John K. Lattimer
Physician at Nuremberg

Ian Allan
PUBLISHING

First published 1999

ISBN 0 7110 2700 5

Published by Ian Allan Publishing

An imprint of Ian Allan Publishing Ltd, Terminal House,
Shepperton, Surrey TW17 8AS.

Printed in the United States of America.

Contents

ACKNOWLEDGMENTS

I owe my good fortune in having access to the Nuremberg Trials to our then Lutheran chaplain, the Reverend Henry Gerecke, of my 98th U.S. Army General Hospital in Munich. He persuaded me to come with him to the prison interrogation center at Mondorf, in Luxembourg, where the top Nazi leaders were being selected for trial. He said, "You mustn't miss this," and he was right. Having him as a sponsor and an advocate, and then finding that psychiatrist Kelley and psychologist Gilbert were both from Columbia University and that psychiatrists Goldensohn and Dunn, who came later, were all New Yorkers, was a great stroke of luck.

I am also indebted to Dr. Abraham Lieberman, of the Barrow Neurological Institute, for his comprehensive 1995 monograph, *Hitler, Parkinson's Disease and History.* He also brought to my attention the works of Drs. Haaglund and Gibbels, who had documented Hitler's Parkinson's disease. Ben Swearingen, of Lewisville, Texas, had done a vast amount of research on Göring's suicide, as recounted in his excellent book, *The Mystery of Hermann Göring's Suicide.* The many members of the legal staff from the trial have shared their views, personally, and in their many books, notably Telford Taylor and Drexel Sprecher.

In the immediate postwar years, I put the experiences of the wartime era on the back burner, while I plunged into the business of building a career in the stimulating postwar climate of medical research and development. It was only the vigor of the fiftieth anniversary celebrations, plus the new data about Hitler's Parkinson's disease, that have stimulated me to write this book at this time.

The expertise of the Department of Photography of the College of Physicians and Surgeons of Columbia University is apparent throughout this book.

I also wish to acknowledge the help of Linda Barth and Dr. Eliahu Loar in translating from the German.

As always, I am indebted to my highly capable secretary, Edna Di Paolo, for her precise and skillful preparation of this manuscript with its numerous expansions and contractions.

DEDICATION

This book is dedicated to the memory of the late Ben Swearingen, foremost among the students, researchers, and collectors of World War II memorabilia. It was he who helped me gather most of the items you will see depicted here.

My wife, Jamie, my daughter Evan and my two doctor sons, Jon and Gary have advised me and have tolerated all the hardships associated with this effort to contribute to the history of the war in Europe.

Chronology of World War II

1920   Hitler becomes Chairman of the Nazi Party.

1923   A Putsch against the Bavarian government is attempted in Munich and fails. Hitler is arrested and spends about a year in Landsberg Prison writing *Mein Kampf,* along with Hess. Göring is wounded and recovers in Italy.

1933   Hitler is appointed Chancellor of the German Reich.
Japan and Germany quit the League of Nations.

1934   Non-aggression Pact signed between Poland and Germany. Von Hindenberg dies and Hitler declares himself Führer of Germany.

1935   The Luftwaffe is established illegally.
Military conscription is established illegally, violating the Versailles Treaty. Britain agrees to permit the German fleet to be built up to be 35 per cent of the power of the British fleet.

1936   Hitler occupies the Rhineland.
Spanish Civil War starts and is used as a testing ground for German military training and aircraft.

1937   Hitler declares the Versailles Treaty void.
Hitler declares that he will dominate Europe by force.
Italy withdraws from the League of Nations.

1938   Hitler misleads Chamberlain at Munich.

1939   Russian-German Non-aggression Pact is signed.
September 1, Germany invades Poland.
England and France declare war on Germany.

1940   April 9, Germany invades and occupies Denmark and Norway.
May 10, Germany invades Holland and Belgium and attacks France.
May 28, Dunkirk falls but the British Army is permitted to escape.
June 14, Paris falls.
September 27, Germany, Italy and Japan join a Tripartite Pact.
Hitler isolates himself about this time, foregoing the massive public demonstrations and appearances which had brought him to power.

1941   Lend-lease agreements between the United States and Britain begin, but the U.S. does not supply the British free of charge.
Germany invades Greece and Yugoslavia.
Hess flies to Scotland to try to persuade the British to negotiate peace with Hitler.
June 22, Germany invades Russia.
December 7, Japan attacks the United States at Pearl Harbor.
December 11, Germany declares war on the United States, unnecessarily. Italy declares war on the United States.

1942   Montgomery stops Rommel at El Alamein.

November 8, the United States lands troops in North Africa.

November 27, Toulon falls and the French fleet is scuttled.

1943   The large German Army in Stalingrad is defeated by the Russians.

Rommel's last units surrender in Africa.

Mussolini is overthrown.

September 9, United States troops land in Italy.

Italy declares war on Germany.

1944   June 4, Rome falls to the United States Army.

June 6, Normandy is invaded by the Allies.

July 20, a bomb attempt to kill Hitler fails but leads to the murder of a large number of German generals who are alleged to have been involved in the plot to kill Hitler.

August 15, southern France is invaded by the Americans.

August 25, Paris is liberated from the Germans.

December 16, Hitler attacks the Allies through the Ardennes Forest, in a surprise assault, taking 80,000 prisoners the first day.

December 28, the German attack is halted and reduction of the bulge in the Allied line is started (known as the Battle of the Bulge).

1945   March 7, the U.S. First Army crosses the Rhine at Remagen when the bridge fails to fall.

April 12, President Franklin Roosevelt dies.

April 21, Berlin is attacked by the Russians.

April 28, Mussolini is shot by Italian partisans.

April 30, Hitler, Eva Braun and the Goebbels family all commit suicide in the Bunker in Berlin.

May 8 and 9, German forces are surrendered by Dönitz and Keitel.

August 6, the first atom bomb is dropped on Hiroshima.

August 8, the Soviet Union declares war on Japan.

August 14, Japan surrenders to the Allies, with a formal ceremony on September 2 on the Battleship Missouri.

November 20, the main Nuremberg trial opens.

CHAPTER 1

The Deadly Road To Nuremberg

Fig 1—John K. Lattimer, MD., SC.D.
Dr. Lattimer, a surgical specialist, now became a hospital train commander whenever his army hospital moved. He was one of the few medical officers who had been a commander of troops.
Evan Lattimer Collection.

After the bombing of Pearl Harbor and the subsequent declarations of war, I was among thousands of young American doctors who volunteered to support the American Army in our massive war against Germany, Italy and Japan. Everyone, specialists and academicians alike, were included (figs. 1 & 2). Starting in 1942, a network of U.S. Army general, evacuation, and field hospitals was gradually built up in Great Britain to care for the enormous numbers of casualties that were going to result from the forthcoming assault on the heavily fortified German positions along the French coast (figs. 3 & 4). Hospital trains and ambulance convoy routes were organized to ferry the wounded from the British coastal (invasion) ports to these hospitals. When the D-day assault actually occurred on June 6, 1944, this system worked well. The landing craft that had taken the troops across brought back thousands of battered bodies (figs. 5 & 12). Each general hospital had highly qualified specialists in every field, and hospital "centers" for the most frequent problems, such as orthopedics and rehabilitation medicine, were augmented as their increasing needs became obvious. An airlift back to the United States took care of the long-term cases and many hospital units were ready to move to France.

The slaughter we endured on Omaha Beach, and to a lesser extent on Utah Beach, was no surprise. We knew we had to endure it. We poured in so many men that the Germans practically ran out of ammunition mowing them down, as it appeared to me.

Some of the combat engineers we sent over first—to sweep up the mines and the barbed wire obstacles—had their feet cut off by shell fragments which came under their tanks. I had three men in adjacent cots, all with no

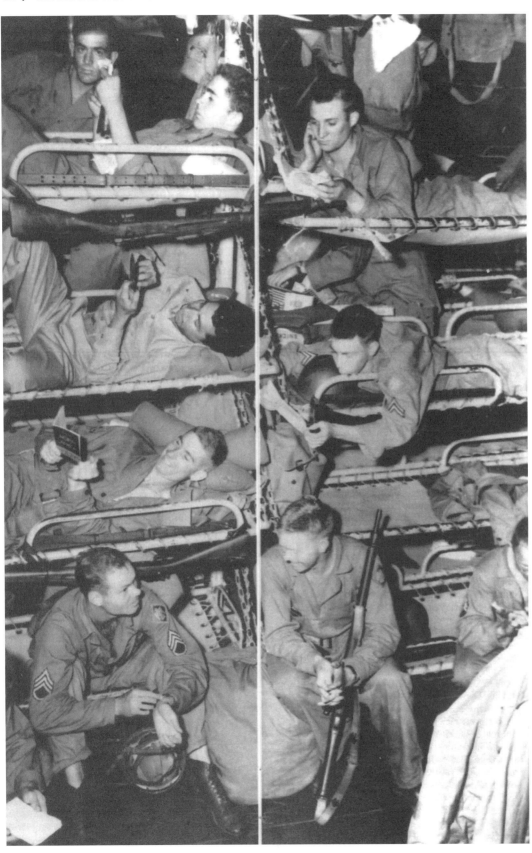

Fig 2—Millions of young Americans were packed into troopships *Our bunks were so close together you had to be careful in turning over, lest you hit the springs of the bunk above you. If we had been torpedoed, we could not possibly have gotten out alive.*

Fig 3—U.S. Army nurses training for the Normandy battlefields. *In villages like Llandudno along the Welsh coast, we prepared for the coming ordeal.* Evan Lattimer Collection.

Fig 4—The author's drill team of nurses could match the Rockettes. *Churchill and Eisenhower came to watch them as we trained for the Normandy Invasion, in Welsh villages like Llandudno, shown here.* Evan Lattimer Collection.

Fig 5—Offloading into landing craft—Normandy, June 6, 1944

Fig 6—Hitler began randomly killing English civilians with V1 flying bombs and later rockets.
The destruction of residential apartment areas like this one in London in 1944 by each German flying bomb or rocket. The rockets came over once every hour, so you could sleep in between them.

Fig 7—Hitler killed innocent Belgian civilians with his V2 rockets after a hail of flying bombs.
Christmas shoppers in Antwerp in 1944 were killed by the hundreds.

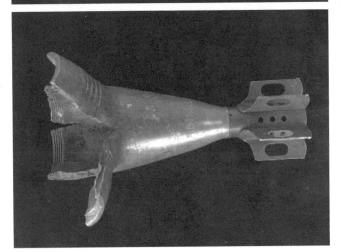

Fig 11—Five-story apartment houses became just piles of bricks
Wreaths and notices in memory of families buried there, were everywhere. The author reads this one in Kassel, Germany. Evan Lattimer Collection.

Fig 8—A huge "Teller-Mine" Bomb (Top)
These were 4 inches thick, in the sand and up on posts, all over Omaha Beach. Evan Lattimer Collection.

Fig 9—A German Hand Grenade (Middle)
These were shaped like old-fashioned "potato-mashers" and were piled everywhere, in case we got close. Their fragments were deadly. They were stacked in piles. Evan Lattimer Collection.

Fig 10—A Mortar Bomb (Bottom)
These created hundreds of shards of steel when they exploded, injuring everyone within a large radius. The Germans had every spot "zeroed-in" for mortar shells, like this one. They caused our most frequent wounds. Evan Lattimer Collection.

Fig 12—Our wounded being returned on landing craft
They were distributed by ambulances and hospital trains to hospitals all over England. A few were put on hospital ships.

Fig 13—The effects of our assault
Every major German city was reduced to rubble as you see in this picture of Frankfurt. The streets were just paths among the piles of smashed apartments and other buildings. There was no power for street lights at night and every rain made a quagmire of these streets and many shell holes. Germans were living in occasional rooms which were intact inside the wreckage. Evan Lattimer Collection.

Fig 14—I lived briefly in the other end of this bombed house in Kassel, Germany

If you opened the door on the second floor corridor, you fell off into the wreckage. Evan Lattimer Collection.

Fig 15—The cost to us was high

Germany was littered with the wreckage of our American bombers like this one. Each one was a monument to the ten young Americans who undoubtedly died with it. Evan Lattimer Collection.

(above right) Fig 16—Paris is surrendered by the German Commander

General von Choltitz orders the commanders of his Paris strong points to stop all resistance immediately. This was one of the strips of paper (top) delivered to each German strong point (Stützpunkt) by a team made up of 1 German, 1 American and 1 French officer. A typist typed the same message several times, and cut the sheet into strips like this, after von Choltitz had signed each one. I kept this one. It reads as follows: "Befehl - der Widerstand in dem Stützpunktbereich und Stützpunkten ist sofort einzustellen" ("Order - Resistance in the strong point areas and at the strong points is to cease immediately.")

                                Von Choltitz, General of Infantry

The medal (bottom) given to Dr. Lattimer by French Army Veterans, to commemorate the 50th anniversary of the Liberation of Paris, in 1944. Evan Lattimer Collection.

feet. They were the only ones who had survived from a whole company of engineers.

But then we began to see that we were fighting a madman. When I saw the piles of bodies that had been innocent Christmas shoppers in the town squares in England and Belgium, killed by V bombs that had no military purpose, I was sickened (figs. 6 & 7).

We also saw the effects of Hitler's direct orders to his soldiers who butchered helpless prisoners like those at Malmedy and adjacent towns (fig. 17), during the Germans' desperate "last gasp" attack—the Battle of the Bulge. That month-long debacle (December 1944-January 1945) occurred when a massive German force, made up of all the remaining men the German Army could gather, killed thousands of young Americans and took some 80,000 prisoners. This gave us a terrible taste of what devastation an intact German Army would have caused us. When the German offensive in this area finally failed, the German Army had very little strength left and collapsed under the pressure of the Allied and Russian offensives on both fronts. Fortunately, our massive bomb raids, now unopposed by the decimated German Air Force, weakened the capability of the German soldiers by wrecking their ammunition factories, their gasoline manufacturing capabilities, and their transportation system.

At that time I was one of the Army's qualified surgical specialists in urology. I also had broad general surgical experience and was made the chief of all surgery in various hospital units during emergency conditions. I was also one of the few medical officers who had been a commander of troops in our training battalions and had experience with ballistics, so I was kept busy. I was attached to the U.S. Third Army for a period and then finally to the U.S. Seventh Army, during the assault on Germany itself.

As the army advanced into Germany, we encountered some of the shriveled, starving escapees from the death camps. At first you just didn't believe it. Their limbs were so wasted that it felt like the feathers of a sparrow touching your arm; they had no weight. We still could not believe that this was deliberate starvation until one day one of our lead units overtook a stalled freight train that had been *en route* to Dachau. Every freight car was full of emaciated dead bodies clothed in the pitifully thin blue-and-white striped "pajamas" issued to the prisoners (figs. 18, 19, & 20). Each freight car had a bucket for excreta, but no other facilities whatsoever. The odor of feces and dead bodies was overpowering. When it came to the camps themselves, the dead littered the area. The corpses and the living prisoners looked alike, except that the living were still moving. Each day the dead from each building were pushed out into the road and later carried toward the crematorium (fig. 25). More bodies came from the shower rooms (Brausebad) where cyanide gas from Zyklon was used to kill the prisoners (figs. 22 & 23). Outside the crematorium buildings the bodies were piled like cordwood. Inside each crematorium there was a large room with whitewashed walls just before the furnace room piled with bodies (fig. 21). On the walls of this room there were bloody finger marks where some of the still-living victims had clawed their fingers into bloody stumps. The furnaces had obviously been unable to keep up with the death rate and the bodies were piled deep (fig. 24). In their sector, the British found it necessary to bulldoze the mass of bodies into large pits in a most startling and horrifying fashion (figs. 26 & 27). People from many of the towns adjacent to the death camps were recruited to help gather the bodies. All of the civilians professed complete ignorance of what had been going on in the camps in their neighborhood, even though the odor of burning flesh from the crematoriums was overpowering.

Meanwhile, as long columns of German troops hurried west to escape the approaching Russians, huge piles of rifles, pistols, machine guns, and artillery pieces began to accumulate at designated locations. In addition, worry over the rumor of "Fortress Europa," where the Germans might make a last-ditch stand in the area around Berchtesgaden, slowed our advance; but as resistance crumbled, a race was on to see who

Fig 17—The murders at Malmedy as Hitler's SS men began killing prisoners

The bodies of unarmed American prisoners are being dug out of the snow and identified. This was only one of several mass shootings of prisoners by the Germans during the "Battle of the Bulge." Here orders were communicated directly to the SS troopers from Hitler rather than coming from their officers, as was revealed at the inquest at my hospital. This changed the tenor of the war.

would have the honor of capturing Hitler's Berchtesgaden retreat. The bridges over the last river (the Salzalk) had all been dynamited except for one. This fell into the hands of the 3rd U.S. Infantry Division under General "Pappy" O'Daniel. He sent his tanks across and told them to turn down toward Berchtesgaden, and declared that he would not let anybody else across until he heard on the radio that his men had captured Hitler's house. The tanks were on their way when General Le Clerc arrived with elements of his 2nd French Armored Division, intent on getting to Berchtesgaden first. The sentry at the bridge called the general and reported Le Clerc's presence. He said that Le Clerc threatened to shoot his way across if necessary. General O'Daniel neatly solved this problem by telling the sentry to let General Le Clerc across, but none of his men. Thus while the elements of the 501st Parachute Infantry Regiment from the 101st Airborne Division had been designated as those to have the honor of capturing Berchtesgaden, the 3rd Division tanks got there a few hours beforehand, and some elements of the French Armored Division also converged on the house in a mad race. However it was the 101st Airborne troopers who pulled down the German flag and ran up the Stars and Stripes, even though the French troops and the 3rd Division had gotten there earlier (fig. 30).

Meanwhile, the garrison of SS troopers had pulled out of the Berchtesgaden Berghof (Hitler's home) and set it afire. They had, however, given the servants and the populace of Berchtesgaden a number of hours to loot the house and carry off any of the tons of food and treasures locked away in the massive hoards in the basement and air-raid tunnels. (Only the secure rooms called the "archives," a reinforced room in the attic, and two in the basement, were not looted.) As a consequence, the town of Berchtesgaden has become a treasure trove of memorabilia in the hands of the natives.

After the surrender, I was ordered back to Munich to help reorganize the large German civilian hospital in the northern neighborhood of Schwabing. It was rebuilt into an army hospital, designated as the 98th U.S. Army General Hospital (fig. 31). The construction of covered walkways between various hospital buildings was immediately commenced. We were amazed that the Germans had been wheeling their patients on gurneys from one building to another, out in the rain, without any hesitation.

At this time one of my old units, the 101st Airborne Division, was capturing some of the most wanted Nazi leaders such as Robert Ley and Julius Streicher, who had been hiding out in this part of Bavaria. They were among those prisoners who, it was thought, might be tried at a Nuremberg criminal trial, and in preparation for this, were transported to Luxembourg and interrogated at a large spa-hotel called Mondorf-Les-Bains. It was referred to by our army as "Ashcan." A similar collecting and interrogation facility in the British zone was referred to as "Dustbin."

Chaplain Henry Gerecke (fig. 32), our Lutheran chaplain at the hospital, had been asked to serve as the Protestant chaplain for the prisoners at Ashcan. They were very appreciative of his services and when his time to go home arrived, the prisoners petitioned him, and the staff, and also his wife (by mail) to let him stay for the duration of the trial. Chaplain Gerecke was in a quandary over this, but finally decided that he would indeed stay as the Protestant chaplain until the end of the trial. He eventually walked the prisoners to the gallows.

He encouraged us to come and visit him, introduced us to the various prisoners, and pointed out what an important event this trial would be. He urged each of us to come often and to volunteer as part of the medical staff. After the prisoners were moved to Nuremberg, it was easier to drive up the Autobahn to Nuremberg and not only observe the trial, but also help Dr. Ludwig Pflücker, the POW doctor (and a urologist), with the urological care of some of the patients, such as Funk and Dönitz. Some of the senior jurists and generals also had urological problems and appreciated advice and treatment.

I was delighted to discover that a number of the doctors who were assigned to the prison had come from New York. Indeed the two most prolific interviewers of the prisoners had trained at Columbia University when I was there. Dr. Douglas Kelley, a very likable psychiatrist, had initially been sent to Ashcan by General Eisenhower's headquarters to evaluate Göring and later took over the psychiatric care of all of the prisoners. He was very hospitable to me and readily shared his impressions and findings. Dr. Kelley was so highly thought-of that having him as a "friend at court" made visiting very easy and very satisfactory. Dr. Gustav Gilbert, a psychologist who also had trained at Columbia, came to the prison just after the indictments had been delivered. He replaced the intelligence officer who had been acting as Colonel Andrus's interpreter and also as his inside man with the prisoners. This was Lieutenant Dolibois. When he had first arrived, Göring made a guess that Dolibois was a "welfare" officer assigned to the prison to be sure that the fine points of the Geneva Convention were observed. The administration continued this masquerade, permitting this officer (whom they now called Lt. Gillen) to gain the confidence of the prisoners by pretending to be interested

Fig 18—We overran a train full of bodies
These had been bound for concentration camps but never made it.

Fig 19—The trains were long

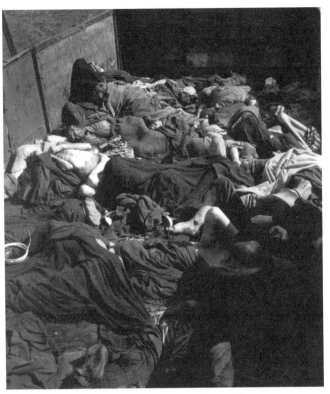

Fig 22—The label from a can of Xyklon (Cyanide) powder
This was the powder which released potassium cyanide gas and was used to kill most of the concentration camp inmates in so-called "shower" bathrooms (Brausebad). This is the kind of gas Albert Speer claims he tried to obtain to dump into the air intake of Hitler's "Führer-bunker" in Berlin, but was foiled by Hitler's precautions against a gas attack by the Russians.

Fig 20—The only facility was the pail on the lower left.
It was full of feces, but the floor was also covered.

Fig 21—Bodies awaiting cremation at Dachau
The bloody finger marks on the white cement walls (upper left), showed that they were not yet all dead, when they arrived for burning.

Fig 23—Brausebad (Shower Bath) rooms *These were packed with naked victims and sealed. Then live steam or cyanide gas (as Zyklon-B) was introduced, killing all the occupants in a few minutes.* Evan Lattimer Collection.

Fig 24—Bodies for cremation after Zyklon-B at Dachau, when we captured it *These were in the ready room just before the gas furnaces.*

Fig 25—The dead from one night

Fig 26—Huge pits had to be bulldozed for the bodies

Fig 27—Sometimes the bodies were bulldozed into these pits
This was done in the British zone. It was sickening to watch.

Fig 28—The gas-fired crematorium furnaces
There was a row of these furnaces, each with a long tray which would slide out and permit bodies to be piled on it. Then it was slid back inside and the gas turned on. The bodies were consumed surprisingly quickly. The odor of burning flesh permeated the camp and the vicinity as well.

Fig 29—Waifs of the War
Our army treated children well. As Norman Rockwell said: "Simple human decency made an impression on everyone." Evan Lattimer Collection.

Fig 30—Finally we came to Hitler's house
The Berghof, in Berchtesgaden, had been looted by the local populace, at the invitation of the Commander of the Garrison, as he withdrew. Then it was set afire. Here the men of my own Seventh Army are pulling down the Nazi flag to run up the Stars and Stripes.

in their rights. He was actually from Luxembourg and spoke German, just as did Dr. Gilbert who had learned it in school in New York. While "Lt. Gillen" continued to visit the prisoners occasionally, under the guise of being an historian assigned to compile a history of the war, Gilbert took over as the interpreter and as Colonel Andrus's observer. Part of Gilbert's job was to assess the mood of the prisoners to make sure that they were not so depressed that they would try suicide. He was

very skillful at this and a great source of information about what the prisoners had to say on this score.

When the judges decided which of the top Nazis they would try in the first, most important, showcase trial, the prisoners were transferred by airplane or ambulance to the prison at the Palace of Justice in Nuremberg on August 12, 1945. Each man was now placed in solitary confinement in a barren, depressing cell. This was the first rude shock for the prisoners. Then on October

Fig 31—The large German civilian hospital at Schwabing (A Northern neighborhood of Munich)

This was now converted into the 98th U.S. Army General Hospital. Our Chaplain (Gerecke) and several doctors were asked to help with the care of the Nazi leaders in the prison at Nuremberg, straight north, up the Autobahn.

Fig 32—Prison chaplain Henry Gerecke

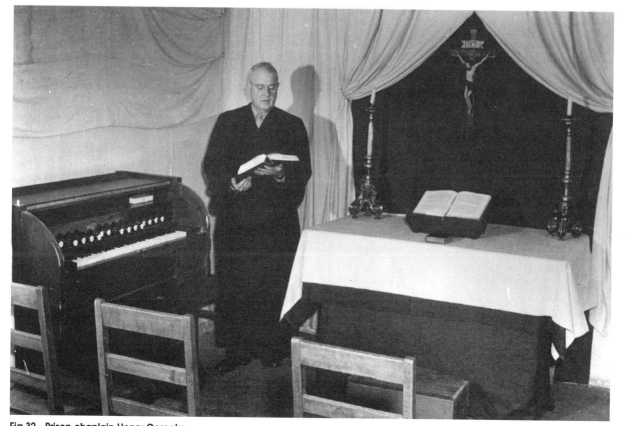

He was from Dr. Lattimer's 98th U.S. Army General Hospital and ministered to the Protestant prisoners in Nuremberg. They begged him to stay on with them. He walked them to the gallows. Raymond D'Addario Collection.

20, 1945, the four indictments were read to the prisoners. Each was accused of conspiring to wage war, planning and executing a war of aggression, committing war crimes, and of crimes against humanity.

It occurred to me that the Roman General Tacitus had been correct when he said, "You don't know what war is really like until you have fought the Germans."

For the first time, it became obvious to all of them that they faced a possible death penalty—diplomats, bankers, administrators, as well as the military men. German lawyers were found to represent them, but the indictments were a second rude shock.

The trial officially opened on November 20, 1945, with a long, well prepared speech by Mr. Justice Robert Jackson, on leave from the U.S. Supreme Court. Dr. Gilbert recorded each prisoner's reactions in great detail. He not only interviewed each man, using the techniques he had developed as an intelligence officer and a professional psychologist, but he asked each man to write down his thoughts about each event. The book he produced, *Nuremberg Diary*, is a valuable, well documented account of his findings throughout the trial.

Let us look first at the three top Nazis, and the medical problems which racked each of them. Then let us look at the other defendants and at the fragile security arrangements at the prison and at the trial.

CHAPTER 2

Hitler's Preoccupation with an Early Death

Fig 1—Hitler's silver-framed portrait
Hitler gave his picture to favored people in these monogrammed silver frames. This one he gave to Inga Arvad, a Danish beauty queen reporter, who he had sit in his box at the Berlin Olympic Games. Hitler's inscription read's "To Inga Arvad with friendly regards, Adolf Hitler." When she came to Washington, young Jack Kennedy became so intent on marrying her that his father had him assigned to the South Pacific to break up the romance. It nearly ruined JFK politically. Ben Swearingen Estate.

Listening to the testimony at the Nuremberg war crimes trial, it became obvious that Hitler, after devastating Europe in 1939 and 1940, was on his way to an infinitely larger devastation of England and the Middle East when he suddenly came to a halt. He had won his war, as it appeared to me, driving the British Army into the sea at Dunkirk. All he had to do was invade and occupy England. Furthermore, he could then have given Rommel the troops he needed to drive the British out of Africa and take over the Middle Eastern oil fields, with disastrous results for the Allies. Instead, he threw victory away and decided to attack Russia right then, in a desperate and foolish effort to secure world domination in one fell swoop. He knew the perils of a two-front war very well. I was curious as to why he changed course so abruptly. I could get no coherent explanation from the prisoners. It sounded to me as if he had suffered some sort of severe mental blow which had completely changed his agenda.

The first clue to his fatal behavior came during my long talks with the extremely perceptive Albert Speer, Hitler's personal architect. He told me that Hitler repeatedly expressed a worry that he might not live to achieve his goal of world domination. (I had no hint as to the reason for his fear of an early death, although I knew he took great precautions against assassination. I was much more impressed by the success of his military machine in steam-rolling the opposition.) Speer related that Hitler would philosophize about the fact that if he dominated the world, he would be known as the greatest military leader of all time, whereas if he lost, he would be condemned, vilified, and denigrated.

At that time we had no knowledge that Hitler had deteriorated seriously, since this was kept not only from us but also from the German people.

Only now, more than fifty years later, has it become clear to me what had happened to Hitler to bring him up short. We now have clear evidence of his severe Parkinson's disease and the likelihood that it was not just ordinary old-age Parkinson's disease, but rather a faster moving post-encephalitic Parkinson's disease. His efforts to keep his tremor concealed from the public had been eminently successful until the very last days of the war when a newsreel crew photographed him and showed his "pill-rolling" tremor for the first time. In retrospect, it became obvious that Hitler had been suffering from Parkinson's disease for several years. Back then there was no treatment for Parkinson's and it is my feeling that someone told him in 1940 that he had an incurable disease and that his time was very limited. He then decided that he would have to move up his timetable for world domination by attacking Russia sooner, rather than later, which he did, with disastrous consequences. In these pages, I will show the gradual evolution of his illness upon which these conclusions are based.

The revelation that his days were numbered must have come just about the time of the British evacuation at Dunkirk. It was clearly a devastating mental blow. He decided to forget England and to gamble at overrunning Russia before he had secured the Middle Eastern oil fields. Despite the numerous perils, Hitler took the chance—and lost. Only recently have we seen the clear-cut evidence for Hitler's disease, but let me tell you about the details as I saw them.

Hitler's Disastrous Confrontation with His Incurable Disease

As the incredible details about Hitler's rise to power unfolded at the Nuremberg trials, it slowly became obvious to me that Hitler had not only turned Germany into a superpower, he had also won his war. By 1940 he controlled most of Europe, the notable exception being the Soviet Union. His army was superb, while the British had lost their armor and their artillery, and their aircraft factories had been damaged. They later acknowledged that they had been at his mercy. His rear was cleverly protected by the nonagression treaty with Stalin. He could have given Rommel the troops he needed to seize the Middle Eastern oil fields. Spain and Italy were on his side, as was Japan.

His Progressive Downfall

Inexplicably (at the time), Hitler made a number of disastrous decisions. First he stopped his army from capturing the helpless British Expeditionary Force at

Fig 2—The Zepplin Stadium in Nuremberg, filled with Hitler's fanatical soldiers

Hitler (center-foreground) has marched in silence, except for the beating of a drum, from one end to the other, has saluted the Nazi memorial and will march slowly back to the podium, to begin his address to the multitude. This was most impressive.

Fig 3—Hitler suppressed the tremor of his left hand.

Even in 1932 (upper left) he was gripping one hand with the other, to suppress his tremor. If he tightened the muscles to his left hand, it checked the shaking. He therefore carried in it a rolled-up magazine, or pair of gloves, or the dog's leash, or kept his trembling left hand in his pocket. In groups he stood out because he would be the only person with his hands together. Often he would grip his belt buckle with his left hand.

Dunkirk. Then he failed in the invasion of England where American bomber bases and troop-staging areas would later be his undoing. He stopped Göring's destruction of the RAF, focusing instead on devastating London in retribution. Later he personally crippled the German world-beating jet fighter program that could have decimated our bomber formations. Then to cap it all, he made the fatal mistake of invading Russia in June 1941, plunging Germany into a two-front war—a move which he himself had condemned in *Mein Kampf.* What had happened to him?

By this time he had developed a tremor in his left hand which he went to great pains to conceal. He stopped using his left hand to gesture during his histrionic speeches as far back as 1934, when he was 45 years old. Then he began to hold one hand with the other, or use his left hand to grip the buckle of his Sam Browne

belt to keep his hand from trembling (fig. 3). In every group photograph after 1940, this is highly noticeable. He also began carrying something in his left hand much of the time, since the trembling stopped when he made the muscular effort to grip something such as a pair of gloves or a rolled-up paper. By 1940, he discontinued the powerful public appearances that had been so important for his image up to that time. The party rallies, like those of 1938, had been impressive moves on his part (fig. 2), but he gave them up rather than expose his now obvious, pill-rolling tremor to the world, lest it be seen as a manifestation of senility.

Hitler's giving up of his previously highly successful public-speaking techniques was so striking as to suggest that he had suffered a medical or mental disaster of some type.

Now, after more than fifty years, a persuasive explanation for Hitler's disastrous mental reversals has become apparent. Neurological experts such as Abraham Lieberman and others (see reference list) have postulated and demonstrated that Hitler was definitely suffering from then-untreatable, progressive, post-encephalitis Parkinson's disease. I believe some doctor, perhaps Dr. Brandt, told Hitler that he only had 4 or 5 more years to live just before Dunkirk.

Surprisingly enough, even after he had initiated the assault on Russia, he might still have beaten them had he not let his Nazi machine "give in" to the coldly homicidal, psychopathic fury that was part of his and their methodology. The oppressed populations of much of Russia had welcomed the Nazi soldiers as liberators from the yoke of Communism, which they hated. This was especially true in the Ukraine where many enlisted in Hitler's military battalions to help overwhelm the Communists. Instead of accepting this collaboration, Hitler and his minions brutalized and slaughtered many sympathetic Russians and Ukrainians in retaliation for any deaths of German soldiers by partisans or anyone else.

This was not his only bad policy move. Hitler's other mistake, according to Albert Speer, was in not permitting him (Speer) to use German women in his war-production factories earlier in the war. This might have released enough skilled German men, in that day of the mechanized military machine, to provide enough divisions to defeat the Russians. Yet Hitler steadfastly refused to do this; it was part of his obsession that every German woman regarded him as her "husband," and he refused to put them at hard labor in his factories.

Dr. Abraham Lieberman, Medical Director of the National Parkinson Foundation, whose masterful article "Hitler, Parkinson's Disease and History" presents an excellent account by an outstanding neurologist, has permitted me to quote him extensively. Dr. Lieberman has pointed out that Hitler was well aware that the trembling of his left hand would be regarded by his public as a manifestation of advancing age and infirmity, and, took great pains to conceal it. Newsreel photographers were restricted to views where they would not show his shaking left hand. Even home movies taken by Eva Braun never showed his hands. In early 1945, however, when censorship was relaxing, a newsreel team finally released some motion pictures of Hitler greeting young soldiers in the garden of the ruined Chancellery, which showed the gross tremor of his left hand.

At the end of World War I, Hitler had had an episode of blindness and was hospitalized. Later he had a second episode of blindness while still in the hospital. Records of his illness have all been destroyed and we have only Hitler's word that a chlorine gassing by the British caused the blindness. This might well have caused the first episode, but hardly the second.

It was at that time that viral diseases were sweeping the world. Influenza was the most common of these epidemics, but polio and encephalitis also became widespread. But let me quote Dr. Lieberman directly.

A Time of Onset of Hitler's Parkinson's Disease

Dr. Lieberman quotes two acquaintances of Hitler, J. Recktenwald and W. Masur, who describe episodes of tremor in 1923, when Hitler was 34 years old and still in prison following the abortive Beer Hall Putsch. Hitler again had an episode that began in November 1923 with a left-side tremor that lasted until December 24, before his release from prison. After reviewing some 300 hours of video tapes of Hitler, Dr. Lieberman recognized that Hitler began to use his left arm less and less as the day wore on, especially during the filming of Leni Riefenstahl's epic motion picture, *Triumph of the Will*. This did not become apparent until the afternoon of the filming, when the benefit from the previous night's sleep had worn off. It became much more obvious by that evening when Hitler had stopped using his left arm completely. As noted above, this was in 1934 when Hitler was 45 years old.

After 1940 it became obvious that Hitler always held one hand with the other or gripped something in his left hand, which would have stopped the tremor (fig. 3). While the tremor in his left arm became very notice-

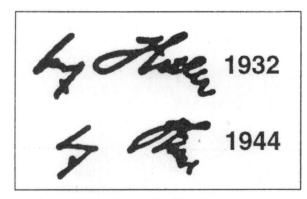

Fig 4—Micrographia in advanced Parkinson's.
Hitler's tiny lower signature, from 1944, compared to his upper signature from 1938. This characteristic development of micrographia is evident in Hitler's signature on his wedding certificate, signed shortly before his suicide. It is also evident on other documents signed in 1945. It shows that the involvement now affected both his arms, as Dr. Lieberman points out here. Abraham Lieberman Collection.

able in the autumn if 1942, it had undoubtedly been noted by *him* much earlier, when he began to take obvious measures to suppress it.

When the tremor was only in his left arm, it would have been Stage 1 on the rating scale proposed by Drs. Hoehn and Yahr. Subsequent to this, weakness was noted in Hitler's left leg, then tremor of his head and "micrographia" in his right-handed writing, which would have made his condition Stage 2. Next, he began to drag his left leg, which would have placed him in Stage 3, with a slight gait difficulty. The upper part of his body now tended to incline forward. In 1945, he showed definite micrographia in writing (fig. 4). When standing up, he was forced to cling for support to his conversation partner, which put him into Stage 4, implying bilateral involvement with postural instability. In 1945, it became necessary to position benches on which he could rest every few feet in the bunker corridors.

Autonomic Dysfunctions

In addition, Hitler developed the autonomic dysfunctions characteristic of Parkinson's: constipation, excessive sweating, flatulence, and abdominal distension. He also developed a change in his sleep pattern, going to bed *very* late and then sleeping extremely soundly for a short period. The very early onset of these symptoms is much more suggestive of post-encephalitis Parkinson's disease than it is of the idiopathic or "old age" type, which is more likely due to arteriosclerosis, according to Dr. Lieberman.

Hitler held very strongly to the opinion that as the leader of Nazi Germany he must *never* show *any* signs of infirmity. He even forbade photographers from taking his picture while he wore his reading glasses. He would wear gold-rimmed glasses during the briefing sessions each day, but when the photographers appeared to record the sessions, the glasses would be put away. He occasionally used an enormous round "reading glass" to inspect maps and other exhibits at the twice-daily military conferences, but he even tried to discourage photographers from showing the reading glass.

He also began to have other signs suggestive of Parkinsonianism, including painful eye spasms. These are known as oculogyric crises. According to Dr. Lieberman, they are more common during or following post-encephalitis Parkinsonianism than with old-age Parkinson's disease. Dr. Lieberman wrote that in September 1938, during the Munich conference, Prime Minister Edouard Daladier of France observed in Hitler a possible oculogenic spasm. He said, "Hitler's dull, blue eyes developed a hard strained look and suddenly turned upwards." Von Schirach, the head of the Hitler Youth organization, also described an episode that sounded like an oculogenic crisis, and Dr. Stolk presented a 1939 film clip during which Hitler's face suddenly became expressionless as he struggled against a spasm of his eyes. He twitched his eyebrows and tilted his head to the right. He kept glancing in the same direction.

Rage Attacks

Dr. Lieberman also points out that rage attacks, for which Hitler was notorious, were another symptom of post-encephalitis Parkinson's disease. Many people thought they were contrived, but he was described as stamping his feet and banging his fists on the tables and walls while he foamed at the mouth, panting and stammering in uncontrolled fury. Hitler was an alarming sight with his hair disheveled, his eyes fixed, and his face distorted and purple with blotches. Then he would smooth his hair and resume a normal manner. He had at least one such episode when speaking to General Guderian in 1943. He also startled both Göring and Ribbentrop on occasion with these attacks.

Dr. Walters, an encephalitis expert, commented that a few epidemic encephalitis victims, following their illness, exhibited new capacities for leadership and even a certain charisma. We also know that Francisco Franco, Chairman Mao, Pope John Paul II, and Attorney General Janet Reno have or had Parkinson's disease. Certainly Hitler had been a failure the first 30 years of his life and was not promoted past the rank of corporal during World War I because his superiors thought he "lacked leadership qualities." In 1918, of the 80 million Germans who swore revenge against the Versailles Treaty restrictions, Hitler would have been thought among the least likely to become famous. Dr. Walters speculated that something happened to transform this obtrusive, argumentative know-it-all into a shrewd, skilled, and charismatic orator. After the war ended, Hitler became a beguiling actor who learned to sway and fascinate the masses in a manner that has puzzled and confused psychologists, political scientists, and historians. Alan Bullock, a well-known historian and Hitler biographer, described Hitler's rise to power, including his asocial behavior, as amorality and psychopathology, saying that Hitler had one supreme and fortunately rare advantage: he had neither scruples nor inhibitions. He was swept along by a genuine belief in his own inspiration to such a degree that he deliberately exploited the irrational side of human nature, both in himself and others, with a shrewd calculation. Whether his encephalitis had anything to do with this transformation is hard to say.

His own description of experiencing being gassed, described in *Mein Kampf*, is as follows:

On the night of October 13 the English gas attack burst loose. A few hours later my eyes had turned into glowing coals; it had grown dark around me. Thus I came to the hospital at Pasewalk in Pomerania.

In November 1918, I had been getting better. I was given grounds for hoping I would recover my eyesight. In any case, I was on the road to improvement when the monstrous thing happened [meaning the Armistice]. Again, everything went black before my eyes. There followed terrible days and even worse nights. I felt that all was lost. In the days that followed, I decided to go into politics.

The records of Hitler's hospitalization in 1918 have been lost. Initially, he may have been blinded by the irritation of chlorine gas, but then he recovered. His subsequent episode of blindness has never been explained. While it might have been a delayed toxic effect of the gas, or hysteria, it is also very possible that Hitler had contracted encephalitis. Six percent of patients who were hospitalized for encephalitis, according to Dr. Lieberman, reported blindness.

The Differential Diagnosis of Hitler's Parkinson's Disease

Dr. Lieberman also points out that a dementing or motor disorder can also occur in patients with vascular risk factors for arteriosclerosis or strokes. In June 1944, when Hitler was 55 years old, Speer described an episode during which Hitler fumbled for words and became confused and distracted in midsentence, in front of 100 people. This episode might possibly have been a transient ischemic episode of the brain. In February 1945, Hitler's own Dr. Giesing described a similar event. Hitler was said to have had electrocardiographic evidence of a myocardial infarction and borderline hypertension, but he was a vegetarian and did not smoke, factors that would have reduced his risk of vascular disease to some extent.

The insidious onset of Hitler's symptoms when he was only 46 years old (and possibly at age 34), however, plus their slowly progressive nature and the presence of a "resting" tremor, argue against the more common arteriosclerotic or "idiopathic" type of Parkinsonianism. Neurosyphilis would be unlikely to cause Parkinsonianism, and furthermore, Hitler had a negative Wassermann test and none of the pupillary

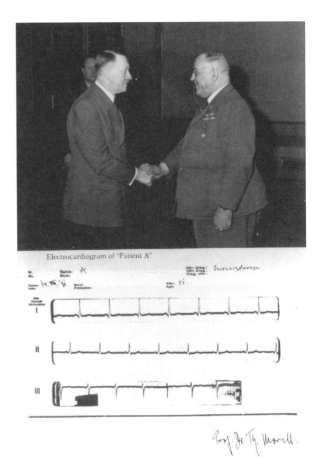

Electrocardiogram of "Patient A"

Fig 5—Dr. Morrell, Hitler's favorite doctor
Hitler shaking hands with Dr. Morrell, the quack who pleased him. Dr. Morrell injected Hitler with all manner of stimulants, sedatives and mild narcotics to meet his every imagined need. Several of these contained potentially toxic elements such as Strichnine. Hitler's other doctors tried to warn him about the perils of these remedies but Hitler would hear none of it until the Strichnine gave him hepatitis. One of Hitler's electrocardiograms (above) taken by Dr. Morrell, read as showing left coronary insufficiency.

abnormalities associated with neurosyphilis. According to the detailed roster of pills and injections kept by Dr. Morrell (fig. 5), Hitler, each day, certainly used a large number of tablets containing caffeine (which might aggravate a tremor) as well as a bromide, off and on. He also was given pentamethylenetetrazol, cardiozol, and pyridin-B-carbonic acid. And after 1942, Dr. Morrell sporadically injected him with two cardiac stimulants: diethylamide and coramine.

All of these preparations were begun in 1942, after the onset of Hitler's tremor. While it is true these drugs can *exacerbate* tremor, they could not have *induced* Hitler's unilateral resting tremor. It has also been suggested that Hitler's tremor, because it was initially intermittent, might have been just an exaggerated physiologic tremor or an hysterical tremor. However, the unilateral onset of Hitler's tremor, its association with other features of Parkinson's disease, and its progressive nature argue strongly against those two causes, according to Dr. Lieberman.

Hitler's effort to control his tremor, and to deprecate its importance, were part of his effort to maintain an invincible image. After the assassination attempt on July 20, 1944, he was astonished immediately thereafter to discover that his tremor had apparently disappeared. Alas, the tremor reappeared all too soon.

It seemed especially foolish, as I have said, for him to fail to occupy England, and fail to drive the British out of North Africa and the Middle East oil fields when his rear was well protected by his clever nonaggression treaty with Russia and by Stalin's suspicions of the Allies. Hitler had by this time (1940) developed a tripartite treaty with the Japanese and the Italians, and he might very well have persuaded the Japanese to prepare to attack Russia in the east, thus relaxing pressure on the Germans. Then when the Japanese unexpectedly attacked the United States at Pearl Harbor in 1941, Hitler foolishly declared war on the United States, removing any restrictions on American thinking about attacking and bombing Germany.

Lt. Colonel Bernhardt Frank (fig. 6), who at that time was the commander of the garrison guarding the Berghof, wrote that he was shocked to observe that Hitler had deteriorated severely during the last year of the war, and that it was apparent to him that the knowledge of Hitler's deterioration was being kept from the German public by Goebbels. Frank's description of Hitler's tremors, his shuffling gait and leaning posture, was classic for Parkinson's disease. Others, including Albert Speer, noted that Hitler's tremor now began to appear in his head and in his right hand as well, and that he would spill food down his previously immaculate uniforms without appearing to notice. Others noted that he would sometimes have to grasp the person with whom he was talking in order to maintain his balance. These progressions are the hallmarks of the stages of advancing Parkinson's disease.

An intelligence officer named Boldt, assigned to Hitler's staff, said that in February 1945 the Führer shuffled slowly toward him with his head shaking, his left arm hanging by his side, and his left hand trembling perceptibly. Still other officers wrote that both his hands shook. We also know that his handwriting became minute (another Parkinson's symptom) on documents in 1944 and even on his own wedding certificate in 1945. While Hitler, with Goebbels' assistance, strove to keep up the pretense of being a vigorous energetic leader, he was failing rapidly. Professor Maximillian de Crinis, a German neurologist, without examining Hitler but merely seeing a German newsreel in 1944, informed General Walter Schellenberg, Himmler's chief of staff, that Hitler had Parkinson's disease. Schellenberg, in turn, informed Himmler. This is what led Dr. Lieberman to speculate that Himmler then undertook to betray Hitler by starting peace negotiations through the Scandinavians, without Hitler's knowledge.

As far back as 1935, Dr. Karl Brandt, one of Hitler's personal physicians, had urged him to have a complete medical examination, but Hitler had refused, sensing he could ill afford even hints of physical incapacity. (He would never let doctors examine him with his clothes off.)

As described above, Hitler took huge amounts of tablets and injections, given to him by Dr. Morrell. He

Fig 6—S.S. Lt. Col. Bernhardt Frank
Commander of the garrison guarding the Berghof and surrounding compound. He was shocked to see Hitler's physical deterioration. He realized this was being hidden from the German public and says so in his book, "Hitler, Göring and the Obersalzberg."

would take as many as twenty Coster's "anti-gas" tablets which contained large amounts of belladonna and strichnine. He had started taking them on his own and insisted on continuing. It has been estimated by Dr. Lieberman that he took between one and a half and four milligrams of atropine a day and twenty to sixty milligrams of strichnine a day. These were considered responsible for an attack of jaundice in 1944, after which Hitler discontinued these tablets. The atropine would have suppressed his tremor and his tendency to heavy sweating, which had caused him to change his clothes several times a day. This may have explained his persistence in taking these medications over the protests of all of his other doctors, except Morrell. Hitler also welcomed the injections of amphetamines and glucose that Morrell gave him in large amounts both intramuscularly and intravenously. Mild narcotics were given freely to Hitler by Dr. Morrell: codeine and nasal cocaine were given for colds and, occasionally, morphine for his cramps.

Mental Changes

Speer often stated that while Hitler had originally let his experts assume full responsibility, he began in 1938 to avoid discussion. He became very suspicious and was very little inclined to adopt anyone else's ideas, never recovering the mental agility of his earlier years. He lamented his inability to think out large-scale concepts and began to worry that he would die before he could achieve his goals. He began to agonize over his indecisiveness and inability to deal with important problems. During some of his late night sessions, Speer thought that Hitler gave the impression of being mentally impaired.

This has been remarked upon by others. Field Marshal Gerd von Rundstedt said that "formerly the general staff would present their plans and there would be intelligent counter-questions. Previously, Hitler had loathed details; now he would even question whether pill boxes were fortified." In *Hitler: A Study in Tyranny*, Alan Bullock pointed out that several of his associates noted that after 1942, Hitler lost the flexibility and innovation that had marked his earlier military thinking. Again and again, Hitler's rigid insistence on "no retreat" became the cornerstone of German strategy, despite pleas from his military commanders and the catastrophes that followed. Furthermore, the Hestons, in *The Medical Casebook of Adolf Hitler: His Illnesses,*

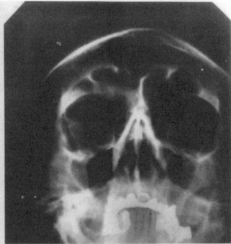
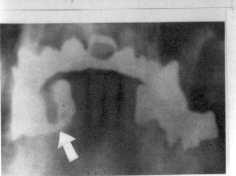

Fig 7—Hitler's head x-ray and portrait, showing his distinctive denture
This x-ray was taken during the fall of 1944 and revealed sinus inflammation in Hitler's left antrum, which was more cloudy than the right. His dental bridge work was unique. He hated dentists and most of his teeth had been replaced with huge gold bridges as seen here. Note the distinctive apperance of his left upper incisor. This was merely a gold frame with a thin porcelain facing. It was different from his other false teeth in this area. He is also seen smiling broadly, which he rarely did. Here the different color of the left medial upper incisor is obvious, due to the porcelain frame construction. Note also the gold semi-circle in his lower right denture (arrows). This was the type of evidence which allowed Russians to identify his lower denture in his corpse. Evan Lattimer Collection, L. Bezymanski, and H. P. Frentz.

Fig 8—The church of St. Mary of Victory, in Vienna
A watercolor painted by Hitler as a postcard during his early days, when he was attempting to become a commercial artist. It is fairly accurate but the perspective is exaggerated. Evan Lattimer Collection.

Fig 9—A Hitler Watercolor
This church in Vienna (the Kaiser-Kirche) is easily recognizable but the painting has the problem that the various upright structures all lean in slightly different directions. The columns across the facade lean in still a different direction. Evan Lattimer Collection.

Fig 10—A Hitler painting
A painting of St. Basil's Cathedral in Vienna depicts the structure fairly accurately but it is worrisome to see the adjacent building on the right leaning in different directions. This is the only painting I have found by Hitler in which any effort was made to draw animals and persons as more than match-stick figures. Evan Lattimer Collection.

Doctors, and Drugs, wrote that early in the war he had "strongly advocated basic research in weapons development, but he failed to grasp the importance of jet airplanes, atomic energy, heat-seeking rockets, sound-seeking torpedoes, ground-to-air missiles and radar. All of these decisive technological advances were well within the grasp of German research and development but all were aborted or delayed by Hitler's neglect or interference. Hitler was clinging to a single alternative (secret) weapons system, long-range flying bombs and rockets, and he did this long after it was clear that the rockets were too limited in payload and accuracy to play any significant role. His rigidity effectively froze German research, with disastrous effects."

All of these mental lapses appear to me to be due to his Parkinson's disease and the realization that it was not only progressing, but that there was no hope for a cure.

Hitler's Fear of Dentists

Hitler was so anxious to avoid dentists that he permitted his teeth to deteriorate badly. His left-upper, central incisor was visibly different (fig. 7). It was capped with a false tooth that, by X ray, had a distinctive frame-like metal rim with a thin central panel of porcelain. It finally became necessary to make upper dentures for him, which had to be anchored to the remnants of the remaining stumps of his central incisors on the top. He was always embarrassed about his teeth and could rarely be enticed to smile broadly, even for his official photographer, Heinrich Hoffmann. In fig. 8, the different shade of white of the left-upper, central incisor is obvious. His lower-jaw bridgework (the bone of the upper jaw was destroyed by the effects of cremation) was also distinctive enough to lead the Russians to conclude that one of the partially burned bodies exhumed in the garden of the Chancellery was indeed Hitler. They quickly tracked down the dentists and dental technicians who had made the dentures and who verified their work, satisfying even the suspicious Russians.

X-Rays of Hitler's Head

During the trial, head X-rays were introduced as exhibits and revealed the obviously sorry state of Hitler's teeth (fig. 7). They also revealed that he had suffered from sinus trouble of moderately severe degree, as of November 18, 1944 when X-rays were taken to evaluate his sinusitis. The fact that he had sinus trouble did not surprise any of us who were serving in Germany. I personally remember the war in northern Europe as two years of cold, snow, and rain.

Hitler was never one to pamper himself by going south during the winter, even though he apparently suffered from sinusitis a great deal. A vacation on the Riviera, or in southern Italy, or in Greece would have done wonders for his sinus trouble, but he was not so minded. There was always too much tension from the war to permit him to leave home for long. There is an impressive lack of photographs of him in bathing costume or relaxing anywhere, except drowsing briefly in his own dining room or in his plane or car.

Hitler as Artist

Hitler was tenaciously interested in art, and strove to be an artist and an architect. As a youth, he had applied to an art school in Vienna and had been rejected. It has often been speculated that had they accepted him and diverted him into a lifetime of artwork, the world might have been spared the savagery he unleashed upon it. In the period 1910 and 1911 he painted postcards of churches and public buildings in Vienna to sell. Several of these watercolors are preserved in various collections. He also went on to record in both watercolors and in oil paint many of the public buildings, churches, and palaces in and around Vienna (figs. 8-10). While these are reasonably accurate, there is a persistent defect throughout much of his artwork in that many of the buildings have a tendency to be slightly crooked. Even his mammoth churches tend to lean slightly to the right or left, rather than sit squarely on their foundations. The other striking thing about his paintings is that the human figures are very poorly done. It was clear that depicting people was not one of his interests or capabilities. They were usually a collection of very thin lines or, at best, matchstick figures. There are those who read a psychological failing into this inability to depict the human figure. In fact, Hitler was only a little better at depicting horses. However, flowers were no problem (figs. 11 & 12).

After Hitler came to power, and money was no longer a consideration, his grandiose architectural ideas became possibilities. Once he had discovered Albert Speer, a superb young architect who was very skillful in creating spectacular effects, his plans burgeoned. He began to sketch massive concert halls, opera houses, and public buildings for all the principal cities of his new empire (figs. 13-17). Even his hometown of Linz, Austria, was to have a massive opera house, monuments, and public buildings. Hitler claimed that great men in the past have been memorialized by the giant monuments they left behind, such as the Pyramids. Speer wrote:

Fig 11—A Hitler painting
An interior with flowers by Hitler. This is a reasonably attractive painting except that here again even the panes of glass in the door are crooked. Evan Lattimer Collection.

Fig 12— Hitler painting
A painting of a floral arrangement by Hitler. Again, attractive enough, except that the container in the right foreground is not sitting upright. Evan Lattimer Collection.

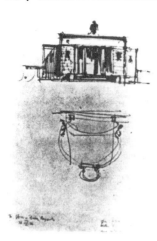

625
Theater in Bayreuth
July 1936, pencil/paper
PC: D 2; F: P
Sketch done on July 26, 1936.
No. 27 from the Speer
collection.

Fig 13—Hitler sketch
The Entrance and a plan for a theatre for Bayreuth, drawn July 26, 1936. It is number 7 in the Speer catalogue of sketches by Hitler. Evan Lattimer Collection.

(Below) Fig 14—An Architectural sketch by Hitler
This is sketch #9 made in the presence of Albert Speer at the Obersalzburg in the spring of 1939. It is a sketch for a library in Linz. The ground plan shows an open hall with plinths for sculptures along the main walls. This hall was to lead to the central room, which in turn led to two large reading rooms and numerous smaller ones. This sketch is listed as #9 in the catalogue kept by Otto Apel in Speer's office. It is listed as the "Linz Library Building, Obersalzberg" Spring 1939. Evan Lattimer Collection.

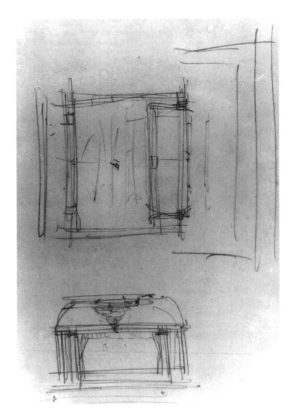

(Above) Fig 15—A Hitler architectural sketch
A sketch by Hitler for a private theatre he intended for the new building of the Führer Palace. The stage proscenium was to be 14 meters in width. In front of the stage was the orchestra pit and auditorium. The theatre was intended for Hitler's private entertainment and also for operatic performances on state visits. There were about 8 rows with comfortable seats for between 80 to 100 guests and Hitler. This sketch is listed as #63 in the catalogue of Hitler's drawings made in the presence of Albert Speer in December of 1937. The Catalogue started in 1937 and was continued until the end of the war by Otto Apel, Chief of Speer's office of architecture. Evan Lattimer Collection.

77

Fig 16—
Architectual
sketch by Hitler
*A Hitler sketch
of a tower and
arcade, drawn
in the presence
of Albert Speer
and clarified by
him.* Evan
Lattimer
Collection.

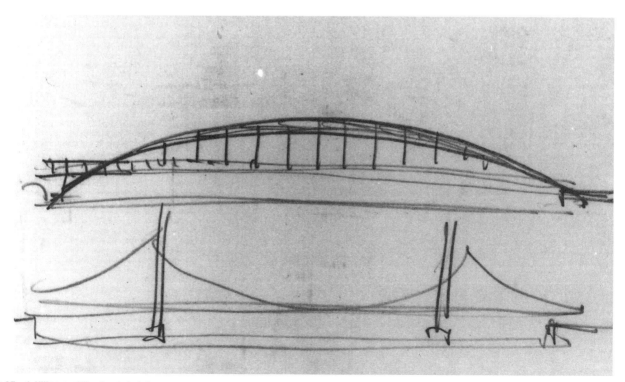

Fig 17—A Hitler architectural sketch
A quick sketch of two different types of bridges made in the presence of Albert Speer. He had certified this. Evan Lattimer Collection.

In conferring with me over plans, Hitler perpetually drew sketches of his own. They were casually tossed off, but accurate in perspective; he drew outlines, cross-sections and renderings to scale. An architect could not have done better. Some mornings he would show me a well-executed sketch he had prepared overnight, although most of his drawings were done in a few hasty strokes during our discussions.

I kept these quick sketches of Hitler's, noting their dates and subjects, and have preserved them to this day. It is interesting that of a total of 125 such drawings, a good fourth of them relate to Linz building projects, which were always closest to his heart. Equally frequent are sketches for theatres. One morning he surprised me with a neatly drawn design for a commemorative shaft for Munich, which was to be a new symbol of the city, dwarfing the towers of the Frauenkirche. He regarded this project, like the Berlin Triumphal Arch, as his very own, and did not hesitate to make revisions, based on his own sketch, in the design of a Munich architect. Even today these changes strike me as real improvements, providing better for the transition between the static elements of the base and the dynamic thrust of the column.

As he sat with Speer designing fantastic monuments to himself and to his empire, Hitler often sketched ideas for the façades of monumental buildings, usually fronted by a mammoth colonnade. While Speer excused these rapid sketches as concepts rather than detailed artwork, the common characteristic of many of these drawings was the tendency of the columns to lean to one side. Speer had his architectural assistant, Apel, keep these sketches and collect them in a sort of catalogue. He was quite tolerant of Hitler's architectural exercises, and the Führer was far more reasonable in accepting suggestions from him or from other architects than he was with his political associates or his staff, with whom he was brutally rude, overbearing, and cruel.

Considering Speer's success in building mammoth exhibition structures such as the giant Zeppelin Stadium in Nuremberg that was used for Nazi rallies (fig. 2), it would have been interesting to see what would have resulted from Hitler's ideas and Speer's abilities had they been permitted to continue. Hitler's determination to build monuments to himself, with Speer's expert help and his own grandiose ideas, would have resulted in some impressive structures, had Germany not lost the war. The Zeppelin Stadium at Nuremberg (the only monument to be completed) is a truly astonishing example of the kind of projects Hitler and Speer had planned together. Large enough to encompass several football fields, it had a beautiful white marble colonnade along one side, a quarter-mile in length, and marble grandstands were arranged all the way around it. Speer commandeered 150 antiaircraft searchlights to make columns of light, straight up, around the periphery, with tall red Nazi banners at focal points, for the nighttime Party rally of 1938. The floor of this enormous stadium was a solid carpet of helmeted soldiers on that occasion. The total effect was stupendous. The whole world took note.

When General Patton's troops overran it, Patton immediately had the Nazi swastika dynamited off the top of the colonnade and replaced with a giant letter "A" (the emblem of Patton's Third U.S. Army) on the front of the podium (fig. 18). We all posed on Hitler's podium.

Despite Hitler's deference to Speer in architectural matters, he was obstinate in underestimating the enormous war production potential of both the Soviet Union and the United States. This may have merely reflected his provincial outlook: he had never been abroad except to Liverpool as a boy, and later to Rome with Mussolini. He deprecated Speer's accurate analysis of American war production capabilities. Speer said that when he had heard the estimated numbers of ships and tanks and bombers the United States could manufacture per month, he knew the war was lost. He knew the Americans could do just what they estimated and advised Hitler to stop the war while he was ahead. Hitler condemned these opinions as traitorous.

His Personal Image

Hitler had made a policy decision to continue being "every man's" soldier, the unpretentious corporal he had been in World War I. His uniforms, for example, reveal his avoidance of any ostentation (fig. 19). These were custom tailored of a good but ordinary military quality, with none of the embroidery or gold bullion laid on by Göring, Frick, and the others. He used mostly pin-on insignia and badges of the simplest type. He wore clip-on neckties (fig. 20), and his servants darned his socks (figs. 21 & 22). His chauffeur, Erich Kempka (fig. 23), kept Hitler's suitcase stocked with extra clothing (figs. 24 & 25), which he authenticated after the war. As mentioned above, Hitler perspired profusely and had to change clothes often. Kempka also carried Hitler's rain cape and modest scarf (figs. 26 & 27).

Hitler was careful not to invite the old aristocrats or the officer corps to meet at dinner with his little group of inner-circle courtiers. He was apparently afraid the

Fig 18—The author on Hitler's favorite podium

The large "A" on the front of Hitler's podium is the insignia of General Patton's U.S. Third Army. We all undertook to ridicule Hitler, but I must say that the Zeppelin Stadium was very impressive. Evan Lattimer Collection.

(Below) Fig 19—Hitler's green uniform jacket

This was of standard good quality military fabric, with no gold braid or embroidery of the type favored by Göring, Ribbentrop and even Frick. It was custom made by Holters of Berlin (see label from inside breast pocket). Pinholes from his Party badge and ironcross were visible. It had been kept at one of his field headquarters. Evan Lattimer Collection.

Fig 20—Hitler's neckties

Here you see two of his Khaki neckties, one on each side of his picture and his white tie worn with his tails on the occasion shown above. Here von Neurath, in his elegant diplomat's garb, appears to be lording it over the master, a dangerous tactic which may have led to his downfall. Evan Lattimer Collection.

Fig 21—Hitler's socks
These were of very modest materials and had been "darned." His housekeepers were no doubt keeping the state budget in mind and Hitler apparently never noticed. He was surpringly frugal in many small ways. Evan Lattimer Collection.

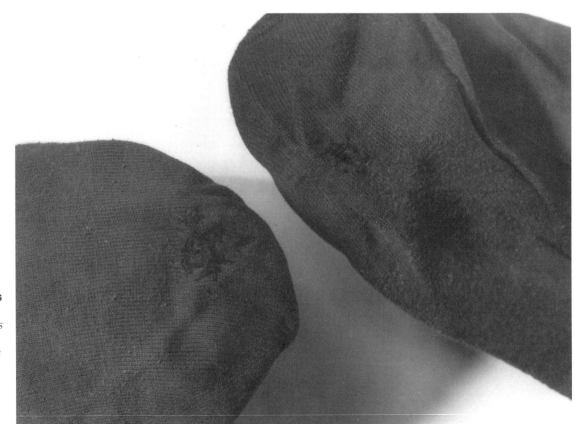

Fig 22—The darns in Hitler's socks
He spent billions on memorial monuments, but his housekeeper economized on socks. Evan Lattimer Collection.

Fig 23—Hitler riding with his chauffeur Erich Kempka

In his open Mercedes touring car. At times Hitler would wear an aviator's helmet to enjoy their 100 mile an hour drives up and down autobahns. Kempka kept a large reserve of clothing for Hitler, who perspired heavily, due to his Parkinson's, and changed clothes often. Kempka had a large stock of memorabilia to sell after his release from prison.

Fig 24—Hitler's suitcase

This is a fine quality fitted leather case made for a special compartment in the large Mercedes touring cars favored by Hitler. His chauffeur Erich Kempka, seen with him above, was charged with keeping emergency clothing in these suitcases, in each of the cars used by Hitler. He had a substantial stock of Hitler memorabilia by war's end. Kempka attached shipping label as seen in Fig 25. Evan Lattimer Collection.

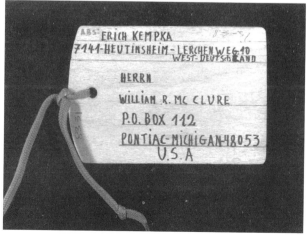

Fig 25—Kempka's shipping label

This was on Hitler's suitcase, filled with Hitler's clothing, to William McClure, the author's friend in Michigan, who had been a guard at the U.S. Embassy in Berlin. Evan Lattimer Collection.

Fig 26—Hitler's rain-cape
This was carried by his chauffeur Erich Kempka in case of unexpected precipitation. It was of light-weight tightly-woven, rubberized fabric. Here you see Hitler leaving the back of the enormous Zeppelin Stadium in Nuremberg, above. At the bottom left he was wearing it when he greeted Mussolini. Evan Lattimer Collection.

Fig 27—Hitler's scarf
This was a very modest scarf, compared to the scarves of Göring, Ribbentrop and other members of the entourage. Hitler rarely used it and was oblivious to details of that type. Dr. Morrell urged him to wear it, but he did not do so. Evan Lattimer Collection.

old aristocracy would recognize his friends for the sycophants they were. His tendency to stay awake far into the night is common among people with Parkinson's disease, although the amphetamines prescribed by Morrell may have contributed to his sleeplessness. He claimed that he acquired this habit as a messenger in the army during World War I, but it probably indicated the early advent of his disease.

Similarly, he avoided meeting Charles Lindbergh and his wife when our Army sent them to visit and evaluate Germany, lest he be compared unfavorably with this "clean-cut genuine hero" and his aristocratic wife.

His refusal to get married permitted him to be considered as the figurative husband for every German woman, or so he thought. Eva Braun was kept in the background, except for his inner circle and the household servants and the staff, who knew her very well. His early womanizing was superficial and took strange turns. His attempt to make his niece, Geli Raubal, his mistress ended with her suicide, using his pistol in his apartment (fig. 28). Though he claimed he did not need to carry a pistol because everyone loved him, it was discovered later that he had the pockets of every pair of trousers relined with leather pockets so he could carry a small pistol in them (figs. 29-31).

The Berghof, Hitler's Mansion at Berchtesgaden

Hitler had been born an Austrian in Braunau (near Linz). He hated his father, a local official, because he was cruel to his mother, who sheltered Adolf. When

Fig 28—Hitler's revolver used by Geli Raubal

Hitler's .22 caliber revolver with which his niece Geli Raubal committed suicide in his apartment. This caused him tremendous distress for approximately a year.

Fig 31—Hitler personal 7.65mm Walther ppk

This was presented to him by the Walther Company on his 50th birthday, April 20, 1939. This is the type of pistol he used to kill himself but it is doubtful that he used this fancy specimen. For some time he had carried one of these in a pistol holster on his Sam Browne belt, but as his confidence grew, he began to hide the pistol in his leather lined pocket and claimed he did not need one. The jacket originally had a leather stain from his earlier method of carrying the pistol in a holster.

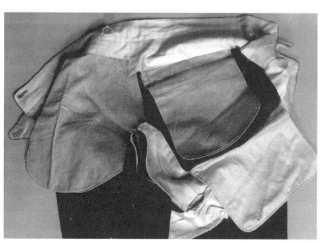

(Left) Fig 29 & 30—Hitler's leather pockets for carrying a pistol

While Hitler claimed he did not need to carry a pistol because his people loved him so, he had his trousers pockets lined with leather, so the serrated front sight on his pistol would not cut through. This pair of trousers was at the tailor's to have the last (left) pocket replaced with leather (as the others were, see fig 31) and so escaped the destruction of all his clothing that had been ordered. Evan Lattimer Collection.

Fig 32—Hitler's first cottage on this site in the Obersalzberg *Hitler was delighted with the area and had it annexed to Germany, even though it was originally part of his native Austria.*

Fig 33—Haus Wachtenfeld *Hitler tore down the cottage and built a fairly large alpine type home called the Haus Wachtenfeld, which is pictured here. It soon proved inadequate and was replaced by the final "Berghof."*

Hitler began to rise in the Nazi Party, he first rented (1925) and later "bought" a tiny cottage in Austria on the mountain overlooking the town of Berchtesgaden (fig. 32). In 1933, he had a substantial chalet on this site, called Haus Wachtenfeld (fig. 33). Eventually that, too, became inadequate for his now supremely powerful situation. In 1936 and 1937, he therefore had it rebuilt and enlarged, under his personal supervision, into the huge edifice, thereafter called the Berghof (fig. 34). Other powerful Nazis, such as Göring, Speer, and Bormann, also built houses near Hitler's. Guest-houses were built nearby to accommodate guests. A huge barracks complex for the garrison of guards and antiaircraft gunners was also built nearby and the entire complex was fenced in with a heavily guarded perimeter. This was expanded as needed. Antiaircraft guns were installed on the surrounding mountaintops and the valley could be filled with a chemical fog on very short notice if enemy bombers were reported en route to the area (fig. 35). The entire area was formally annexed to Germany and the air-raid tunnels connecting all of the buildings were air-conditioned and stocked with food and ammunition in the later phases of the war. This complex was an imposing sight when I first visited it at the end of the war, and again more recently. Now it has been destroyed (fig. 53).

The main room of the Berghof had at one end an enormous window whose glass pane could be rolled down completely out of sight (figs. 36 & 37). This left an unobstructed view of the huge mountain across the way, which pleased Hitler greatly. The view was more awe-inspiring than it was beautiful. Private dining rooms existed in the Berghof and in the Eagle's Nest (fig. 38).

An enormous stock of different patterns of linens, glassware, and silverware with Hitler's favorite monogram were used for state dinners (figs. 39-41).

Among the many decorations was a Viking ship model in sterling silver, a present from Vidkun Quisling (fig. 44). It was burned and crushed during the destruction of the Berghof and the fragment pictured here is all that was left. The inscription to Hitler on the plaque at the bottom, however, is clearly visible.

As noted above, the garrison permitted the populace to loot the house and its extensive storage areas of food, furnishings, and personal belongings of Hitler and Eva before setting fire to it, in anticipation of its capture by the Americans and the French. The Allies found it still smoldering (fig. 49). The terrace in front of the picture window, on top of the garage, had been a favorite gathering place for the Nazi hierarchy (fig. 50). British bombers bombed the area after the German Air Force had been destroyed and the early-warning network was no longer working. One entire side of the Berghof

Fig 34—The Berghof at Berchtesgaden, in the Obersalzberg
Hitler built this huge home in a series of stages, in an area of Austria which was a favorite alpine area for both him and Göring during their youths. It was not only his home, but it had a magnificent main room for official functions, as well as headquarters for each of his military adjutants. It was connected underground to bomb-proof shelters and to the homes of the other Nazi leaders which were nearby.

Fig 35—Smoke screen could hide the Berghof
When enemy bombers were reported approaching, the valley could quickly be filled with smoke. The top photo is after 10 minutes of smoke generating, the middle photo is after 15 minutes and the bottom photo is 20 minutes after the smoke generators were turned on. By April 25, 1945, the early-warning apparatus had broken down. The devastating British bombers encountered no smoke and hit the Berghof hard, as well as the mansions of Göring and Bormann, plus the huge barrack complex.

Fig 36—The main room of the Berghof
This is the huge living room where most of the entertaining was done. The large tapestry on the right hides a movie screen which was often used in the evening. The fireplace on the left was the site of gatherings in the evenings, with Hitler holding forth, as usual.

Fig 37—The retractable picture-window
The view looking towards the huge window at the end of the main room of the Berghof. The view from the window was not nearly as "beautiful" as it was "awe-inspiring." The large window could be rolled down out of sight, so that you could have an unobstructed view of the mountain across the way. This pleased Hitler greatly.

Fig 38—Hitler's private dining room in the "Eagle's Nest" (the Kehlsteinhaus)
This painting may have been made by Hitler himself. The heavily fringed tablecloth is also in our collection. Evan Lattimer Collection.

Fig 39—Beige linen tablecloth and napkins
These are from Hitler's apartment at the Berghof. Evan Lattimer Collection.

Fig 40—The Berghof's silverware

The vaults of the Berghof contained a large variety of different patterns of silverware. All of them bore Hitler's initials and his favorite Nazi eagle and swastika. There were place-settings by the dozens. These vaults were raided by the populace, when the military guard left. The guards invited the citizens of Berchtesgaden to carry away away this loot plus all of the food stored there, since it was about to fall into the hands of the enemy, anyway. Evan Lattimer Collection.

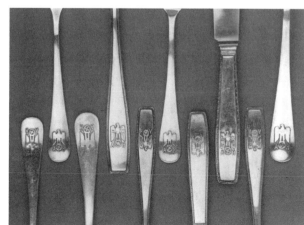

Fig 41—Hitler serving platter
A large silver tray from the Berghof bearing Hitler's initials and the Nazi eagle and swastika. A large roast beef was obviously carved upon this silver platter judging from the knife marks on the bottom. Evan Lattimer Collection.

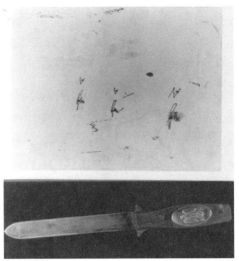

Fig 43—Hitler's desk blotter and letter opener
Several reversed images of his distinctive signature paraph can be made out on the blotter. His letter opener from his desk at the Berghof bears the same initials and eagle as his formal dinnerware. Evan Lattimer Collection.

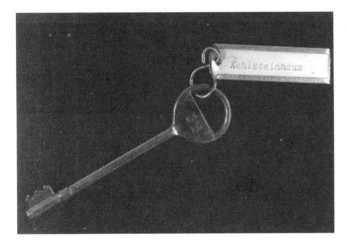

Fig 42—The key to Hitler's personal office
At the "Eagle's Nest", officially known as the Kehlsteinhaus. Evan Lattimer Collection.

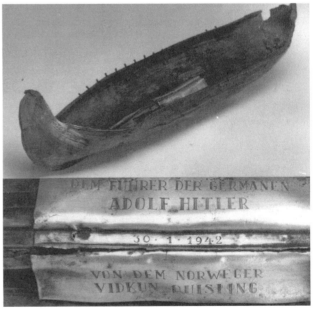

(Above right) Fig 44—A viking ship model from Vidkun Quisling to Hitler
This was carefully crafted out of sterling silver and given as a present from the Nazi ruler of Norway to Adolf Hitler, January 20, 1942. This beautiful specimen, one of the hundreds of fancy presents at the Berghof, was trampled and burned when the building was set on fire by the retreating SS troopers. The model was burned on the ends and crushed by being stepped on by a heavy foot. Its delicate workmanship is still recognizable, as is the presentation plaque in the bottom. Hundreds of treasures were burned or damaged in a similar way, when the Berghof was partially gutted. It had been somewhat damaged by the British bombers, in the last days of the war. The vaults of furnishings were fairly intact, however, and thus became a treasure trove for the people of Berchtesgaden, except for two strong-rooms. Evan Lattimer Collection.

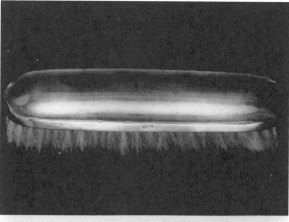

Fig 45—Body brush from Hitler's bedroom
This bore the 800 mark of the jeweler Wellner, marking it to be of the highest quality, as was everything in the building. Evan Lattimer Collection.

Fig 47—A funeral ribbon in watered silk, bearing a Nazi swastika, an eagle and a note personally signed by Hitler
Hitler's memorial ribbons for funeral wreaths were notably more modest than those of Göring, whose name was splashed in gold very prominently on his memorials of this type. Evan Lattimer Collection.

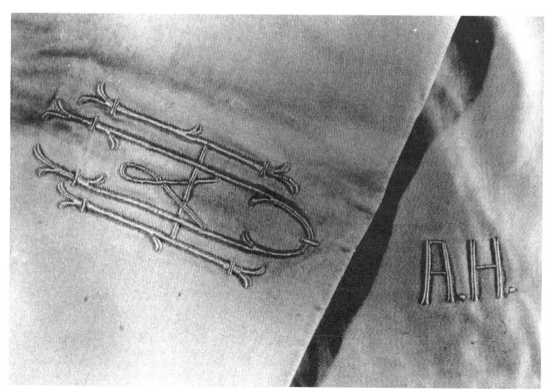

Fig 46—Hitler's personal pillow case
It had his initials in two different styles and was an extravagantly large and handsome piece of linen. Evan Lattimer Collection.

Fig 48—Hitler worried children
Here, two children are posed with Hitler but looked very skeptical about this "honor." It made you wonder what they had heard about the great man at home, that made them look this worried. Great efforts were made to make Hitler look like a benign grandfather with children gathered around him, but the reaction many times was very much like this. Göring's daughter reacted similarly.

Fig 50—Hitler's terrace
The author standing on the terrace in front of the Berghof, a favorite gathering place. It was on top of the garage section. Evan Lattimer Collection.

Fig 49—The Berghof as we found it
What was left of the Berghof after the bombing had been fairly well cleaned out by the staff and by the citizens of Berchtesgaden. Then it was set afire by the garrison, as they retreated before the Americans and the French.

Fig 51—British bombs damaged the Berghof
One entire side of the main building was blown off by the British bombs and "adjutants" wing was destroyed. Most of the building was burned out and appeared like this by the time we reached it in May. Evan Lattimer Collection.

Fig 52—A gas mask from Hitler's apartment
The author holding a German army gas mask in "new" condition, found in the rubble of Hitler's apartment in the Berghof. Hitler had been gassed in WWI and worried about gas. Evan Lattimer Collection.

Fig 53—The Berghof dynamited

The Berghof being demolished by the German government so that it would not become a shrine to the Nazis. This was done on April 30, 1952. Note that the garage on the right was not demolished and still remains. Your author has climbed inside those windows even though they are overgrown by brush and tall trees by now. A few basement rooms remain. The terrace was on top of the garage and was one of the popular gathering places during the summer weather, for Hiiler and his entourage.

was blown away (fig. 51). The German government dynamited the ruin after a number of years in order to prevent its being made a shrine to Hitler (fig. 53).

Not only did Hitler have huge stocks of beautiful linens and silver but he had hammered silver frames made up for his portrait, to give to favorite guests (fig. 1). Göring had to outdo everyone else and had an even larger hammered silver frame made for his portrait of Hitler. Hitler's adjutant, Martin Bormann (who succeeded Hess), had an elaborate teahouse built on the very top of an adjacent mountain, at tremendous expense, thinking it would please Hitler. Tunneling into the rock of the mountain and then straight up to the teahouse was unbelievably expensive, but Bormann was sure it would please the Führer. As it turned out, Hitler did not like it and rarely went there. The reason is apparent when you look down from it. The entire area appears miniscule, rather than grandiose, as it

looks from below. The teahouse, called the Eagle's Nest, is the only relic that was not dynamited by the German government. It is now a tourist attraction of sorts (fig. 54).

Hitler's Power

Hitler was an egocentric psychopath who had the German people in his complete control. He was the first dictator who had the advantage of using the radio and the public address system in a masterful way to dominate an entire populace. He correctly estimated the need of the Germans for a leader who would lead them away from the oppressive terms of the Versailles Treaty of 1918 and restore their self-respect as a nation. His good luck in enlisting financial geniuses like Schacht, who convinced Franklin Roosevelt and the other Allied leaders to cancel the oppressive war-debt reparations, annex the peripheral, German populated territories. When the Allies indeed failed to react, he then overstepped. He overran Poland, whereupon Great Britain and France surprised him by declaring war. Then he overran Denmark and Norway, the Low Countries, and finally, France. His armies proved to be brilliantly equipped and led. While he never expected Britain and France to declare war, he nevertheless cleverly protected his rear with a treaty with the Soviet Union.

As stated, some mental aberration, starting in 1940, led Hitler to fail to follow through and invade England, and then to make the ultimate mistake of invading the Soviet Union. After that, everything was downhill. Hitler sent hundreds of thousands of Germany's finest young men to their deaths in suicidal last stands, which he demanded in his pathologically rigid philosophy of "never retreat." Stalingrad was the worst example of this philosophy. Furthermore, he let the German cities be turned into charred ruins by our bombers. In the end, he even ordered the German civilian establishment to be destroyed, along with the cities. Fortunately,

Fig 54—The Eagle's Nest, above the Berghof
The Eagle's Nest was an unbelievably expensive "teahouse" built by Bormann, Hitler's "toady," adjutant in an effort to please him. A long tunnel was chiselled into a nearby mountain, and an elevator shaft tunneled upwards through the solid rock to the teahouse. The large bronze elevator was in two parts. It would stop at the top and the guard unit would disembark. If no bomb exploded, then Hitler's segment of the elevator would come up and he would come out. The view from this height makes everything seem diminutive. Hitler was not overly pleased with this and visited the lavish bauble only a few times.

Fig 55—Hitler's Belgian Shepherd Dog "Blondi"
He had his staff demonstrate the effectiveness of one of the cyanide capsules on her (middle photo). Hitler's application for yet another dog, in 1929, is shown at the bottom. Evan Lattimer Collection.

earned him a tremendous following. Using the radio, his message went right down to the personal level of every German, rather than depending on filtering orders and concepts down through a hierarchy. This increased his power tremendously. His propaganda expert, Goebbels, was also very skillful with this medium. Buoyed by his absolute control of Germany, Hitler had made several shrewd guesses early in the game. He guessed correctly that the Allies would not stop him from illegally rearming, and that they would let him

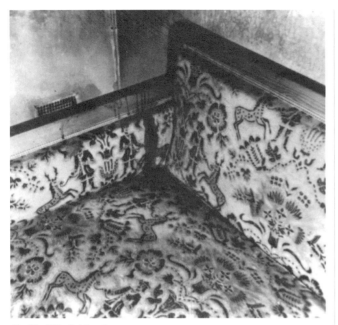

Fig 56—Hitler's blood
Hitler's blood on the arm of the chair in which he shot himself. A piece of this blood stained fabric was given to a reporter by the Russian guard at the scene. It was later acquired by Ben Swearingen. Pictures of it were published in an article by Swearingen in "After the Battle" magazine.

Speer was able to countermand many of these orders at great personal risk to himself.

Germany's disastrous downhill rush, beginning in 1943, might even then have been reversed, as I saw it, if Hitler had turned over the government to Göring and Speer. Instead, his technique of pitting the strong and vicious rivals in his entourage against one another, (Himmler, Göring, Bormann and Kaltenbrunner, for example) fell apart at the end, when each wanted to double-cross him by surrendering on their own and becoming the new leader.

Himmler was also trying surreptitiously to establish an industrial empire throughout conquered Europe, run by his SS organization. His SS men were incompetent at industry and interfered with Speer's, war production apparatus at every turn. Furthermore, each rival was actually trying to assassinate the other whenever opportunity presented itself. Speer was targeted by others for possible assassination. They planned to declare him ill and then announce that complications had set in, which had led to his untimely death. Luckily, Speer's wife was able to forestall this by appealing to Hitler's personal doctor (Dr. Brandt) to take over his care when he fell ill with post-operative phlebitis and pulmonary emboli.

Another blunder that hastened Hitler's fall, as I saw it, was the Nazis' practice of importing, and then starving to death, their millions of slave laborers. Had they

Fig 57—The site of Hitler's first grave
The shell crater immediately outside the exit door from the bunker to the Führer's headquarters in Berlin. It was in the walls of this crater that Hitler's and his wife's bodies were buried after being partially burned by several hours of soaking with gasoline. The Russians dug them up and identified them by their dental work, after being told by witnesses who they were.

organized and utilized more of them in their own countries, as Speer wanted to do, rather than displacing them to Germany, the Germans could have gotten far better production from them and preserved the food producing ability of all Europe, as well as Germany itself. Hitler's destructive policies toward the people he controlled, including the Germans, were already failing. The whole machinery could have been run in a way that would have permitted Hitler to dominate the world. Göring could have done it for him, for example, as he himself declared. Speer also could have helped him do it.

Hitler's Ardennes Offensive (The Battle of the Bulge)

Late in 1944, Hitler came up with a wild proposal that greatly upset Speer and the military commanders. He proposed to mobilize all of the remaining reserves for a desperation thrust to cut the Allied armies in two, aiming for the port of Antwerp. This plan ended any confidence Speer or von Rundstedt had in Hitler, since in the opinions of his advisors, it would deprive all of the other elements of Hitler's army of their reserves and would have very little chance of success. Speer was appalled at this notion, but Hitler said that if he could score a big victory with a surprise attack, he would then be in a strong position to propose a peace. This made sense to Speer, who then supported him, despite his misgivings.

Hitler was adamant about his plan, and successful total secrecy was preserved during the buildup. Field Marshal von Rundstedt was then brought back from his third forced retirement by Hitler. He told me that he and Field Marshal Rommel had already told Hitler that the war was lost in July of 1944, after the successful Allied landings. In fact, they had told Hitler that it was probably lost after the Stalingrad defeat in 1943. Von Rundstedt said that the Battle of the Bulge, attributed to him as the "von Rundstedt Offensive," had absolutely nothing to do with him, but was planned and insisted upon by Hitler and by Hitler only. He told me, further, that the execution of Allied prisoners in and about Malmedy was purely a function of Himmler's SS men and not of his regular German Army (the Wehrmacht). (I had assisted with the inquest into the massacres.) von Rundstedt pointed out that any general orders to the effect that prisoners should be killed would have been known to him and to Rommel, and that they would have insisted that this not be done. He said that they had captured something like 80,000 Allied prisoners in the Battle of the Bulge and that, if it had been a policy to kill prisoners, there would have been far more incidents than just in the vicinity of Malmedy. All of the soldiers involved had indicated that they understood that the orders came directly from Hitler to "Fight like savages and to show no mercy."

Eva Braun

Eva Braun, an assistant to photographer Heinrich Hoffmann, was the ideal companion for Hitler (fig. 59). She was attractive and kept herself in good physical shape by swimming and by skiing, which she was later ordered to give up, much to her regret (figs. 60 & 61). She was always available as a hostess, when she was wanted, but knew enough to disappear when she was not. Apparently she had no political views. She was not only nubile, but she was supposedly agreeable to any of the bizarre sexual practices in which Hitler was rumored to indulge. During the long periods when Hitler was away, she enjoyed the Berghof. She loved her two Scotty dogs plus numerous kittens, white rabbits, and other pets, but had no social life. When Hitler finally agreed to let her take vacation trips to Italy and Paris, she went with the Speer family, Dr. Morrell, and some of the other wives. Eva favored Parisian perfumes and accessories (fig. 62). Her toilet articles were of the finest quality and her dresses were beautifully made (figs. 67 & 68). For Christmas 1938, Hitler gave her a gold fountain pen with his signature inscribed on it, made by Gold-Fink of the Mont Blanc company (fig. 69). When the other Nazis found out that Hitler had given fountain pens, they all gave fountain pens for Christmas that year. Speer designed a clever monogram for her, combining her initials E and B, back-to-back, to make a "four-leaf clover" or a "butterfly." Her French evening bag and accessories were of the finest materials, marked with this monogram.

At the end of his life Hitler, was almost certainly impotent as a result of his Parkinson's disease. Speer said Hitler had told Eva that she was released from any obligation to him since he could no longer act towards her as he had done in the past. It was Eva's own dedication to Hitler that caused her to join him in the bunker and to die with him, after their last-minute wedding.

Eva elected to die by cyanide rather than by cyanide plus shooting, as Hitler had declared he would do, and apparently did. In the discussions about the topic among the women during the last days in the bunker, she had said that she did not wish to be shot because she wished to be a "beautiful corpse." The Russians found a partly burned body, along with Hitler's partly burned body, in a shell crater in front of the entrance to the "Führerbunker" in Berlin (fig. 71). The dental work

Fig 58—Hitler's corpse

The box containing the partly burned body of Adolf Hitler, dug out of the walls of a shell crater by the Russians. It was identified primarily by the dental work, since the Russians were quickly able to identify Hitler's dentist and the one who took care of Eva Braun as well. The allegation in the Russian autopsy report that Hitler only had one testis may well be true, but there was never any supporting evidence for this allegation, during his lifetime. Several doctors indicated a normal physical examination, but there was never any specific description of the scrotum nor of its contents that we can find. Hitler did query Dr. Morrell about hypospadias, a deformity of the penis.

Fig 59—Hitler and Eva Braun at the Berghof

Eva was a dignified and pleasant consort for Hitler for all non-political events at the Berghof. This was no secret among the members of Hitler's staff. She would disappear discreetly whenever political matters came up.

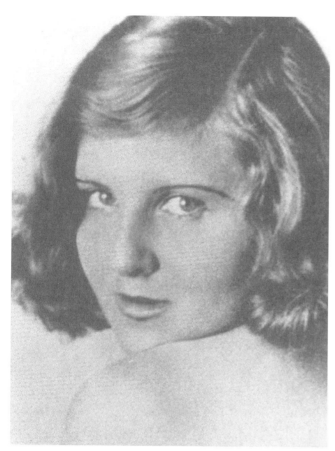

Fig 60—Eva could be glamorous
Her old employer, Hitler photographer, Hoffman knew she could be an ideal companion for Hitler.

was five years away. If Germany had invaded the Middle East, the Jewish people in that region would have suffered the same horrendous fate as the Jews of Europe. The state of Israel may never have been formed.

Suspicious of the Allies and worried about an attack by the Japanese, Stalin may have made a deal with Hitler, as he had done in the past. If England had been taken over and the British government forced into exile, the British and Americans would have been offered a compromise, just as the French had been, and as Stalin had accepted.

With the slave labor, facilities, and raw materials gained by such a conquest, Hitler's empire could have been enormously powerful.

If Hitler had occupied England and had achieved bases in South America from cooperative governments there, it would have been very difficult for the United States to mount any real resistance to the Germans. Hitler's ever expanding hi-tech submarine fleet would have made sea lanes difficult to maintain.

It is not easy to ascertain who explained to Hitler that he had only a few more years to live, due to his progressive, untreatable disease. It was rumored that one of the SS doctors told Himmler to initiate talks about an armistice with the Allies.

Both Speer and Dr. Morrell said that Hitler began to verbalize his worry that he would not live long enough to complete his grand plan, but none of them realized the significance of his preoccupation with an early death. None of the top Nazis that I interrogated about

in the mouth was the same as Eva's although it has been suggested that perhaps someone else's body was substituted. The Russian prosecutors were satisfied that it was Eva, but have offered no details since that time. As noted above, Hitler's dental work clearly identified his charred body (fig. 58).

The Russian autopsy report on Hitler's body was unremarkable except that he had only one testicle. The brain had been destroyed by the gasoline-fed cremation, so no evaluation of his Parkinsonianism was possible. The bridgework of the lower jaw was well preserved and matched his distinctive dental work.

Some conclusions

In 1940 Hitler had most of Europe under his control. England verged on becoming his for the taking. There were not enough Allied troops deployed to keep him out of the Middle Eastern oil fields, if he had chosen to reinforce Rommel. America had not yet joined the war and was not mobilized. The American atomic bomb

Fig 61—Eva kept in excellent physical condition
Here we see her in her bathing suit. She trained like a ballet dancer.

Fig 62—Eva's monogrammed evening bag from Paris
Eva favored Parisian accessories and perfumes. In the lower photo-graph you see her monogram of the four-leafed clover inside the evening bag, which is marked "Made in France." Evan Lattimer Collection.

Fig 64—Eva's body brush, bearing her conventional initials
Evan Lattimer Collection.

Fig 65—One of Eva's mirror and brush sets
This set was not one initialed but was of the highest quality, as were all her things. Evan Lattimer Collection.

Fig 63—A compact Eva gave to her sister
Eva shared her good fortune with her friends and gave them expensive presents like this at Christmas time. Evan Lattimer Collection.

Fig 66—Eva's lipstick holder
A nicely made golden bauble, shown with one of her calling cards. Evan Lattimer Collection.

Fig 67—One of Eva's hand-some afternoon dresses
It was made of very expensive dark red silk with a tiny black flower in it. An intricate system of hooks and eyes underneath the fabric made it fit perfectly. Her dresses were all custom made for her. Evan Lattimer Collection.

Fig 68—Eva's black silk sheath evening-dress
The pockets were stiched with gold thread and there was a peach colored silk lining. It too was custom fitted. Evan Lattimer Collection.

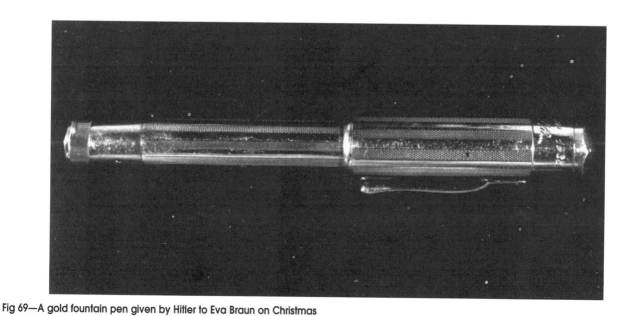

Fig 69—A gold fountain pen given by Hitler to Eva Braun on Christmas
It is a small pen of the most popular design of the day. Hitler's name is engraved at top, with "Weihnachten 1938." It is a "Mont Blanc" fountain pen, which is of excellent quality, of 14 kt gold, of their Gold-fink line, marked "585." Once Hitler started giving pens, the other Nazis all started giving pens, at least that year. Evan Lattimer Collection.

Hitler's failure to invade England had a logical answer. Now, however with firm evidence of his severe Parkinsonism, we have a very probable explanation for his failure to invade England and his subsequent disastrous downhill course. We can thank goodness that he got Parkinson's disease before there was any treatment for it.

Fig 70—Eva's French vanity case
It contained elegant hand mirrors, brushes, shoe-horns, etc., in a well worn case used by Eva Braun when travelling. Each of the items bears her "four-leafed clover" monogram. Evan Lattimer Collection.

Fig 72—Eva Braun's dentures from her corpse
These were in the mouth of her corpse when the Russians did her autopsy. They matched her dental records.

Fig 71—Eva's partly burned corpse
This box contained the partly burned corpse of Eva which the Russians dug out of the walls of a shell crater near the door of the bunker. The gold bridgework in the mouth matched Eva's enough to satisfy the suspicious Russians, despite suggestions that it might be the body of someone else.

CHAPTER 3

Reichsmarshal Hermann Göring

Fig 1—Göring had indeed been handsome
In his early years, as seen in this signed photograph, he always wore not only his iron crosses but his "Blue-Max," Germany's highest military award. Evan Lattimer Collection.

Hermann Göring was impressive (fig. 1). He was highly intelligent, very capable, very flamboyant and a consummate actor. He was nobody's fool, not even Hitler's, as our agents rapidly discovered. Most important, it quickly became apparent to me that he was clearly the only one of the top Nazis who could have deposed Hitler when Hitler began to disintegrate mentally. He could have then either stopped the war or continued it as the leader of the mighty empire and the mighty army that Hitler had built up. In his aggressive early days he might very well have done this, it seemed to me. He could have run Germany so much better than Hitler that there would have been no comparison. The question in my mind was: what had happened to him? The answer became apparent as his problems began to unfold at the trial.

My First Impression of Göring

When Dr. Kelley, my fellow Columbia University alumnus, first took me to see Göring, I did not know what to expect. He was someone whose minions I felt had been actively trying to kill me, personally, for the past two years. I was ready to squash him like you might squash a black widow spider. I was amazed to see what looked like an overinflated blimp from the Macy's parade (figs. 3-6). His 300 pounds made him look unreal. When we entered his cell he was lounging on his bed like an overweight but still dangerous tiger, ready to crush anyone who came within reach. The instant metamorphosis when he saw Dr. Kelley was impressive; he became charm itself. His excellent English surprised me. He patted his bed and chair, urging us to sit down and talk. He expressed eagerness to help with anything

(Left) Fig 2—Book by Göring
Göring's book: Growth of a Nation was found by Dr. Goldensohn in a stack of Nazi books being "purged" from a Nuremberg library. Evan Lattimer Collection.

Fig 4—Göring playing tennis
Even after he got embarrassingly fat, he continued to play tennis, although he could not get around the court well enough to dominate the play. He did love to hit the ball very hard, however. In this costume he could still wear a confining corset around his huge abdomen, under his tennis clothes. By contrast he never let himself be photographed, in bathing trunks where the corset could not be worn.

Fig 3—Göring's wedding feast
After his marriage to Emmy Sonneman, a well known actress, in 1935, Göring entertained at a lavish banquet. Hitler, his best man, is seated on Mrs. Göring's right. In this picture Göring wears a selection of his numerous decorations, including the pour-le-Merite, around his neck, as always. Raymond Zyla Collection.

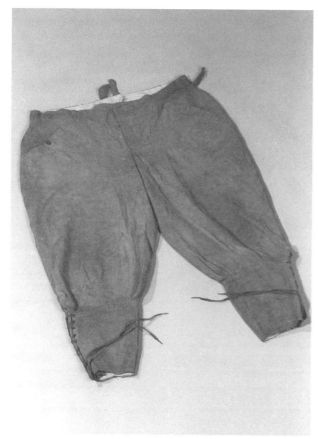

Fig 5—Göring's gigantic Lederhosen
Enormous leather trousers worn by Hermann Göring as part of his hunting outfit. They are of the very finest suede leather and of a size to encompass his 300 pound obesity. Evan Lattimer Collection.

we wanted to discuss. He denied any need for a urologist "at least for now." He said he certainly hoped that the trial did not last so long that he might develop a need for one. He thought both Funk and Dönitz needed a urologist right then, however, and he was right. In any case, he said that he was glad that I was there, especially if I was a friend of Dr. Kelley's. He was amazingly knowledgeable about a wide range of topics and eager to talk.

In that very first visit, he brought up the fact that he had a skin condition that required a lot of attention. I did not recognize the significance of this remark at the time, but Dr. Kelley already knew about it and merely reassured him that it would be taken care of. His fat thighs did rub together and chafed the skin. This is called "intertrigo." However, even after he had lost so much weight that the chafing had disappeared, he continued to talk about his skin condition. When I pointed out he no longer had a skin condition, he responded, "That is because I take such good care of it with my

skin cream." This sounded reasonable, and assured his access to jars of skin cream in his luggage whenever he asked for it.

Göring was clearly the star of our menagerie and everyone wanted to see him. He acknowledged this evidence of his leadership position: "Of course," he said. Even visitors who were sent to interview some other prisoner, such as Hess, always wanted to see Göring as well. He was well aware of his dominant position at all times.

Our Allied propaganda machine had painted Göring as a debauched eunuch, intent mainly on looting museums. In fact, when we watched him matching wits against the world's top prosecutors, he was brilliant. He had occupied a host of very important positions in the German government, including being Hitler's deputy, President of the Reichstag, Prussian Prime Minister, head of the Four-year Plan, commander not only of the German military Air Force, but also of all airline activity in occupied Europe. He had an extensive industrial empire in all of the occupied countries called the "Hermann Göring Works," which made him a multimillionaire and required a great deal of administrative work. He was also President of the Prussian State Council, Reich Governor of Prussia, Reich Forestry and Hunting Minister, Chairman of the Secret Cabinet Council, and Reichsmarshal (figs. 7-13).

Fig 6—Göring's expandable hunting coat
A hunting coat of Göring's, custom made by Stechbarth of Berlin of the finest green and black tweed favored by the Bavarians, with a green velvet collar. The back and shoulders were for a very large man, but the back was also pleated so that it could be expanded to permit his stomach to grow. Fig 16 shows Göring wearing this coat during a stag hunt on his estate. The RAF borrowed this coat in order to get the true measurements for Göring for reenactments they were creating on the 50th anniversary of the battle of Britain. Evan Lattimer Collection.

Im
Namen des Reichs

verleihe ich

dem Hauptmann a.D.

Hermann Göring

den Charakter als General der Infanterie.

Berlin, den 30.August 1933

Der Reichspräsident

gez. von Hindenburg

Der Reichswehrminister
gez. von Blomberg

Der Chef der Heeresleitung
gez. Freiherr von Hammerstein

für die Richtigkeit

Generalleutnant und Chef
des Heerespersonalamts.

Fig 7—Göring's commision as an Infantry General
Göring's appointment as a General of Infantry, by then-president Von Hindenburg, signed by Keitel Aug. 30, 1933. This was only one of his several official titles in the Nazi hierarchy. Evan Lattimer Collection.

Fig 8—Cuff band from a member of the Hermann Göring Infantry Division
This type of cuff band was worn by the men of this division. Since he was a General of Infantry, he "naturally" had a division named after him. Evan Lattimer Collection.

Fig 9—Göring wearing his officer's sword
This beautiful engraved sword is being worn by Göring (left) to show that he could be a "member of the team." Evan Lattimer Collection.

Jm Namen
des
Deutschen Volkes

Jch befördere

den Reichsminister der Luftfahrt und Oberbefehlshaber der Luftwaffe

Generaloberst G ö r i n g

zum Generalfeldmarschall.

Berlin, den 4. Februar 1938.

Der Führer und Reichskanzler

Für den Reichsminister der Luftfahrt
und Oberbefehlshaber der Luftwaffe.
W.A.Nr.100/38   W P.

Auf Grund des Gesetzes über den
Staatsrat ernenne ich Sie hiermit
zum

Preussischen Staatsrat

Jch vollziehe diese Urkunde in der
Erwartung, daß Sie nach Gesetz und
Recht Jhre Pflichten zum Wohle des
Volkes erfüllen und das Vertrauen
rechtfertigen, das Jhnen durch diese
Ernennung bewiesen wird. Zugleich
sichere ich Jhnen meinen besonderen
Schutz zu.

Berlin, den *15 September 1933*
Der Preussische Ministerpräsident

An Herrn

in   *München*

(Left) Fig 10—Göring's commission as General-Feldmarschall, and Air-Force Chief
This bears Hitler's signature and is dated 4 February, 1938. Later he was made the one-and-only Reichsmarschall. Evan Lattimer Collection.

Fig 11—Göring's staff
Sturdy three-foot-long staff bears Göring's crest as a Reichsmarschall and was a favorite stick of his. His family crest is engraved on the knob. Evan Lattimer Collection.

Fig 12—Göring used his title as Prussian Minister President
An official document signed by Göring in September 1933, on which he used his title of "Prussian Minister President." Later on he dropped "Prussian" because it made this title too long and unwieldy. Evan Lattimer Collection.

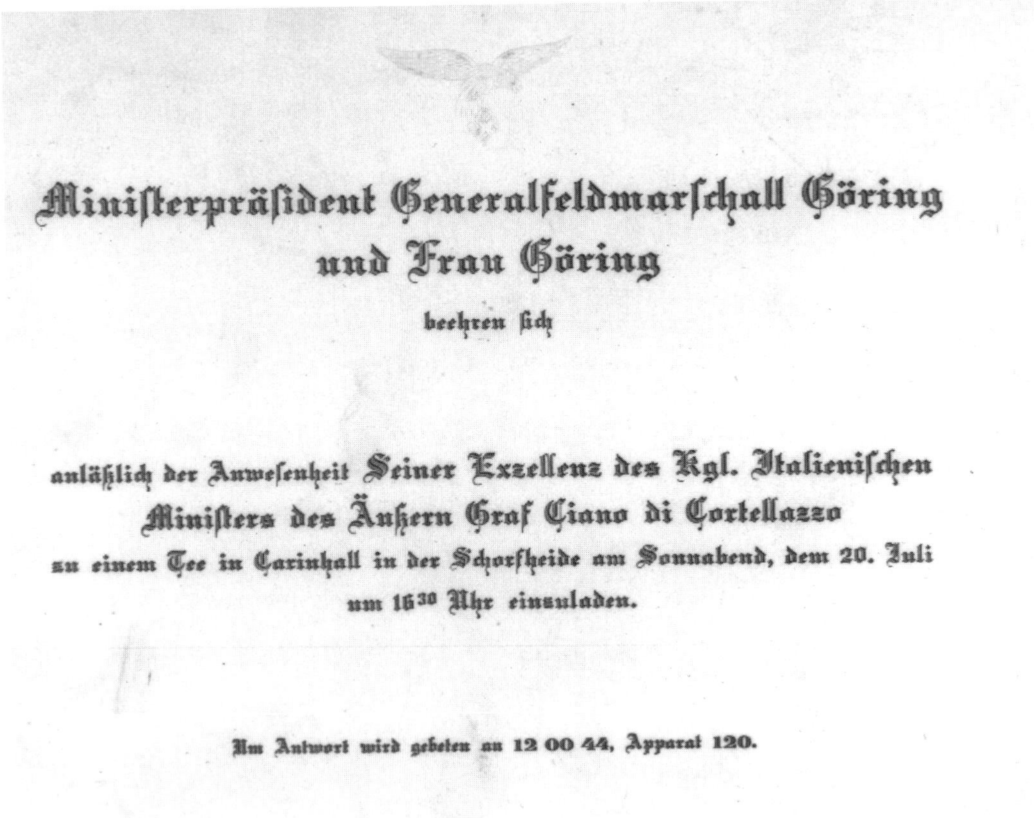

Fig 13—Combining his various titles
Here Göring combines several of his titles (but drops the word Prussian) as on this invitation to meet Count Ciano at Karinhall. Evan Lattimer Collection.

Ministerpräsident Generalfeldmarschall Göring und Frau Göring

beehren sich

anläßlich der Anwesenheit Seiner Exzellenz des Kgl. Italienischen Ministers des Äußern Graf Ciano di Cortellazzo zu einem Tee in Carinhall in der Schorfheide am Sonnabend, dem 20. Juli um 16³⁰ Uhr einzuladen.

Um Antwort wird gebeten an 12 00 44, Apparat 120.

It turned out that he actually worked hard at each of these positions, putting in very long days. When it was noted that he was not the womanizer that some of the other top Nazis were, Dr. Kelley remarked that he spent all of his energy on his many jobs, and did not have time left for womanizing. He also built an enormous hunting lodge in the forest east of Berlin, where he was happy to entertain anyone from other governments who visited the Reich. Hitler was glad to have him do this, because Hitler himself disliked entertaining and realized he was not good at it. This was despite the tutelage of von Ribbentrop's wife, who tried to educate Hitler in the niceties of social entertaining and acted as his hostess on many occasions. When people commented on the excesses of Göring's hunting lodge, Hitler said "Leave Göring alone, he entertains so well." One of his excesses was a pet lion which roamed the halls, but which consumed enough meat to supply an entire village during the days of severe rationing (fig. 19). Karinhall, the hunting lodge, was named after his first wife, the Baroness Carin von Kantzow, who died of tuberculosis in 1931 and whose ornate mausoleum was on the grounds.

Göring's experience in the various government posts and his dominance over the other top Nazis was so obvious that I asked him over and over why he did not depose Hitler when his disintegration became inevitable. Especially since Göring had declared to me, on many occasions, that his main ambition in life had been to lead Germany. He said that of all the movements to rebuild Germany after the Versailles Treaty, only Hitler's Nazi group appeared capable of succeeding, so he had joined them. He declared over and over that their ideology and anti-Semitism did not appeal to him, but their power did.

At one point during the trial when Göring was raging at some of the other defendants who had participated in the plot to kill Hitler with a bomb, the crusty (figs. 20 & 21), fragile, old diplomat von Papen said to him, "Göring, you let us down. We put you, the war hero, into power with Hitler with the idea that if he got out of line, you would take him by the scruff of the neck and throw him out, but you failed us."

Each time I asked Göring why he did not eliminate Hitler, just as he had eliminated Röhm, who (as Göring declared) "had gotten in his way" in his climb to the top, he said it was a matter of honor. You did not betray your leader. When his wife also began to complain about his ridiculous loyalty to Hitler, even after Hitler had condemned Göring, his wife, and his child to be shot, he merely said, "Women did not understand about a man's honor."

Fig 14—Göring was an excellent speaker
He made a very strong leadership model, as a war-hero and a vigorous patriot.

Fig 16—Göring wearing his expandable hunting coat
These photographs, taken out of Göring's Minox camera which he had with him when he was captured, show him standing over this stag, holding a huntsmen's symbolic spear. This does not imply that he killed the stag with the spear but he is obviously proud of the very large rack of antlers on this beast. His rustic hunting lodge at Karinhall, east of Berlin, was decorated with dozens of racks of antlers like these. While he would hunt enthusiastically, he would be outraged at any word that animals were being used by anyone else, as for medical experimentation. He kept a large menagerie, including a half-grown lion, on his estate, feeding them enormous amounts of meat, even as the population of Germany was suffering severe protein deprivation. His ambivalence in these matters was hard to understand but was one of his characteristics. He is wearing our expandable hunting coat (see Fig. 6, page 69) in this picture. Evan Lattimer Collection.

Fig 15—Karinhall
Karinhall, the enormous hunting lodge in the forest, northeast of Berlin, where Göring spent more and more of his time as the war progressed and his prestige deteriorated. In fact he was building onto the lodge on a tremendous scale, making it into a huge art gallery for his looted paintings, when the Russians began to advance toward it and caused him to abandon it. In the beginning, Hitler had him entertain state visitors there so Hitler did not have to bother with them. He said "Göring entertains so well!"

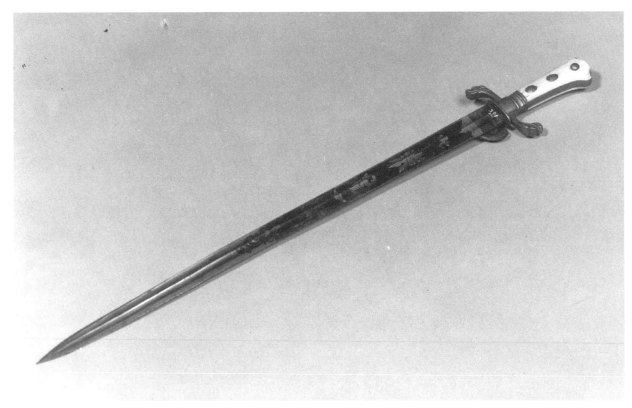

Fig 17—An antique hunting sword carried by Göring at Karinhall
This is a classical design appropiate to his grandiose hunting estate. Evan Lattimer Collection.

Fig 18—Huge racks of antlers at Karinhall
The lodge must have had a hundred of these fine specimens hung on the walls. Perhaps Göring was now killing off most of the game, since the Russians were about to take over the area. Evan Lattimer Collection.

Fig 19—Göring's pet lion
This beast ate huge amounts of scarce meat, but was impressive for visitors to Karinhall. Even Göring was a little afraid of it, as is evident here.

Fig 20—Göring at Nuremberg harassing the other defendants
Göring would harass the other prisoners unmercifully. He would do this at the mid-morning and mid-afternoon breaks, if their testimony had displeased him. He continued this harassment at lunch time.

Fig 21—Göring made to eat alone, after this
Göring initially was permitted to eat with the other Nuremberg defendants such as Rosenberg, Funk and Fritzsche, as you see here. He used these occasions to harass the others so violently and so effectively that he was made to eat by himself after mid-February. This was at the suggestion of Speer and put in effect by Dr. Gilbert. Göring was furious at this restriction of his opportunity to influence the others.

Fig 22—Göring carrying his loaded revolver
This was just after the assassination attempt on Hitler's life in the summer on 1944. He was the only one of the inner circle near Hitler with a loaded pistol and could very easily have shot him, as well as Himmler and Bormann, had his drug addiction not made him so complacent, as I saw it.

Fig 23—Goring and von Richthofen's Fokker triplane
Here Göring is talking to a group of his fellow pilots in front of one of the Red Baron's Fokker Triplanes (taken from an English design) when he took over von Richthofen's squadron late in World War I. While it was very maneuverable, the triplane was abandoned for the faster Fokker D7 shown in Fig. 57. This in turn was eventually abandoned by Göring, in favor of a still faster monoplane.

Fig 25—Göring's lock of the Red Baron's hair
This was Göring's personal keepsake of the legendary Baron von Richthofen, whose famous "flying circus" Göring took over. He kept it in a locket with this, and also a "miniature" of the Baron, which showed his reddish blond hair. Evan Lattimer Collection.

Fig 24—Göring with von Richthofen's favorite walking stick
Göring has just taken over command of von Richthofen's famous squadron. He is standing beside the "hot" new Fokker biplanes of the day. Note the machine guns with which he shot down so many opponents.

Göring was the only one allowed to openly carry a pistol in Hitler's presence (fig. 22). He could have easily gotten Hitler, Himmler, and Goebbels in the same room and shot them all. Then he could have declared it a mass suicide. But he apparently never even considered this.

Why Then Did Göring Not Depose Hitler?

I attributed his failure to displace Hitler to his drug addiction and its effects. It soothed his normal aggressiveness. Besides, he saw that others were plotting to kill Hitler and he knew that he was the designated successor, in case anything did happen to Hitler.

After we had gotten him off the drugs and several months had passed, however, he gradually began to acknowledge the possibility that he should have done something about Hitler. He explained that he would have had to get three German psychiatrists to agree that Hitler was insane and no German psychiatrist would even think of doing that. They knew that Hitler's Gestapo would murder them instantly. This was, absolutely true. When we told Göring that the Western press all considered the Nazis to be a group of yes-men, he said, "Well that was certainly true, but show me a no-man who is not six feet under the ground."

Fig 27—Extravagant ribbon attached to a wreath sent by Göring in memory of some special person who had died
Characteristic of Göring, it had a great deal more printing and listed his title with the Air Force, so no one could have any doubt about who sent it. Evan Lattimer Collection.

Fig 26—The Castle at Mauterndorf where Göring grew up
The Nazis imprisoned him here, briefly, at the very end, before his own paratrooper bodyguards rescued him from Bormann's SS troopers.

Göring's Background

Not only was Göring a prominent war hero after World War I, but he had a background which made him highly acceptable as a German leader (figs. 23-27). His father had been a diplomat representing Germany in various countries. He was serving in Haiti when Göring was about to be born. His wife returned to Germany to have her child on German soil, but left the baby with relatives while she returned to her husband's side. Göring grew up without parental supervision and became a strong willed, rebellious youngster, widely known among the other children as a bully. As a result, he was sent to a military school for discipline.

During his youth, Göring had climbed many of the more difficult mountain peaks in and around the Berchtesgaden area, where later the Nazis made their large homes. In his diary he describes his adventures in this area in exactly the way that was popular with the German youth of that period. All of this would have increased his popularity, had he taken over the country and run it in place of Hitler.

When World War I broke out, he enlisted in the infantry but was fascinated by the fighter planes he saw at a nearby aerodrome, so he switched to the Air Force and rapidly became famous as a daring fighter pilot. He was noted for his chivalrous conduct towards disabled opponents. When the supreme hero of German aviation, Baron von Richthofen, was killed, Göring was appointed to replace him in his command, over the heads of several other worthy candidates. This caused some resentment toward him, but he was so daring and successful that he became a national hero. When the war ended, he refused to surrender his fighter planes but instead flew them back to Germany.

After the war, Göring tried to advance the cause of commercial aviation and went to Scandinavia to put on air shows and promote airlines. There he met the Baroness Carin von Kantzow, of the von Fock family. He convinced her to divorce her husband and marry him (figs. 31 & 32). She and her husband had already been on the point of divorce. After their marriage, she persuaded him to return to Munich and attend the university, especially for education in political science.

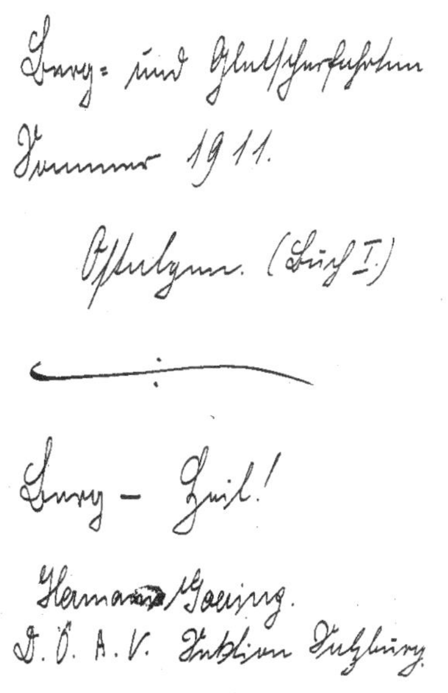

Fig 29—Göring loved mountain climbing as a youth
Göring's mountain-climbing route up the side of this very sheer wall was typical of his weekend recreational jaunts. Crampons, pitons and ropes were often necessary. His favorite very rugged mountains were in the same area around Berchtesgaden where the Nazis later made their palatial homes. He had photographs of himself like this in his diary of 1911.

Fig 28—Göring's diary of mountain and glacier tours, summer 1911
Eastern Alps (Book I)
Good Mountaineering!
Hermann Göring
German-Austrian Alpine Club
Section on Salzburg
Evan Lattimer Collection.

During this time he met Hitler and participated in Hitler's 1923 abortive march to take over the Bavarian government in Munich by force. Hitler's group included not only Göring but another war hero, General Ludendorff. Hitler never thought the police would fire on these two distinguished figures but they did, wounding Göring severely in the thigh. He was smuggled away for medical care, but Hitler was arrested and put in the Landsberg Prison where he wrote *Mein Kampf* with the help of Rudolf Hess, who volunteered to come and share his prison term.

Göring's Drug Addictions

Göring's pain was so severe after being shot that he became addicted to morphine during this period. During his convalescence, Hitler persuaded him to go to Italy and try to convince Mussolini to join forces with the German Nazis. He spent a good deal of time at the Brittania Hotel in Venice, run by an admirer and financed by Carin's mother, but Mussolini's advisors rebuffed him. His wife, now the former Baroness, finally persuaded him to return to Sweden with her and undergo a cure for his addiction. This consisted of his being placed in a locked ward, which was the standard

[handwritten diary text]

Fig 30—From Göring's mountain climbing Diary of 1911
Evan Lattimer Collection.

Fig 31—Carin and Hermann in his beloved mountains
The baroness Carin Von Kantzow, his new wife, had had tuberculosis and was not up to climbing but did enjoy beautiful scenery. Here the two of them are relaxing in the mountain climbing country. Evan Lattimer Collection.

Fig 32—Carin rests by a mountain shrine
Carin's tuberculosis made it difficult for her to breathe easily at high altitudes, but she wanted to please her Hermann. Evan Lattimer Collection.

Fig 33—A slender Göring in the early Nazi days
Wearing his medals as a war hero, plus an early Nazi armband, Göring cut a trim and handsome figure. After things began to crumble and he fell out of favor with Hitler, he began to eat compulsively. By the time of his marriage to Emmy in 1935 he was grotesquely obese.

technique in Sweden at that time, and was successful in curing him of his morphine addiction.

In due time he was recalled to Germany to assist Hitler in his meteoric rise to the top. Carin meanwhile deteriorated rapidly from tuberculosis and died in Sweden in 1931. Göring was so critically involved in Hitler's activities that he was not present at her bedside when she died, much to his chagrin. After the Nazis consolidated their power, however, he had her body brought to Germany on a warship and held a state funeral for her. She was buried in a special mausoleum with stained-glass windows and grand decor on Göring's feudal hunting estate, thereafter called Karinhall (fig. 34). Sadly, when the Russians overran it at the end of World War II, they defiled it and scattered Carin's bones about. These were eventually collected and taken back to the family cemetery in Stockholm by a Swedish prelate.

In 1935, Göring married the well-known German actress Emmy Sonnemann (fig. 3). They had a daughter, Edda, who grew into a handsome youngster and was five years old at the time Hermann died (fig. 35). As an infant, Edda had rebuffed Hitler (fig. 37).

Meanwhile, due to Hitler's power, Göring was appointed head of all the huge organizations mentioned earlier. This made him the second most powerful man in Germany. He entertained lavishly at Karinhall. It was here that he became Hitler's principal host of state visitors. Since he also was the Chief Huntsman and Forester for the Third Reich, he especially enjoyed the hunting lodge (fig. 39). He remained very popular with the German populace, as we saw at the end of the war at the time he was captured. Whenever he would pass a group of German prisoners of war they would all cheer him and shout *der Dicke* after him, meaning "the fat one," with obvious friendly implications.

All of these factors would have enabled him to run the German government with great efficiency and comprehension, in contrast to Hitler's capricious decisions which were often based on biases and insufficient information. He claimed that he did not approve of the concentration camp concept. His own factory workers he preferred to keep in their native countries where they could be much more efficiently utilized, even though security would be more difficult. This was in keeping with Speer's concepts of how labor should be used.

After being cured from morphine addiction, Göring complained of pain from the many battle wounds he had received during his dogfights as a World War I fighter pilot. He said he also had begun to have pain in his teeth of a neuritis type which bothered him greatly. At this time he started taking a synthetic codeine called dihydrocodeine (or paracodein), manufactured in Germany, and found it gave him great relief. On the other hand, since it was a mild pill, he had to take a great many of them. He would pour out a hundred pills in the morning and eat them like peanuts all day long.

Not only did dihydrocodeine control his discomfort, it also obviously relaxed him to the point where his normally aggressive and tense personality did not rebel against Hitler's oppressive type of leadership. For me it was so obvious that he would have done himself and his country a great deal of good by overthrowing Hitler and replacing him, that it is easy for me to believe that it was the rosy glow induced by the codeine that kept him from being aggressive. This same speculation was expressed by others who knew him, I discovered, when he came to us at the Mondorf collecting point in Luxembourg where the prisoners were all brought during the selection process to determine who would be tried at the first large trial.

Göring brought with him a huge amount of baggage and personal effects. He had clearly expected to be interned in a neutral country the way the Kaiser had been after World War I. He had started out with seven-

Fig 34—Carin's mausoleum at Karinhall
The underground mausoleum for Carin's body, which he had built on a rise overlooking the lake near Karinhall, had stained glass windows and was very impressive. When the Russians overran it they desecrated it and scattered Carin's bones about. One of her own Swedish clergymen later came to Karinhall and collected her bones. He returned them to a burial place in the family plot in Lovo, Sweden.

Fig 35—Edda became a very attractive child
Edda, Göring's daughter grew rapidly into a handsome youngster even as the war and then the trial progressed. She was the apple of his eye. Göring had his wife bring the child to the prison several times and both seemed to benefit from it. At one point the child asked if it was true that he wore his medals in the bathtub and asked if she could see them after he was released. She asked if they tickled. He was pleased with the lack of bitterness on her part. Steven L. Carson Collection.

Fig 36—Letter to Onkel Pilli (Gen. Koerner) from Emmy and Edda
Both sign with great affection. He tried to be very helpful to them while they were in prison. Steven L. Carson Collection.

Fig 37—Baby Edda rebuffs Hitler
Here is Göring holding his handsome little daughter Edda and trying to get the child to accept Hitler's vain attempts to be friendly. She was rejecting his advances, much to the embarrassment of her mother and father and the discomfiture of Hitler, which is obvious.

ADOLF HITLER

BERLIN, im April 1942

Fig 38—Hitler's thank-you note
It is dated April 1 1942 to thank "Frau Reichsmarshall" for entertaining him at Karinhall, even in spite of Edda's rejection of him. Hitler did not interact well with children. Evan Lattimer Collection.

Nehme meinen Geburtstag zum Anlaß, Ihnen und der Frau Reichsmarschall sowie an allen Beteiligten auf Karinhall für das Entgegen kommen mit so warmer Empfindung für mich, meinen Dank auszusprechen.

Fig 39—Göring as head huntsman of the Third Reich
Hermann Göring in his costume as the head huntsman of the Third Reich. He is wearing one of our pairs of his huge leather "knickers" of very soft, very good quality chamois-type leather.

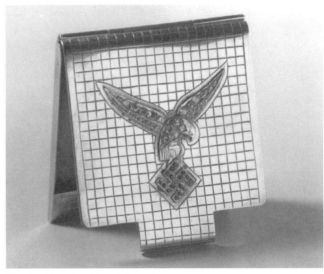

Fig 40—Göring' gold match-book cover
This handsome solid gold cover for a "book" of paper matches, had on it the Luftwaffe eagle, in diamonds. The eagle is carrying in its claws a Swastika set with rubies. This was given to another guard officer (Lt. Sanford) who Göring had worked hard to "butter-up." We have notes written to Lt. Sanford from Göring asking permission for Göring to get from the baggage room, his large blue leather-covered notebook, his sponge, comb, mouthwash and shaving materials (Fig. 49). He certainly got the distinctive blue notebook, with which he later appeared in court. He obviously knew he would not get his entire toilet case, with its scissors and razors, but in getting the notebook without causing any trouble, he "opened-the-door" to the concept of easy and legitimate access to his baggage. He was disappointed when Sanford left Nuremberg to go home, but easily made other friends in Dr. Kelley and Lt. Wheelis. He could be very charming, and was very interesting in his conversations, so he could attract anyone he chose to work on. Evan Lattimer Collection.

Fig 41—Göring's gold seal ring
Göring's seal ring commemorating his ascension to the post of Reichminister President. It bears his family crest with the familiar raised mailed fist and has goldsmith's marks on the back. Göring had seal rings made for each of his high government posts. Evan Lattimer Collection.

Fig 42—Göring's marzipan moulds
Göring favored rich marzipan as a dessert, and these were in a velvet box, obviously much used by his cooks. Several were missing, probably in use at the time of his arrest at Hitler's orders. Evan Lattimer Collection.

(Below) Fig 44—Göring's gold tableware
One gold fork bears the handsome decoration of a woodland bird. It does not compete with Hitler's silverware but it is golden, whereas Hitler's was only silver. The other fork bears Göring's crest. Evan Lattimer Collection.

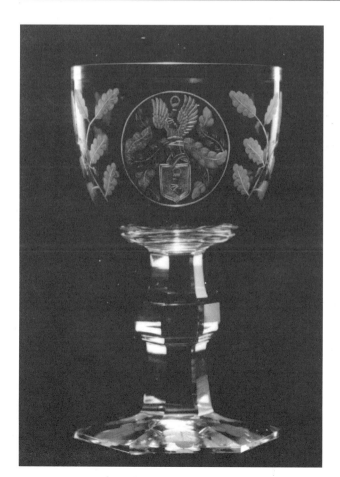

(Left) Fig 43—Göring's crystal ware
Crystal glasses of the finest quality, etched with his family crest, were in the wreckage of his house, on his personal train and in the mass of fine household equipment he brought with him when he assumed he would go into exile, as had the Kaiser in World War I. Evan Lattimer Collection.

Fig 45—Göring's plates (two)
Dinnerware made by the Sevres firm (left) in France, of the finest quality, was abundantly decorated with gold leaf and bore the Göring family crest. A new edition of this china was presented to him on his 50th birthday and was carried by him in quantity in his convoy of vehicles at the time he surrendered to the American Army. Also shown above (right) is a white plate with its coat-of-arms. Evan Lattimer Collection.

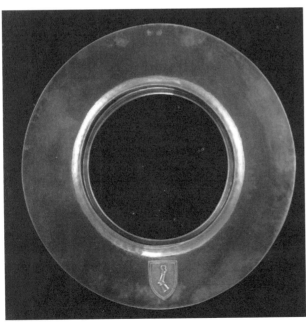

Fig 46—Göring's silver wine caddy
A hallmarked silver wine bottle caddy, bearing Göring's familiar coat-of-arms with the mailed fist. Evan Lattimer Collection.

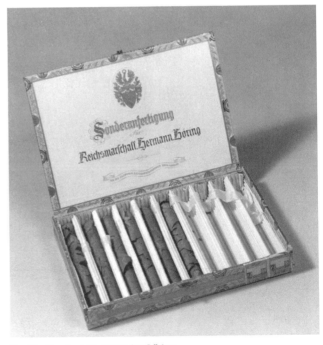

Fig 47—Handmade cigars for Göring
The box is beautifully decorated with his coat of arms and these very special cigars are extra long, in keeping with his exalted status. Evan Lattimer Collection.

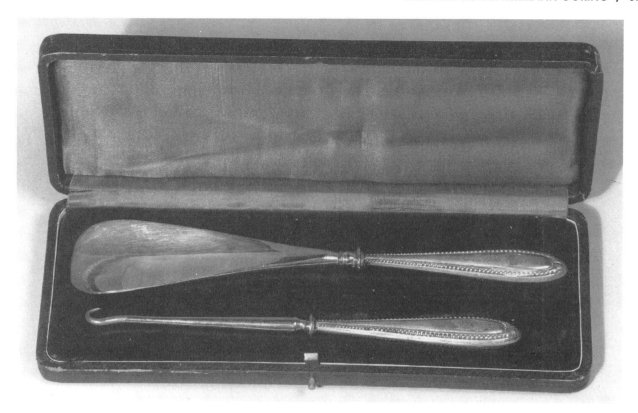

Fig 48—Göring's silver button hook and shoehorn
This shoehorn and button hook set, bearing his family crest, was part of his gear in his toilet case. Evan Lattimer Collection.

Fig 49—Göring's monocle
This is Göring's monocle which he occasionally affected. It was broken when retrieved from his personal train. The magnification is minus 1.00. Evan Lattimer Collection.

Fig 50—Göring's glasses
He disliked wearing his glasses and had not bothered to get the bow fixed. Evan Lattimer Collection.

Fig 51—Göring's Berchtesgaden villa wrecked by British bombs

At the end of the war, after the early-warning network had been destroyed and there was no German Air Force, the British came over in broad daylight and bombed the houses of Hitler, Göring and Bormann into wreckage. Here you see Göring's villa after a bomb-hit. Only the underground air-raid shelters were left intact. With the breakdown of the early-warning communication system there was no time to fill the valley with smoke, as had always been done successfully in the past, to hide the buildings.

Fig 52—Göring's huge suitcase was full of paracodeine

This expensive leather suitcase, with his initials on the side, was one of 17 pieces of luggage he had, when captured. This one was full of pills of the synthetic narcotic "paracodeine." He was consuming 100 pills of it each day, eating them like peanuts, all day long. It can be seen in photo of the prison baggage room (Fig. 91). Evan Lattimer Collection.

teen vehicles filled with all manner of luxurious trappings such as crystal ware, ornate linens, silver, and other accouterments for regal living (figs. 53-62). As it turned out, Göring liked American things. He had an American Smith and Wesson revolver (fig. 22) and a Stetson hat (figs. 65-67). One of his large handsome leather suitcases, embossed with his initials, contained what was probably the world's entire supply of dihydrocodeine, since it was produced only in Germany. The hundreds of thousands of tablets would have lasted Göring the rest of his life.

A sample of the drug was sent to the laboratories in Washington, where it was determined that the dose was relatively small and that withdrawing from it fairly quickly would probably not induce a severe reaction. It was therefore decided to cut him down to twenty pills in the morning and twenty pills at night and then gradually to reduce the amount by one pill each day, in each group. As soon as he discovered this reduction he complained bitterly to the authorities, but the die had been cast. Then he had a sudden attack of tachycardia (rapid heartbeat) after a lightning strike just outside his window. His reaction was so severe that Colonel Andrus feared it would be blamed on the drug reduction, which was therefore suspended. He went back to his eighteen pills in the morning and eighteen at night, for a period of several weeks until it was determined

that his electrocardiogram was normal. Thereafter, the reduction was again resumed and he was completely off the drug by mid-August 1945, the time of his transfer to Nuremberg.

Although Göring complained bitterly of the neuritis and pains that returned when he was off the drug, Dr. Kelley was very successful in appealing to his vanity by convincing him that he had the strength of character to get off the drug anyway, whereas some of the weaker types (such as Ribbentrop, whom Göring despised) would not have had this strength. He was simultaneously being cut back on his rations to the point that he was losing weight very quickly. As a consequence he was far better off physically and made a much better appearance, all of which flattered him.

It was obvious Göring was very amenable to psychological encouragement by Dr. Kelley. However in his analysis of Göring, Kelley was fairly pessimistic about the future. He said that personalities like Göring, who wanted instant gratification, were very likely to drift back into drug abuse, especially if they were returned to places of power where they could control what was being done for them or to them. When he was off the drug, Göring was so brilliant in court that it was indeed impressive: the increase in his mental agility and astuteness was obvious, and quite remarkable. Had he displaced Hitler, Göring's biggest problem would have

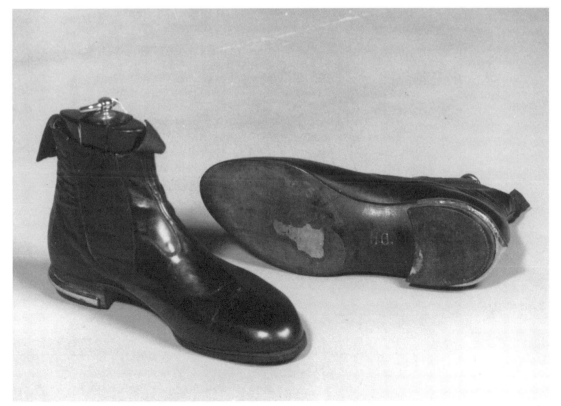

Fig 53—Göring's fine shoes
Göring's "congress-style" (or jodphur style) "boots." These beautifully made shoes also had a tiny decorative silver-colored spur on each heel in keeping with Goring's tendency to embellish everything he had. They are size 9 by American standards. Evan Lattimer Collection.

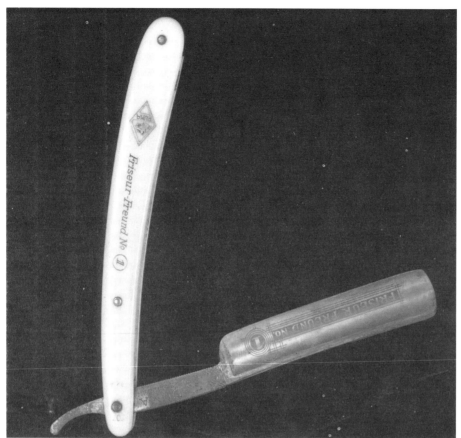

Fig 54—Göring's razor
This is a straight razor with which Göring was shaved every day when he was in his own private train. It was a Friseur-Freund and No. 1.
Evan Lattimer Collection.

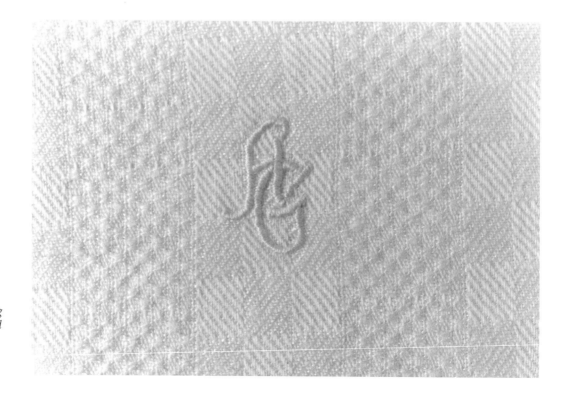

Fig 55—Göring's mono-grammed linen
Everything that Göring had was monogrammed one way or another.
Evan Lattimer Collection.

Fig 56—Göring's gray silk hose
They are of the finest quality and accommodated his size 9 feet and his enormous calves. Evan Lattimer Collection.

Fig 57—Göring's undershorts
These enormous silken undershorts are of superior quality, with blue piping around the edges. Evan Lattimer Collection.

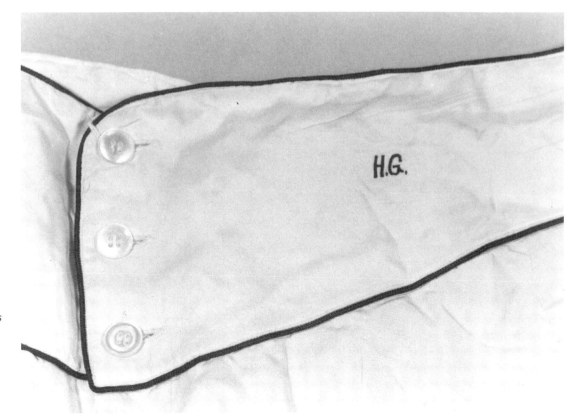

Fig 58—Göring's necktie
Like most of the Nazis, Göring used a pre-tied, military-type necktie with tabs to go under his collar. In this, he was for once following the example of Hitler. Evan Lattimer Collection.

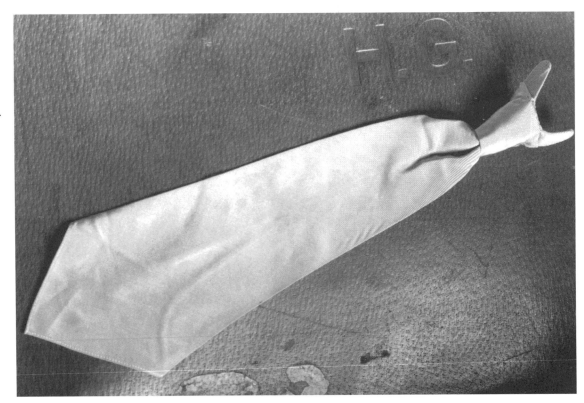

Fig 59—One of Göring's mono- grammed handker- chiefs
One of Göring's expensive handker- chiefs monogrammed with his initials and again of very fine material. He left some of these behind in the outgoing laun- dry just before he committed suicide. Evan Lattimer Collection.

Fig 60—Göring's night shirt
One of Göring's enormous night shirts, removed from the sleeping quarters of his private train. Evan Lattimer Collection.

(Left) Fig 62—Göring's shoulder boards
His various types of shoulder board and collar-tabs, showing his Reichsmarshall's baton, were made of the finest materials, as were all of his many uniforms and accessories. Evan Lattimer Collection.

(Above) Fig 61—Göring protests his drug reduction
In a handwritten note dated 5/28/45 addressed to "First Lieutenant" Göring writes as follows: "I beg of you to see to it that there will be no further shortening of my pill ration, but that I receive the 20 tablets each time. I have been taking three times (3X) this dose daily for many years. The restriction to one third is already now a terrible burden for me and is the cause of some very unpleasant hours of nerve pain every morning and evening. Every further decrease would exacerbate this condition. I want to make these facts known to you confidentially." He just signs it Göring. This was written after he had discovered not only the gross reduction in pills, but that the number was being reduced still further each day. Dr. Kelley finally persuaded him that it was the best course for him to get him off the drugs and that because of his strong character he would be able to stand this program, whereas weaker characters like Ribbentrop and Streicher would not be able to. This pleased Göring, who then cooperated. Evan Lattimer Collection.

Fig 63—Göring grew progressively thinner in prison

Göring now took great pride and satisfaction in his ability to shed the enormous amount of weight he had gained in the past few years, due to his frustrations. He lost weight so fast that there were times when I did not recognize him, after being away for several days. Not only did his clothing hang down on him; his skin hung down in folds. It was necessary to have the prison tailor take in his uniform progressively, as the time went on. He recognized the merit of losing the weight, and participated with enthusiasm. He commented at times that it was not difficult to lose weight on the U.S. Army food, in a sly aside.

(Below) Fig 65—Göring with his Stetson hat

Here he is walking with his adjutant, General Koerner who was a firm family friend. Edda refers to him in her note in Fig. 66 as "Onkel Pilli." Mrs. Göring refers to him as "Pili" in her notes. Evan Lattimer Collection.

(Left) Fig 64—Göring's giant hammered silver-framed portrait of Hitler

While others had silver-framed portraits of Hitler, Göring's family crest below, and the Nazi eagle above. It can be seen in Appendix One, Fig. 3, when he was trying to impress the Lindberghs. Evan Lattimer Collection.

Fig 66—Göring's favorite brown Stetson hat
This hat with the somewhat wide brim characteristic of that period bears the label "John B. Stetson Company, 3x Beaver." There is a small picture of a beaver standing up against the end of the label. A second label in the hat says "C.W. Borchort, Hoflieferant Berlin, W." The size is approximately 7 but may have been slightly larger in its original state. Göring added the small Alpine-style pin seen on the left side of the hat band. Göring liked many American things, including the Smith and Wesson revolver which he carried as his personal side-arm. Evan Lattimer Collection.

Fig 67—Here Göring is wearing the same Stetson hat
But here he is seated on his horse. He liked to wear the front of the brim slightly turned up and the back slightly turned down, which gave it a little more rakish appearance. The horse is being plied with lumps of sugar held by a servant, possibly as a reward for carrying Göring's enormous weight of almost 300 pounds. The horse is extraordinarily large and sturdy. Evan Lattimer Collection.

Fig 68—Emmy and Edda bid farewell to Hermann
In the courtyard of the castle at Fischhorn, they watch Göring depart to surrender to the American army in 1945.

been his vulnerability to becoming re-addicted, once he was back in absolute power.

If Göring had not been on the drug during the last couple years of the war, his natural aggressiveness and capabilities would have stimulated him to depose Hitler and take over the running of the huge empire Hitler had conquered. It was his drug habit that kept him from doing anything along these lines, I believe.

Göring's Medical Condition

Göring had been remarkably healthy throughout most of his life, though his body was peppered with scars from machine gun bullet wounds and secondary missile wounds from his days as a fighter pilot. He could tell you in detail where he had gotten each one of his wounds. Late in the war he had had one episode of generalized, lymph node enlargement, accompanied by a fever which receded without incident and the cause

of which was not obvious. His obesity was his glaring physical problem. It had begun when Hitler started to turn against him. Göring weighed at least 300 pounds at the time of his 1935 wedding to Emmy Sonnemann. Despite that, he still permitted himself to be photographed in tennis clothing but wearing baggy trousers (fig. 4). He never allowed himself to be photographed in swimming attire, however, where his supportive belts would have been visible. His blood pressure was normal when he was captured, but tended to rise severely during any excitement. He also began to have episodes of cardiac palpitation and tachycardia, which gave him substernal pain and which he characterized as "heart attacks." With his weight, of at least 300 pounds, on a frame of 5'7", he was truly grotesque. He could not even see his shoes, much less bend over to fasten them. This was very embarrassing to him and Dr. Kelley was very successful in flattering him that losing weight was essential for his appearance as well as for his health. He agreed to this and did indeed undertake a rigorous diet, with the loss of approximately 100 pounds during the year of his imprisonment (fig. 63).

There is still another very important connection with Göring's medical condition, namely his claims of an alleged skin condition, which made it possible for him to accomplish his brilliant suicidal maneuver.

Göring's Downfall

It was Göring's own impatience that very nearly led to his downfall just before the German surrender. He had been informed by Generals Christian and Koeller that Hitler had made a statement in the bunker in Berlin on April 22 that Göring, rather than he himself, would be the best person to negotiate a surrender. With Hitler in no condition to lead, knowing that the command structure was disintegrating rapidly, Göring made the nearly fatal mistake of wiring Hitler (on April 23) as to whether he might be allowed to take over the country earlier, in view of Hitler's vow to meet his end in Berlin. This message could not have arrived at a worse time. Göring's enemy, Hitler's secretary Martin Bormann, knew that Hitler did not intend to commit suicide quite that early and intercepted Göring's message. He took it to Hitler, interpreting it as a coup attempt on the part of Göring. He presented it in the worst possible way, so that Hitler flew into a rage and demanded that Göring be stripped of all his state duties and that his position as Hitler's designated successor now be stricken from the record. He said he did not want Göring shot just then, because of Göring's many previous good works on behalf of Hitler.

Bormann, who was sending the messages in and out,

Fig 69—Göring's armored limousine
Göring drove to surrender to the American advance scouts, in this armored limousine. He was followed by a long convoy of trucks filled with luxurious trappings. This was a Daimler-Benz A. G. limousine. Evan Lattimer Collection.

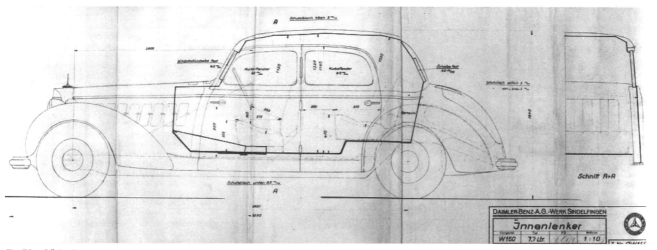

Fig 70—Göring's car armor
Outline of the armor plating (black-line), plus an indication of the extreme thickness of the bullet-proof windows and windshield. The windows could not be opened so a primitive air conditioning system was manufactured for this car. Evan Lattimer Collection.

Fig 71—Göring's car armor
This shows the very heavy armor floor plate for the passenger compartment. This was a protection against driving over a landmine in the road. Evan Lattimer Collection.

Fig 72—Göring's car armor
This shows the extent of the armor plate around the passengers. These photographs and the blueprints for this car were kept in the glove compartment and were captured along with the car. Evan Lattimer Collection.

Fig 73—Göring surrenders
A corsetted Göring had driven to meet the advancing American scouts and was brought to General Stack at Zell-am-See via Fischorn castle. Lt. Shapiro found his convoy stuck in a traffic jam at Radstat, near his castle at Mauterndorf.

then sent a separate message, pretending that it came from Hitler, ordering Göring and his family shot if the Führer died. Luckily for Göring, the commander of the garrison at Berchtesgaden, Colonel Bernhard Frank, went to him and showed him the message about making him a prisoner and stripping him of his rank. Frank cleverly asked Göring what he thought he should do. Göring said, "Well, you have to obey orders." Colonel Frank realized that of all the Nazis, Göring was the most likely to have any favorable contact with the Allied command and would be able to negotiate a more satisfactory surrender. He therefore decided against shooting or imprisoning Göring and removed him to Göring's own castle, at Mauterndorf, because of the rapid approach of the Americans and French towards Berchtesgaden.

Meanwhile, Frau Göring, hearing of this threat, went out through a subterranean passageway and summoned Göring's paratrooper bodyguards to come and rescue him. This they did, relieving Colonel Frank of his responsibilities and worries. Göring then started out on his own in his armored limousine and convoy to seek the advancing Americans, worried that Mussolini's fate might befall them. The convoy became bogged down in the great traffic jam of retreating and surrendering troops, and he was eventually picked up by reconnaissance units from the U.S. Seventh Army, south of Berchtesgaden. They brought him to the castle at Fischorn, where he was held until word came to bring him to Seventh Army headquarters at Kitzbuhel. His wife and child were left behind (fig. 68). After one night of soldier-to-soldier celebration of the end of the war with the conquering U.S. Seventh Army officers, Göring was then turned over to the regular POW sys-

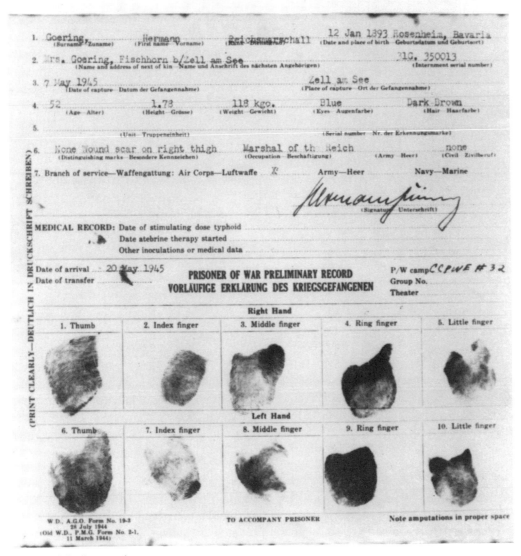

Fig 74—Göring's P.O.W. detention report

It has Göring's fingerprints when captured. It indicates that he was captured at Zell-am-See, (in Bavaria). Actually, he was coming to meet the Americans, on a highway south of Zell-am-See. Göring's official trial photograph for identification purpose, is not as handsome as he usually demanded as a Reichsmarshall, but this ignominy was the same for all the prisoners. Evan Lattimer Collection.

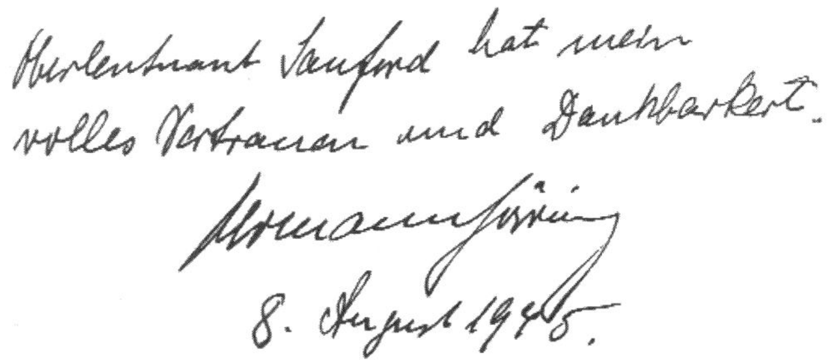

Oberleutnant Sanford hat mein volles Vertrauen und Dankbarkeit.

Hermann Göring

8. August 1945.

Fig 75—Göring butters up guard officer Lt. Sanford
This note was on the back of a photograph of Göring, his child and his wife, was inscribed to 1st Lt. Stanford with his "full trust and gratitude," and dated Aug. 8, 1945. This was part of Göring's policy of gaining the friendship of guard officers who might later let him into the baggage room, where his poison was hidden. Unfortunately for Göring, Lt. Stanford left for home well before the trial ended. Göring covered his chagrin with this pleasant note. Evan Lattimer Collection.

tem and stripped of his rank badges, decorations, and privileges (fig. 75). The newspapers made a great uproar about the friendly reception he had been given when he first surrendered and that precipitated his being treated as a common prisoner.

At this time he was so fat that he could not bend over to pull his boots on and off, so his orderly had to be given back to him for a while until he lost weight. Eventually he was transferred to the detention center at Mondorf, in Luxembourg, where he was held until a decision was made to transfer him to Nuremberg for trial, along with 21 others.

Göring's Spectacular Suicide

The important Nazis all had ampoules of cyanide contained in protective brass coverings made from old rifle cartridge cases. (The markings on the base of the one used by Göring showed that the cartridge had been made by Finower Industries, GmbH in August, 1939.) These were carefully machined with a push-on cover and an expansion groove. They were secure and yet could be opened easily when needed. Both ends of the brass container were sharply knurled so they could be gripped easily when the cover was to be twisted off. Nine hundred fifty of them were delivered from the Sachsenhausen concentration camp and distributed at the Reich Chancellery during the last year of the war, according to researcher and author Ben Swearingen. Ostensibly they were for Reich officials who might be at risk of being captured, especially by the Russians, and might prefer suicide to capture. Himmler used one of the two that he had on him when captured by the British; Goebbels and his wife committed suicide and

put their six children to death with these capsules; and, Hitler and Eva Braun also used them. Shortly before he committed suicide, Hitler wanted to see the capsules' effectiveness demonstrated on his large Alsatian dog, Blondi, who was in the bunker with them. One of his men put the glass ampoule between Blondi's teeth and pushed her teeth together so that the ampoule broke in her mouth. Blondi dropped dead at his feet. Hitler observed this but said that in addition, he wanted to shoot himself and undertook to arrange to do that as well.

When Himmler was captured by the British, two of the brass cyanide capsule containers were found in his pockets. One of them had the cyanide capsule in it and the other was empty. This prompted them to search his possessions and his body carefully but they could not find the missing capsule. They then called for a medical officer who tried to examine his mouth and thought he detected the ampoule lateral to Himmler's upper teeth. When he tried to introduce his finger to feel for the capsule, Himmler bit the capsule and died instantly. There are those, like Gestapo General Walter Schellenberg, who thought that Himmler had been told about Hitler's obvious Parkinsonism by a neurologist friend. He may have therefore been tempted to try to make a separate peace through Count Bernadotte so that he might succeed Hitler. Hitler learned about this and raged against him as well as Göring, in his final hours.

Göring had been observed to be toying with several of these brass, cyanide capsule containers during the last weeks of the war. When he surrendered to the Allies, he had one of the brass, ampoule containers in a can of loose coffee crystals where it was found very

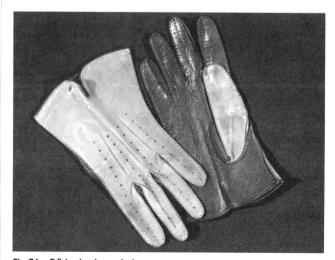

Fig 76—Göring's elegant gloves
A pair of fine gloves which Göring gave to Lt. Wheelis as a future gesture of goodwill. They are beautifully made of the softest leather. Evan Lattimer Collection.

(Left) Fig 77—Göring's valuable chronometer stopwatch

A very expensive wristwatch given to Lt. Wheelis by Göring. This is an aviator's chronometer with small stopwatch dials to help with aerial navigation in the days when the pilot had to do it himself, rather than depend on the radio. It bears the name "Universal" Geneve, and is also a large stopwatch in addition to being a chronometer. It has Göring's name engraved on the back in script. It was listed on an inventory of valuables dated December, 1945 (Fig. 32) which Göring had checked into the baggage room and was mentioned by Colonel Andrus in his list of things Göring brought with him. During the investigation of Göring's suicide, it was stated by one of the guard officers, that the things on Andrus' list were still in the baggage room. The watch was in the possession of Lt. Wheelis, even at that time, making a mockery of the checking by the staff. The watch has a large pigskin band and had obviously had much wear by Göring and later by Wheelis. A gold "Mont-Blanc" fountain pen, with Göring's name on it, was also listed. Both the watch and the pen were apparently given to Lt. Wheelis by Göring. These gifts were "friendly gestures," to assure Wheelis' continuing "good will." Wheelis wore the watch fairly openly, at Nuremberg, among his friends, and enjoyed the notoriety it got him, as a "pal" of the "great Göring." (Col. Andrus did not know he had it.) They hit it off very well, with Göring clearly "buttering-up" Wheelis, hoping for future favors from him. Evan Lattimer Collection.

Fig 78—Göring's name on back of his watch
This was in "script" lettering and was unmistakable. Evan Lattimer Collection.

quickly by the guards. This caused everybody to relax, because they thought they had found his only suicide capsule. He had also hidden two of the capsules in jars of opaque face cream in his case of toilet articles. It was this skin cream to which he asked to have access at various times, obviously as a dry run. He carefully developed a long succession of requests for his skin cream and it was apparently given to him whenever he requested it. Lt. Sanford had obliged him earlier, as had Dr. Kelley. He would return it promptly so that there would be no problem. The mechanism for access to anything in the baggage room was easy and quite clear. The prisoner would make a request to the officer of the guard, who would pass on the request to the baggage room officer, who would arrange for the access.

During the last weeks of their incarceration, there was an obvious relaxation in the tension of frequent surprise inspections of the defendants' cells. If one of them wanted access to his skin cream, there would be very little doubt that the request would be granted, especially since the "poor devils" only had a few days to live and there would be no point in denying them a last comfort of this moderate, innocent type. After the suicide, all of the guards who had the baggage room key in their charge at any time during the last two weeks were interrogated. All of them signed an affidavit that they had let no one in the baggage room. It was perfectly obvious that they would deny this, under the circumstances. It was also obvious that it was a mass signing of the affidavits, which were demanded by the committee investigating the suicide. We do know, however, that the officer in charge of the baggage room during that final period was one Lt. Jack Wheelis (fig. 79).

Wheelis was a large, rugged, friendly type from Texas, who enjoyed talking to Göring about their mutual hunting interests and to whom Göring gave various mementos, such as a pair of fancy gloves (fig. 76) and a handsome wristwatch (fig.77), which was listed among Göring's valuables still in the baggage room (fig. 80). This was indeed a very valuable chronometer with Göring's name on the back (fig. 78). Wheelis wore it publicly and was quite proud of it (fig. 79). At the same time, the inventory of Göring's valuables in the baggage room continued to list the watch even at the time Wheelis was wearing it (fig. 80). Göring became very friendly with Wheelis and wrote him notes about their friendship (fig. 89) and asked him to transfer money to his wife, Emmy, in the routine manner (fig. 81). Normally such a request would have gone through the commandant of the garrison, Colonel Andrus.

During the investigation into Göring's suicide, everyone denied that he had had access to the baggage room, though Wheelis had a note from Göring asking for his blue notebook (fig. 82). Later we all saw Göring

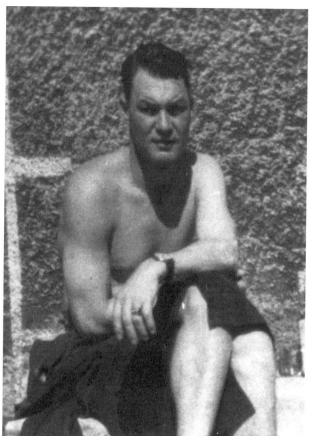

Fig 79—Lt. Wheelis proudly wearing Göring watch
Wheelis was proud of this gift from the great Göring. Col. Andrus and the chief prison guard officer did not know he had it.

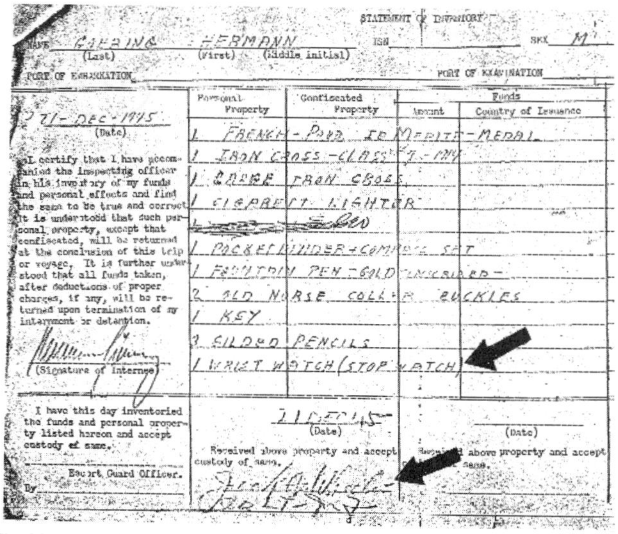

STATEMENT OF INVENTORY

NAME GÖRING HERMANN ISN SEX M
(Last) (First) (Middle initial)

PORT OF EMBARKATION PORT OF EXAMINATION

21-DEC-1945
(Date)

I certify that I have accompanied the inspecting officer in his inventory of my funds and personal effects and find the same to be true and correct. It is understood that such personal property, except that confiscated, will be returned at the conclusion of this trip or voyage. It is further understood that all funds taken, after deductions of proper charges, if any, will be returned upon termination of my internment or detention.

(Signature of Internee)

Personal Property	Confiscated Property	Funds: Amount	Funds: Country of Issuance
1 FRENCH - POUR LE MERITE - MEDAL			
1 IRON CROSS - CLASS 1 - 1914			
1 GREEK IRON CROSS			
1 CIGARETTE LIGHTER			
[illegible]			
1 POCKET BINDER + COMPASS SET			
1 FOUNTAIN PEN - GOLD INSCRIBED -			
2 OLD HORSE COLLAR BUCKLES			
1 KEY			
3 GILDED PENCILS			
1 WRIST WATCH (STOP WATCH)			

I have this day inventoried the funds and personal property listed hereon and accept custody of same.

Escort Guard Officer.
By

21 DEC 45
(Date)
Received above property and accept custody of same.

(Date)
Received above property and accept same.

Fig 80—Inventory of Göring's Valuables
Here, on 21 Dec. 1945, Wheelis has signed (arrow) attesting to the fact that this list of valuables is in his custody. Göring's watch (arrow) is listed as still in the baggage room. Evan Lattimer Collection.

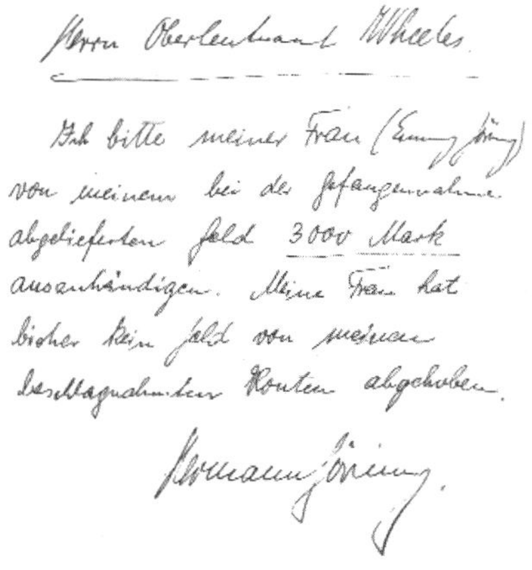

Herrn Oberleutnant Wheeles

Ich bitte meiner Frau (Emmy Göring) von meinem bei der Gefangennahme abgelieferten Geld 3000 Mark auszuhändigen. Meine Frau hat bisher kein Geld von meinen beschlagnahmten Konten abgehoben.

Hermann Göring.

Fig 81—Göring asks Wheelis to transfer money to his wife Emmy
Less than a month before his death, Göring asks Wheelis to arrange for the transfer of 3,000 marks from his impounded funds, to his wife Emmy Göring. This was an established procedure but it is interesting that he appealed to his friend Wheelis rather than to the Commandant Colonel Andrus. This note was written September 18, 1946. Evan Lattimer Collection.

in court with the blue notebook, so it was obvious that he had had access to the baggage room despite the denials. Dr. Gilbert, our prison psychologist, stated firmly that he knew Göring had access to the baggage room in the days just before his suicide. At the time of his suicide (two hours before the time scheduled for the hanging), he had a note in his hand addressed to Colonel Andrus indicating that even if we had found this last capsule, he had another one in reserve in his jar of skin cream (fig. 90). It was indeed there when the cream was probed.

It seemed to me most likely that he had two in the jars of face cream and used one, leaving the other, about which he could write us his sarcastic note. There were many speculations about where he might have hidden the capsule, including in a hollow tooth or in his umbilicus. Neither of these is tenable because the capsule container was much too large. It was approximately two inches in length and approximately one-half inch in diameter—much too big for a tooth or his umbilicus (fig. 85). Another theory was that he had a subcutaneous tunnel built for the capsule, but I can attest to the fact that he had no such subcutaneous tunnel on his body. It was also thought he might have kept it in his rectum. While it is possible that he might have done so just for moments at a time, I say, that it is much too jagged on the ends for the rectum to tolerate it more than a few minutes. It was likely to have been ejected involuntarily. Göring would have discovered that very quickly and would not have taken that chance.

There were some crusts on the outside of the capsule, which an Army laboratory speculated might possibly

Fig 82—Göring asks for (and got) his blue notebook

A note from Göring asking for his blue notebook and toilet articles from the baggage room. He got the notebook, with which he appeared in court later, following this perfectly legitimate request. Thus we know he had access to his baggage. He did not expect to get his toilet articles, naturally, with its scissors and nail files. Evan Lattimer Collection.

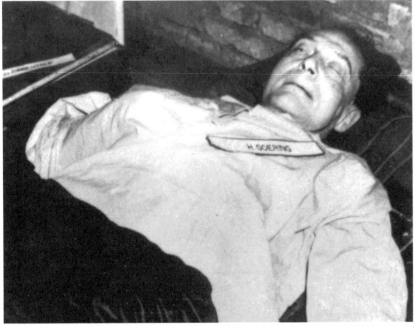

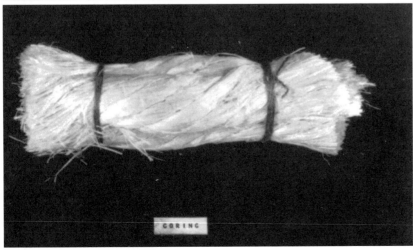

Fig 83—Göring lying dead from cyanide

Only hours after his death, from biting his cyanide capsule, Göring's body was photographed lying on his coffin, as were the bodies of all of the other dead prisoners. Within hours they were all cremated. (Below) A segment of the rope which Sgt. Wood had fashioned into the noose which would have hanged Göring. He cheated the hangman by committing suicide with poison and the noose was burned with his body. Sgt. Wood had carefully cut off a 2 inch segment from the ropes of each of the men who were hanged, as his souvenir. This one was from the rope that was supposed to have hanged Göring. Evan Lattimer Collection.

Fig 84—Uncollected laundry bearing the names of the dead men
This remained in small piles in the baggage room. These were generally of very modest quality except for those of Göring. His handsome monogrammed handkerchiefs can be seen in the lower center, with a note bearing his name in his handwriting. Items belonging to Kaltenbrunner, Keitel, Seyss-Inquart and Ribbentrop and others are visible. The contrast between Göring's clothing and the clothing of the others was impressive.

Uncollected laundry of some of the executed war criminals laid out in the prison laundry room.
(Popperfoto)

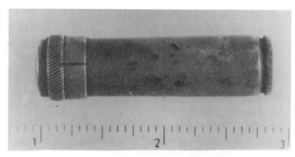

Fig 85—Göring's suicide ampoule container
This contained the ampoule of cyanide he used to kill himself in his cell. It was made at the Mauthausen Concentration Camp from an 8mm Mauser rifle cartridge case (from the Finower Arsenal). It measured 1-3/4 inches by 1/2 inch and had sharp serration's on the ends which would have irritated the rectum if inserted. Evan Lattimer Collection.

Fig 86—Göring asks for headache pills
A note from Göring to Dr. Pflücker asking, "Please, some medicine for my headache!" (as he often did). He would not have hesitated to ask for hemorrhoidal salve. Evan Lattimer Collection.

have been dried fecal material, but this is by no means certain. If Göring had put this sharp-edged object in his rectum, he would shortly have been asking for hemorrhoidal ointment to soothe the irritation. He was never hesitant to ask for medicines, as for headaches (fig. 86). There were no facilities for washing in the cell. To swallow such a capsule container and recover it from the feces repeatedly would have been difficult to the point of being impractical. It is my belief that Göring had his system of hiding the capsules in his skin cream in place; it worked well, and he stayed with it. Mr. Swearingen was of the opinion that Göring might have asked Wheelis, as a friend, to grant him this last favor. But I would think that his system was working so well that he would not have chanced Wheelis changing his mind and denying him this last favor.

Göring was the most prolific letterwriter among the prisoners and had a lot of stationery and envelopes which he used often (figs. 87 & 88). He had the capsule container in an envelope in his hand when he died and had been busy writing letters during the evening. He had access to his stationery and could easily have used it for hiding the capsule container until he needed it. He had interrogated Dr. Pflücker, the German army POW doctor we used as an interface with the prisoners, about when he thought the hangings might start. Dr. Pflücker said he gave him a vague answer that a night might seem short, under the circumstances. As Swearingen points out, Dr. Pflücker had been told at 3:00 P.M. that the hangings would start at midnight, rather than at dawn as the prisoners expected. Dr. Pflücker immediately made a visit to Göring and talked to him at some length. Mr. Swearingen speculates that at that time Dr. Pflücker told Göring or implied to Göring in some way that the hangings might start earlier, rather than at dawn. It seems obvious that Göring had learned that the hangings would start early and was prepared to adjust his plan. I suspect Dr. Pflücker felt that giving Göring this information would not really violate his trust, about which he had been so faithful up to this point.

An official investigation of Göring's suicide was conducted by officers of our own staff and they examined the scene carefully. They realized that there was an entry port for water in the rim of the toilet in Göring's cell, where the porcelain was rolled over to make a thick rim around the top of the toilet bowl. They speculated that perhaps he had hidden the capsule in that water port at some point. The danger about that hiding place was that the capsule might get dislodged and could not be retrieved when needed. Also there had been at least one unscheduled change of cells during the year of the trial, and Göring might have worried

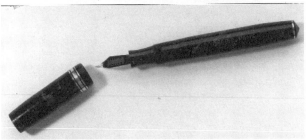

Fig 87—Göring using his much-used fountain pen
The French fountain pen (below) by Mallar (Paris) with which Göring wrote a voluminous correspondence from his cell, during 1945 and 46. He wrote far more letters then any other prisoner in the group. (Mostly to his wife). It has a mottled brown and black and gold barrel and an American gold point. I watched him writing notes with this pen, in his cell. Göring also had a very expensive gold pen by Mont Blanc, in the baggage room but gave this to the guard officer, Lt. Jack Wheelis, as part of his campaign to get into Wheelis' good graces. He needed Wheelis to get him into the baggage room to get out his jar of face cream in which he had the cyanide capsules concealed, for his suicide. When Göring's wife sold this brown and gold pen from his terminal effects, to a collector, her accompanying note says that he had to use this modest pen after the Americans "took" his gold fountain pen. This is not strictly true, since he gave many things to Wheelis, who did indeed help him at the end, to achieve his goal. This may have been inadvertent on Wheelis' part, but there is no doubt that Göring made great efforts to befriend Wheelis, with gifts including not only his (other) (gold) pen but also his very valuable aviator's watch. Wheelis' wife sold this after Wheelis died. Evan Lattimer Collection.

Fig 88—Göring's two-color pencil

A two-color "mechanical" pencil of fine workmanship. It says on it, "Weihnacten (Merry Christmas), 1938" and has a facsimilie of Göring's signature on it. Göring apparently had many of these made up to give as presents in 1938 when he found out that Hitler was giving fountain pens as Christmas presents that year. This automatic pencil will write with either red or blue "lead." While Göring gave away a great many of these as Christmas presents, he was pleased with the mechanics of it and kept some for himself. This is one that he had used but gave it to Keitel. He was fond of initialing or signing government documents and his own correspondence with a colored pencil like this, when in power. General Keitel treasured this gift from Göring at Nuremberg. His wife sold it after his death. Evan Lattimer Collection.

Fig 89—Note from Göring to Wheelis on back of this photograph of them

On the back of this photograph of himself talking to Wheelis, in the prison, (left) Göring has written the following (right) "To the great hunter from Texas, with "Weidmannsheil" (this means returning from the hunt successfully and unhurt.) The two men talked about hunting a great deal, since this was one of Wheelis' favorite preoccupations and Göring was the head huntsman of the Third Reich.

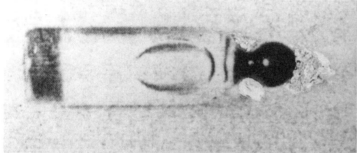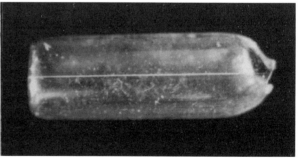

Fig 90—Göring's reserve or "backup" cyanide ampoule

On the left is the glass ampoule of cyanide from his third, or "backup" poison, which he did not have to use. Note the spherical tip of this ampoule, which was of a typical German pattern, quite different from the American ampoules of the day. On the right is the same "backup" cyanide ampoule, after the tip was broken off and the contents verified as cyanide by a U.S. Army laboratory. Evan Lattimer Collection.

that if he hid the capsules there, they would be lost to him if there was a change of cells again.

The third ampoule was taken to a nearby army laboratory and tested to be sure that it contained cyanide, which indeed it did (fig. 90). The brass capsule container that Göring had in his hand when he died (fig. 85) was kept by Colonel Hurless of the investigating team, who later sold it to Ben Swearingen. (Swearingen was canvassing all the people who were at the Nuremberg trials, in preparation for his own excellent book about the event.) Swearingen in turn sold it to me, along with the stopwatch-chronometer and the pair of nicely made gloves that Göring had given to Wheelis as indications of his goodwill. (He had purchased these items from Lt.

Wheelis's widow.) I do not see these as bribes because no direct deal was made. I see them as ways of getting into Wheelis's good graces, so that at the end, when Göring asked Wheelis for his skin cream, Wheelis would be more likely to accede without question.

After the hangings, Göring's body along with those executed was burned in a crematorium on the outskirts of Munich and the ashes quietly dumped into a tributary of the River Iser.

During the trial, Göring defended himself skillfully and vigorously, but with Hitler dead, he stood out among the defendants as the dominant one. The judges found him guilty on all four counts: of conspiracy to wage war, crimes against peace, war crimes, and crimes against humanity, and he was sentenced to death by hanging.

Thus ended the saga of this powerful figure, a gallant hero in World War I, who was so weakened by his drug addiction that he could not overthrow Hitler, as his old friends had hoped he would. Instead, he continued to kowtow to a deteriorating Hitler.

Göring's perceived brilliance in defeating Col. Andrus' boastful confidence that further suicides were impossible pleased the German populace. They had not been happy that Göring's German Air Force had failed to protect them from the Allied bombers, but they still got great satisfaction from his terminal small triumph over the Allies. Col. Andrus was devastated by the embarrassment, which plagued him for the rest of his life.

Fig 91—The baggage room at the prison in Nuremberg
On the upper shelf at the left you can see Göring's two large suitcases (one of which had been full of paracodeine) and a second smaller toilet case, his "blue notebook briefcase" and his hatbox.

CHAPTER FOUR

Rudolf Hess:
The Number-Three Nazi

Fig 1—Hess' official portrait as Hitler's deputy
It carries his confirmation of his official signature, for the court at Nuremberg. Evan Lattimer Collection.

Rudolf Hess (fig. 1) was an idealistic secretarial type, fanatical in many ways. He was dedicated to helping Hitler put his concepts in order and willing to sacrifice himself, as he did at the end. Hess suffered from total amnesia on the basis of depression and hysteria when the British sent him to us at Nuremberg. His frustration at having his so-called peace offer ignored, plus the trauma of four years of prison, were too much for him. Psychiatrist William Dunn called Hess "A dull-witted autistic psychopath with strong hypochondriacal paranoia, who officially sponsored charlatans with nature cures." His psychopathic disorders did actually impair Hess, but he also acted out his "demented" role with great relish. His appointment as the number three man in the Nazi Party was a reflection of the fact that Hitler rewarded old friends, especially when they were no threat to him.

Rudolf Hess, with his psychopathic personality, surprisingly enough was the man the largest number of official inquisitors came specifically to see. Göring may have been the star of the show, but more investigators were sent to try to figure out Hess. He was an enigma. His skill at frustrating communication, whether consciously or unconsciously, was so good that it was impossible to diagnose accurately his mental processes and activity. It appeared to me that Hess was definitely psychologically damaged when we first got him, and that he improved in many ways as the trial went on. He had so many quirks and was so good at rebuffing any kind of analysis that he was supremely hard to figure out.

Hess was born in 1894 to a wealthy German exporter who, at that time, lived in Alexandria, Egypt. Educated in both Germany and Switzerland, he joined the German Army in World War I and was wounded by a rifle bullet through the left lower chest in 1917 on the Romanian front. The wound was verified at his autopsy, despite the skepticism of some. He was hospitalized for a lengthy period but was released in time to join the Air Force and to take some training as a pilot before the war ended. Afterward, he kept his hand in as a flyer, thanks to Willy Messerschmitt.

Hess was 51 at the time the Nuremberg trial began, married, with one son. He had joined Hitler in 1920, when he was a 26 year old idealist, and was of great help to Hitler in composing purposeful directives and intelligent, lucid manuscripts. He participated in the famous march on Munich in 1923 and went into hiding after Hitler, Göring, and Ludendorff were fired upon by the police. However, he turned himself in to be incarcerated with Hitler where, in 1924, he served as Hitler's secretary and wrote most of *Mein Kampf* for him, adding to it a history of the philosophy of science and

of German conquests. Hess was mesmerized by Hitler and by his bold tactics and uncritically adopted Hitler's anti-Semitism.

Hess clearly adopted Hitler as a substitute for his dead father, and in fact, Hitler became his God. His psychiatric state was very difficult to evaluate because he never permitted any friendliness and never answered any personal questions. He continually frustrated the many psychologists and psychiatrists, including the panels of famous psychiatrists evaluating him: three English, three Russians and three American. They verified Dr. Kelley's diagnosis of a dramatic hysterical amnesia. It was their consensus that Hess possessed a strongly schizoid and psychopathic personality. Under the stress of disillusionment and imprisonment, he had developed hysterical reactions and transitory episodes of a psychotic nature. These manifestations were not present to such a degree as to warrant considering him legally incompetent. It was on this basis that he was tried and given a sentence of life imprisonment.

Dr. Kelley was certain that he could not only properly diagnose Hess but bring about an excellent clinical improvement in his condition if Hess would permit himself to be hypnotized. Surprisingly, Hess seemed agreeable to this suggestion and might have permitted it. When he was told that it might require a small amount of pentothal or other injectable sedative, that spoiled it. Hess immediately balked and would have nothing further to do with the whole idea if there were anything smacking of "truth serum" (i.e. pentothal) to be employed. Justice Jackson also objected to anything of this type, If there was any adverse reaction, Jackson felt he would be blamed for the effect on the prisoner for whom he felt responsible.

Hess refused any medical treatment that was suggested, by always asking for an additional consultant. In this way he avoided the dental work that was prescribed by the British and Russian dentists. He insisted, instead, on getting more dental consultants until he found a dentist who agreed with him and advised against having the tooth pulled. He learned that he could utilize an attack of stomach colic (which he called a gallbladder attack) to groan with pain and thus avoid participating in any situation where he was being asked to do something (fig. 3). To interrogators, he merely replied, "I don't remember." He discovered that if he said he did not know, they persisted with questions; but if he said he did not remember, they tended to leave him alone.

He had grown feebler as the war progressed and his psychopathic personality seemed to have come more to the fore. Up to that time he had been a very popular

Fig 2—Hess with Hitler

Hess is standing below Hitler in a protective posture outside the car from which Hitler is reviewing troops. He was Hitler's first ever-present secretary, ready to do the master's bidding at any time or to advise or help in any way he might be needed. He was very popular. When Hitler gripped his belt buckle with his left hand to stop his tremor, Hess did the same, just because the boss did it.

```
                                    March 11, 1938

To The
Commander of the Academy Dresden
Mr. Oberst Kriebel
Dresden N15
Marienallee 11

Dear Mr. Oberst,

    Thank you very much for your letter dated from the 3rd of this
month.  I am honestly sorry that I was not able to keep my promised
speech appointment.  A very acute and serious gallbladder illness
made it impossible for me to attend.  Naturally, I'd like to re-
spond to your wish and once I am healthy again I'll promise to keep
my speech appointment, especially since I will be able then to see
the old Regiment Adjutant.

    My own personal Adjutant will contact you regarding the items
mentioned above.

                                    Heil Hitler!

                                    I H R

                                    /signed/Hess
                                    (R. Hess)
```

Fig 3—Hess' "gallbladder" attacks as an excuse
*Hess used alleged gallbladder attacks to avoid speaking engage-
ments, even as early at 1938. In this letter he writes to his former
adjutant, apologizing for not being able to come because of a serious gallbladder attack. This was long before the trial. At his
autopsy, his gallbladder was innocent.*

```
An den
Kommandeur der Kriegsschule Dresden
Herrn Oberst K r i e b e l
D r e s d e n  N 15
Marienallee 11



    Sehr verehrter Herr Oberst,

    Haben Sie besten Dank für Ihre Zeilen vom 3. des Mo-
nats. Es hat mir aufrichtig leid getan, dass ich meinen
zugesagten Vortrag nicht zum vorgesehenen Zeitpunkt hal-
ten konnte. Eine akute Gallensache machte mir das Kommen
tatsächlich unmöglich. Gern will ich aber Ihrem Wunsche
entsprechen und so bald als angängig den Vortrag nachho-
len, umso lieber, als ich bei der Gelegenheit den alten
Regimentsadjutanten von einst begrüssen kann.

    Mein Adjutant wird sich zu gegebener Zeit mit dem Ih-
ren dieserhalb in Verbindung setzen.

                                    Heil Hitler!
                                    Ihr

                                    (R. Hess)
```

Fig 4—His original letter in German
*Note that his signature during his glory days was very short and
wasted no motions. In prison he began to use his full signature,
especially when he wanted it noticed.* Evan Lattimer Collection.

and enthusiastic introducer of Hitler at rallies, requir-
ing no notes or other help in his public speaking. On
the other hand, if he had to give a long public speech,
as Göring and Streicher both observed, he would

"sweat blood" over the ordeal of having to stand up
before a crowd and speak intelligently.

About 1940, it became clear to Hess that Hitler was
going to get Germany into deep trouble by invading
Russia. This would be contrary to the teaching of Karl
Haushofer, the man in whose home Hess had been
brought up, and the philosopher who had advised so
emphatically against attacking Russia. Hess may have
gotten the idea that he would help Hitler out of this
dilemma by flying to England and persuading the
English to make peace with Germany. He indicated at
one point that an astrologer had told him to do this. He
probably made three attempts before he succeeded in
his remarkable flight, zigzagging to avoid both German
and British fighter planes.

On May 10, 1941, six weeks before the invasion of
Russia, he borrowed a twin-engine Messerschmitt 110
fighter and navigated it very skillfully to the estate in
Scotland of a man he had met at the 1936 Olympic
Games, the Duke of Hamilton (figs. 7-9). Upon para-
chuting (his first parachute jump), Hess asked to be
taken to the duke. After the British let him talk to
Hamilton, their skilled interrogators then took over.
After a lengthy period of indecision as to how to handle this new development, Churchill made the decision
to treat him like an ordinary prisoner. He was thrown
into the Tower of London and thereafter sent around to
various prisons and psychiatric wards. He made two
attempts to commit suicide when he realized that nothing was being done about his proposal for peace. On
one occasion he jumped from the second story of a
house, over the banister and down to the main floor. All
he did was break his hip which resulted in a limp from
then on. (This was noticeable in the courtroom.) He
began to claim that he was being poisoned, and insisted that samples of his food be sequestered for later testing. He brought some of these food samples with him
to his imprisonment at Nuremberg, from his imprisonment in England.

At Nuremberg, Rorschach tests for Dr. Kelley and
intelligence tests with Dr. Gilbert were done, with surprisingly good attention. Because of his lack of cooperation in some parts of anything he did, the true value of
the figures resulting was not dependable, in my opinion. He was given a score of 120 on his IQ test by Dr.
Gilbert, but I suspected that he might have done much
better in the period before his imprisonment. He did
some malingering and some acting and he obviously
remembered a great deal more than he indicated. On
the other hand, it was evident that he did have episodes
of amnesia, especially at the beginning of the trial. On
some occasions he appeared not to recognize Göring at
all, but on other occasions he would snap to attention

Fig 5—Memorial Ribbon
This is from a wreath which Hess contributed to some dignitary's funeral. This was commonly done so that the donor of the wreath would be obvious to the family. His thoughtfulness made him very popular. Evan Lattimer Collection.

Fig 8—ME 110 - Hess' airplane
This is the type of airplane which he flew with surprising skill to Scotland in 1941, in his bid to end the war by negotiation with the British.

Fig 6—Speer was not happy with Hess
Speer is looking at Hess with an expression of disgust. Speer had very little use for Hess, even in the glory days, as we see here.

Fig 9—Hess flies to Scotland with his "peace proposal"
These were British newspaper photographs and headlines announcing Hess' flight to Scotland. This was kept secret for some time but finally released. Note the wreckage of his ME 110 fighter plane with the Nazi insignia.

Fig 7—Hess preparing to take off
Here is Hess in a cold-weather high-altitude flying suit, in front of an ME 110 Fighter plane.

Fig 10—Göring growling at Hess

Göring was often trying to make Hess say something or do something or perhaps stop doing something in court, by growling at him behind his hand as you see him doing here. Hess would usually happily ignore him, looking "goofy."

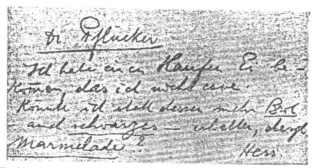

Fig 11—A sample of one of Hess' many notes to Dr. Pflücker

He was always asking for special consideration on his diet. In this one he is asking that eggs be omitted from his diet and marmelade substituted. He would sometimes write notes like this several times a day. Evan Lattimer Collection.

as Göring came along. After the hangings, he was sent with some of the other prisoners to clean up the gymnasium where the hangings had occurred, and saw a spot on the floor which was quite obviously blood. He snapped to attention and gave the Nazi salute toward this dried blood in apparent recognition of its significance.

When the shocking motion pictures of the atrocities were shown, he professed not to recognize anything, but became tense and clasped his hands tightly as the most appalling scenes appeared on the screen. (Dr. Gilbert had gone to some pains to have small light bulbs installed where they would illuminate the hands and faces of the prisoners in the darkened room, without being obvious.) Hess had pretty much convinced everyone that his amnesia was placing him in the position of being dismissed as a psychotic, when suddenly on November 20, 1945, after some urging by the other

(Above) Fig 13—Hess making his final statement in court

On the day everyone was to have their last chance to make a prepared statement to wind up their defense, Hess vowed that he would not make such a statement. However, when Göring finished, and started to pass the microphone to Ribbentrop, Hess seized it, stood up and made a concise statement, after which he went off into a rambling diatribe which finally had to be cut off by the presiding Judge. Here you see Ribbentrop holding the microphone for Hess, which he had expected to take immediately for himself. The others are looking askance at Hess, as he rambles on.

(Left) Fig 12—Hess demands to be tried

Just as Hess was about to be released as mentally incompetent, he demanded a special hearing and as shown here, he stood in court and said his loss of memory was all prevarication. He said he was perfectly competent and understood everything and wanted to be tried with the others. This left the court no option except to grant him this permission, even though he continued to show obvious severe mental troubles.

prisoners, he stood up in court and demanded a hearing (fig. 12). He stated flatly that he had been malingering and that he now understood everything and was responsible for everything and wanted to defend himself. Furthermore, he said that he was capable of standing trial and should indeed be treated as a competent defendant for the remainder of the trial. This left the judges no choice but to continue him as a defendant (figs. 12 & 13). It was quite apparent that he could have, and probably should have, been removed on psychiatric grounds at that point. The fact that he was kept for the rest of his long life in the jail at Berlin mostly reflected the fact that the Russians regarded this as a way to show off a smart drill team of Russian soldiers several times each year, when the guards at the prison were changed. This platoon goose-stepped across the western zone of the city to show off their precision marching and do a little spying as well.

Throughout their careers, Hess was a great thorn in Göring's side. Göring had complained to Hitler that his installing Hess as the number-three man was an insult. Hitler said he had to recognize Hess's early loyalty and stated that if he (Hitler) died, Göring could dump Hess instantly. Göring quoted this as an example of Hitler's genius in handling people. In this way, both men were rewarded but no serious permanent damage could result.

Hess became a little more agitated and paranoid as the trial progressed, but seemed to me to be recovering his intelligence with every passing month. The psychiatrists categorized him as having a juvenile mentality, enchanted by the Nazi uniforms and the great speech-

Fig 15—Hess clenching his fist in pain
He would sometimes do this several times a day, frowning and indicating great pain in the abdomen. While he referred to his gallbladder trouble, it seemed much more likely to Dr. Roska, Dr. Pflücker and myself that he was having intestinal cramps. No significant gallbladder or stomach pathology was found at autopsy.

es of Hitler, and finally making his showoff flight to England. At first, he refused to admit that the Germans had been defeated in the war. When it became obvious that he and Germany had failed in every way, the psychiatrists thought that he might become even more suicidal. They found him to be passive, very suggestible, and very naïve. Whenever he wanted to escape from reality, he would have a severe colicky pain in the pit of his stomach. He would clench his fists and cry out in agony (fig. 15). The psychiatrist concluded that some of his memory loss might be simulated, but that part of it was indeed hysterical. For example, he answered questions about his family perfectly easily and completely, including recollections about his parents. In March 1946, our Navy sent a distinguished psychiatrist, Dr. Francis Braceland, to spend several days studying Hess in an effort to evaluate him, but this very competent man left in frustration with very little data.

Hess's behavior in the prisoner's dock was fascinating. At first he ostensibly paid no attention to anything and would bring a book with him to read (fig. 17). He made frequent, extravagant gestures indicating severe pain in his abdomen. (It should be noted that at the autopsy there was some very mild scarring of his duodenal bulb, as from ulcers, but not much. There was no sign of gallbladder pathology.) Hess would stand up and just walk out of the courtroom. He was permitted to do so, under guard, and would return after varying intervals, depending on how badly he felt and how long he could persuade the guard to let him remain in the bathroom in his cell. He had an enlarged prostate and mild urinary frequency. Sometimes he would stay away from the trial for days.

It appeared to me that Hess had been an intelligent idealist as a youngster who had been fascinated by Hitler as he had by Karl Haushofer. Hess had then gradually become disillusioned and progressively

Fig 14—Changing the guard at Spandau
Every month a new detachment of guards representing one of the four powers, would take over from the other country's representatives who had been running the prison for the preceding month. The Russians enjoyed parading their fancy goose-stepping drill team of honor guards through the British zone to the prison, so refused to discharge Hess, after which the prison would have been closed.

Fig 16—Hess looking and acting normal
After his declaration that he was dissembling, he would chat amiably with the other prisoners and act fairly normal, during the intermissions, as you see here.

Fig 18—Hess joins in thanks to Dr. Pflücker
Here Hess joined in signing a note to Dr. Pflücker as to how much they all appreciated his good care. This was signed by the men who were to go to Spandau from Nuremberg. Dönitz wrote it as a poem, as he often did. Here, Hess signs his full name (bottom) rather than his peremptory initials, as he often did when he was in power. Evan Lattimer Collection.

Fig 17—Hess reading a book in court
I think he did this just to appear "bizarre," although it did look like an apparent gesture of contempt for the court, when he would read books such as "Grimm's Fairy Tales," to show his disdain. After he made his announcement that he was perfectly sane and had been faking his amnesia, he no longer read much in court. He would, however, get up and leave unexpectedly whenever the mood suited him, using his abdominal cramps as the excuse.

Fig 19—Hess at 93
Hess at Spandau at age 93. His son said that he was normal for a man of that age and was optimistic that Gorbachev was considering releasing him, at last. All the other Allied powers had been urging his release. He knew this and was pleased at the prospect.

depressed. We can see how his judgment was affected in that his flight to solicit peace with Britain, while skillfully executed, was based on the ridiculous premise that the Churchill government would make peace with Hitler. It also appeared to me that Hess had very likely been subjected to some sort of severe treatment in England, or perhaps sustained a head injury that resulted in a further derangement of his memory. We may not know anything about this for some time; the British are still very reluctant to release information about this episode. In any case, by the time Hess got to Nuremberg he was definitely amnesic, at least part of the time. He became somewhat more agitated, but on the whole seemed to me to be more normal, though disinterested, as the trial went on.

Once imprisoned in Spandau, he apparently acted more like his old self, according to family members. Speer recounted, however, that he continued to act peculiarly in Spandau, with episodes of screaming, colic, and refractory behavior, whenever it suited him. It was interesting to see that he got away with it in Spandau, just as he had done in the dock at Nuremberg.

Fig 20—Improvised summer-house where Hess died
This screened-in gazebo had been improvised in the prison garden as a place Hess could relax. It was here that he was found in extremis, with an electrical lamp cord around his neck and signs of a struggle. He died the next day in the British Hospital.

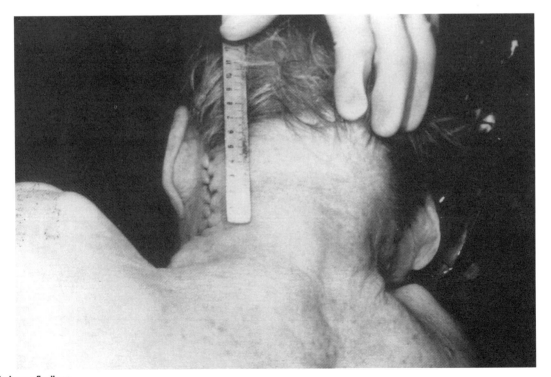

Fig 21—Autopsy findings
The transverse line across the back of Hess' neck after his death at age 93, in Spandau on August 17, 1987. This raised the question that he might have been garroted, rather than had hanged himself, especially since the horns of his thyroid cartilage were broken off, as happens with garroting but rarely with hanging. His son is convinced he was murdered and a repeat autopsy by German pathologists tended to agree with this. A complete release of the British records would help this matter. Full disclosure is always the best course, leaving less to speculation. The British do not plan to release their information, apparently, until after the year 2017.

Subsequent to his transfer to Spandau Prison in Berlin, he began to write entirely intelligent letters to his family and began to accept their visits. It was his son's contention that in the final 20 years of his life he was perfectly normal, except for the debilities of age. Pleas to the Russians to go along with the wishes of the other Allies, who were urging his release, were to no avail until Mikhail Gorbachev came on the scene. It was rumored that the Russians were finally going to relent and allow him to be released in 1989, but the discharge was deferred for some reason and on August 17, 1987, it was reported that Hess had committed suicide. Supposedly, he brought an electric cord to the small gazebo in the garden where he was permitted to walk, and wrapped it around his neck and hanged himself from a window frame. When I first heard this it did not surprise me because he had attempted suicide on several occasions.

The circumstances of his death were very peculiar, however. His orderly and nurse had been out to lunch and when they returned, Hess was lying on the ground in the garden with signs of a struggle all around. There were two strangers present, despite the regulations that no strangers should be admitted to the prison. They were asked to give artificial respiration which they did with great enthusiasm, shocking the orderly by crunching Hess's ribs and sternum when giving closed-chest cardiac massage. At the autopsy, performed by the distinguished British forensic pathologist James MacEwen (the suicide occurred during the time Hess was in the charge of the British), it was revealed that the small structures at the upper end of the thyroid cartilage were broken off. These are called the thyroid "horns." This often occurs when someone is strangled by garroting, but it does not usually occur when a person hangs himself. It is one of the classic clues in the differential diagnoses of the two kinds of strangulation death: homicide versus suicide. The ligature marks across the back of the neck were clearly more or less parallel with the ground, whereas after a hanging the ligature marks usually come down on the sides of the neck from above, across the front of the *upper* part of the neck, and then back up on the other side (fig. 21). It is conceivable that these unusual marks could have been made by some configuration of the suicide noose, but the British are stonewalling the Hess family—they will not release their information about the incident until the year 2017.

The family had a second autopsy done by the well-known, German forensic pathologist, Prof. Dr. W. Spann of Munich. He raised these questions and asked for further information as to the position of the body and the circumstances of the death to see if there some reason why these unusual findings existed in a person who allegedly had hanged himself. Hess's family also pointed out that he could have hanged himself much more easily with a much longer length of cord in the privacy of his own room, rather than in the garden where the cord was very short and the chances of being discovered were much greater. His son, Wolf Rudiger Hess, is trying to gather support for an effort to ask the British government for clarification. In 1995 when I asked him about the motive, Mr. Hess indicated that he suspected that once he was released, his father would have talked about maltreatment he received while a prisoner of the British. He had heard some rumors in the foreign intelligence community that the British had sent their famous SAS troopers to kill Hess to prevent this information from leaking out. Whether true or not, Hess can no longer testify as to what went on in England during his four years' imprisonment.

Fig 22—Spandau prison destroyed
Shortly after Hess died, the entire old prison building was dynamited and the wreckage bulldozed away. Thus ended the period of occupation by four separate military groups.

CHAPTER FIVE

Prison Security:
A Paper Tiger

From the very beginning, a major worry of the Nuremberg prison staff was the shocking lack of real security against an armed military assault to free the prisoners. This was indeed frightening to any of us who had seen the German Army in action. The Palace of Justice, as the prison and court-room complex was called, was huge (fig. 1). A determined group of the deadly German SS commandos—who were numerous among the drifting hordes of discharged German soldiers, and who had worked so effectively under Colonel Otto Skorzeny (who was still at large for a time at the end of the war)—could have raided the prison and liberated all the prisoners. Colonel Burton Andrus, the tough old cavalryman in charge of the 6850 Internal Security Detachment (ISD) for the International Military Tribunal (IMT) was a nervous wreck over this glaring weakness, at least during the first two or three months of the trial (fig. 2). He was seriously understaffed in the beginning. A system of red, white, or blue passes was finally set up by which the personnel could enter only their assigned sections: the Palace of Justice, the prison wing, or the war criminal's wing (figs. 3-6). Even this Mickey Mouse system was hard to run efficiently, and was mainly effective in restricting our own personnel to their assigned areas (much to their annoyance). It would have done nothing, however, to deter a surprise, armed military attack. I can remember how relieved I was when I heard that Skorzeny had decided the war was actually over and had given him-self up (fig. 7).

Nuremberg had been the home base of the dedicated Nazi military and paramilitary organizations, such as Hitler's personal and fanatical body-guard, the SS. While some of these SS troopers were kept in prisoner-of-war cages for a brief time, they were being released by the thousands and were

Fig 1—The Palace of Justice and Prison complex at Nuremberg
The courtroom was in the building at the right center. The prison, with its many wings is at the top of this picture, enclosed by a high wall. Bomb damage was being repaired.

Fig 3—Shoulder-patch and collar badge of the 6850 internal Security Detachment
This shoulder patch was designed by Colonel Andrus, showing the scales of justice, a key for the prison and a broken Nazi eagle at the bottom. It had a field of blue for purity and a section of red and a border of sable. It was to be worn by all of the security personnel at the prison. Evan Lattimer Collection.

Fig 2—Col. Burton C. Andrus, Prison Commandant
Col. Andrus was a regular Army Cavalry officer who had risen through the ranks. He had been an army prison commander for a brief time. After the Armistice he was called back to take charge, first of the interrogation center at Mondorf, and then the prison at Nuremberg. He was a martinet who ran the prisons with an iron hand. This irritated many of the civilian employees, but was accepted by the Germans. He was overly confident of the loyalty of the P.O.W. prison workers and attendants.

Fig 4—A system of passes of different colors was used
At least 5 different types of passes were needed to enter various parts of the Palace of Justice complex. These proved to be tremendously irritating and ineffectual for hundreds of personnel of the trials. They would have been of little use in controlling any enemy effort to infiltrate. The blue pass authorized the bearer to enter the area of the Palace of Justice only. Evan Lattimer Collection.

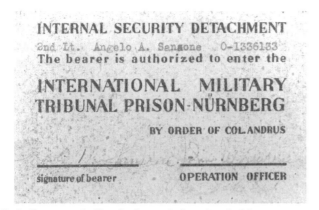

Fig 5—The pass admitting the bearer to the prison building
Evan Lattimer Collection.

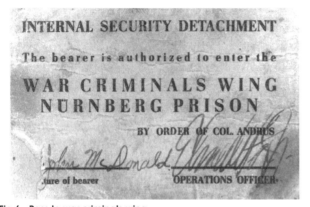

Fig 6—Pass to war criminals wing
This was the most important and closely guarded wing. Evan
Lattimer Collection.

Fig 7—Otto Skorzeny, Hitler's commando
This is the huge, athletic young Austrian who Hitler had com-
manded to kidnap the son of the regent of Hungary, to use as a
hostage. He also kidnapped Mussolini from his guards, after
Mussolini had been dethroned. In the Battle of the Bulge, his men,
dressed in American uniforms, played havoc behind our lines,
turning the road signs around and giving false directions to our
various Army units. On the left is Skorzeny's "German" medal in
silver, awarded by Hitler for his earliest exploits. Later he received
this same medal in gold. Skorzeny was the one man who might
have invaded our prison with ease. I was greatly relieved when he
finally turned himself in. Evan Lattimer Collection.

everywhere. Indeed, some of them were in the work gangs of POWs repairing the bomb-damaged court-room and could easily have hidden delayed-action explosive charges in the woodwork they were repair-ing. This had been done in Munich, some time before. It would have been no trouble at all for them to hide weapons and explosives nearby, in quantities sufficient to raid the prison.

A long, closed corridor was built between the cell-block and the court (fig. 8). Prisoners were always handcuffed to a guard until they got off the small ele-vator to the prisoners' dock in the courtroom.

The Werewolves

Alongside many doorways in Germany, wherever there was a smooth wall area, there was a life-size sten-cil of a lurking man dressed in black clothing and a black Homburg (fig. 9). It had been painted there by a "Hitler-sponsored" organization called the Were-wolves. Their declared purpose was to terrorize the occupying forces, but the total collapse of Germany and the disillusionment and disgust of the war-weary pop-ulace had scuttled this plan. Even so, Germans lurking in the darkness in Nuremberg repeatedly attacked the Soviet enlisted men assigned to the trial unit.

Our own military guard personnel were almost all untrained youngsters fresh from the United States who were sent to the famous 1st Infantry Division through a replacement depot. The combat veterans who had gained so much experience in Normandy and in many subsequent firefights all had enough "points" to go home and were being shipped out daily in their turns. Even though these new youngsters wore the same respected 1st Infantry Division shoulder patch on their uniforms (a big red "1") as did the combat veterans, it was obvious that they had never fired a shot in battle and would have been mowed down in an organized surprise assault by experienced German commandos. Speer was impressed with the patriotism of these young American boys and commented on it, but recog-nized that they were inexperienced "children," in con-trast to our battle-hardened veterans who were all going home.

A tank platoon with five medium tanks and some 35 men was assigned to Colonel Andrus, and put on an impressive show when they arrived (fig. 10). In no time at all, however, these men had been impressed into additional duties such as serving in the PX. In addition, Colonel Andrus could theoretically call on a nearby fighter plane base to help repel any air attacks on the prison. (We wondered whose airplanes might attack us.) An alarm system had been installed to close off the

Fig 8—The jail wings
These 3 jail wings were behind the Palace of Justice and were surrounded by a high wall, between them and the river. The Nazi leaders were kept on the first floor of the building in the foreground and a special weather-proof corridor was built from the end of their jail wing as a passage way to the courtroom via the basement of the Palace of Justice, into an elevator up to the courtroom. The gymnasium where the executions occured can be seen on the right. A special doorway and steps were constructed from the jail wing down to the courtyard and across to the entrance to the gymnasium for the hangings. The other parts of the jail were used to house witnesses or prisoners being interrogated. It was interesting that Streicher had been in this prison previously for a sex offense.

Fig 9—The "Werewolf" sign
This was painted everywhere, as the Nazis retreated. It was Hitler's idea to impress the occupying armies with the fact that they would be attacked by a group of werewolves, who would be invisible but very damaging. Speer was instrumental in stopping this activity, realizing that it would only enrage the occupying armies. I must say that it was quite startling to see this when we first moved in, and it kept us on our toes, especially at night. Evan Lattimer Collection.

Fig 10—A platoon of light tanks was assigned to the trial
In the beginning, a 30 man tank platoon, with five tanks, was assigned to the prison for the support of Colonel Andrus, if necessary. The personnel of this tank platoon were assigned to so many other duties, such as running various Px and other unrelated activities, that it is doubtful that they would have been effective in repelling any surprise attack. They were also unfamiliar with the cannons and machine guns of their tanks, and we suspected that they had never fired a shot in anger, much less at attacking commandos dressed as civilians in crowds. It was said that a unit of fighter planes was on the alert at a nearby airbase, in case of an airborne assault on the jail. The fact that tanks and armored cars were sometimes visible, was regarded as a deterrant, and perhaps it was. It was certainly an empty gesture, as Andrus knew, and as any serious attacker, such as Colonel Skorzeny, would have known in advance. It was this kind of sham exercise which made the whole security situation frightening to any of us who had seen how effective the German soldiers could be in actual combat. Luckily the system of rewards, such as preferential treatment, was far more effective than any military or armed deterrant, in actual fact.

area if it were attacked, but all this was just window dressing, in the opinion of the combat veterans. Colonel Andrus also had a couple of armored cars at his disposal but none of the young soldiers running them had had any experience in using an armored vehicle among crowds of civilians, or against enemy personnel who would have destroyed them immediately with surprise antitank techniques. Our prisoners and the Germans assigned to construction work all talked to these new guards at length and were well aware that they were inexperienced youngsters. They were so fresh from the United States that a few of them even painted crude graffiti on the walls of the prison, indicating how dissatisfied they were with their lot, running a jail. Colonel Andrus stepped on them rudely and hard.

The Appearance of the Guards in the Courtroom

Colonel Andrus did surprisingly well with the appearance of his military police guards in the courtroom and in the prison. Despite his severe manpower shortages, he insisted that the guard for each prisoner must be taller than the prisoner he was escorting. This was a problem with Kaltenbrunner, who was approximately 6' 4" and Keitel, who was 6' 1". There had to be more than one tall guard for each man, since they were forced to stand stiffly at "Parade Rest" with their hands linked behind them for periods of 30 minutes. Not only was it necessary to rotate these guards in the courtroom every 30 minutes, but there had to be allowances for illnesses and absences. Whenever a witness was on the stand, the number of guards in the courtroom was increased from 9 to 12. As it was, the entire group of guards averaged about 5' 10", with several who were taller, for Kaltenbrunner and Keitel. Each guard had his shiny white helmet liner, white belt, and white gloves. They made a good, well-pressed appearance despite the boring duty of standing stiffly while listening to a language they could not understand much of the time. Speer commented to me, nevertheless, on the "smartness" of these youngsters who were far from home, with a dull type of duty. In general, they did a creditable job.

The Palace of Justice had been hit by two or three bombs, and the walls and roofs were badly damaged in several places. When bombs exploded inside the buildings, all the slate shingles of the roof were popped up and off, leaving bare rafters. Our entire courtroom area had collapsed into the cellar, even as it was being refurbished. The fact that the reconstruction was completed in time for the opening of the trial was remarkable. The breaches in the walls and roofs were repaired by POW

Fig 11—Major Robert E. Matteson
Major Matteson, after his single-handed capture of Kaltenbrunner, was brought back to Nuremberg to redesign the security system. He was a CIC officer who was awarded the Silver Star by General Patton for this intrepid and daring action. He brought with him his associate, Sgt. Lloyd Roach, appointing him "Captain," as was the preogative of CIC agents. Matteson and Roach beefed up the security regulations at the prison enormously but demonstrated that they were vulnerable to infiltration, even though Colonel Andrus thought they were ironclad. Evan Lattimer Collection.

work gangs made up not only of regular German Army (Wehrmacht) men but also a substantial number of the fanatics who had become SS troopers. Many of these still proudly wore their "Death's Head" insignias on their caps. These gangs of POWs were guarded by only one American sentry for every 50 German troopers. They could easily have disarmed the sentry and stormed the prison where they were already working. The numbers and training of our troops assigned to guard the prison, both externally and in the courtroom, were totally inadequate to stave off an armed attack from outside. Colonel Andrus had been told he could tap the resources of the 1st Infantry Division which was quartered immediately north of Nuremberg, but this was a fiasco.

He applied for 800 troops. He was actually given 30 and these were the inexperienced youngsters. He asked for 20 officers, preferably West Pointers, because of the importance and delicacy of the mission. He was given no new West Pointers (he already had a few) and only a few inexperienced new officers. Colonel Andrus was desperate for manpower. That was why I was welcomed, even to come and go whenever I would do so. I was careful, however, to avoid getting my feet frozen in his cement. He promised promotions and all sorts of special privileges if I would sign on with him. I told him that Seventh Army headquarters, which had assigned me to help develop a general hospital in Munich (the 98th U.S. Army General Hospital), would want me to continue on detached service to his unit as long as he might need me, but wanted me back. This arrangement worked out nicely. My work in Munich was not demanding, so I could be detached to Nuremberg most of the time.

The Architect of Our Security System— Agent Robert E. Matteson

Because of his outstanding bravery in successfully capturing Kaltenbrunner, Counterintelligence Corps (CIC) Agent Matteson of the Third Army (fig. 11), was rewarded with a battlefield commission and the Silver Star by the U.S. Army. He was the only CIC Agent ever to be awarded a Silver Star (so far as I know) and one of the few to get a battlefield commission for his good work. One should realize that CIC Agents were empowered to assume any rank they found necessary to make their immediate mission more successful, so perhaps the importance of rank did not seem as attractive to them as it did to others. The citation concerning his Silver Star read as follows:

> Award of Silver Star by Direction of the President— 5 June 1945
>
> The Silver Star Medal is hereby awarded Robert Eliot Matteson for gallantry in action in Austria, on 12 May 1945, in connection with military operations against an enemy of the United States.

On this date, after learning the whereabouts of Ernst Kaltenbrunner and his SS guards, Special Agent Matteson organized and led a patrol at night over dangerous glacial terrain. Unarmed, and dressed in Austrian civilian clothes, Special Agent Matteson approached the cabin where Kaltenbrunner and his guards were living. By repeatedly knocking on the door, he aroused the occupants who were preparing to

Fig 12—Lloyd M. Roach
The CIC agent who assisted in the development of the security system and the testing of it, to make sure that it would indeed work. Evan Lattimer Collection.

fight, until they saw other members of the patrol approaching. Breaking down the door, Agent Matteson and his men captured Kaltenbrunner, his aide, and his two SS bodyguards who had two machine pistols, four rifles, two pistols, one machine gun, and a large supply of ammunition. Special Agent Matteson's careful planning and fearless execution of a dangerous mission against an armed enemy of the most vicious and desperate type is a credit to himself and to the Armed Forces of the United States.

Matteson's Battlefield Commission as Major, U.S. Army

On the next day, June 6, 1945, Agent Matteson was given a battlefield commission signed by General George Patton, commanding general of the Third U.S. Army. He was discharged as a Counterintelligence Corps agent and then sworn back in as an officer. His pay was increased to $267.00 a month. He found it strange that because enlisted men now called him "Sir" and saluted. He said, "I now eat in an officers' mess on tablecloths with plates and silverware. No longer do I stand in line with a mess kit to eat out of garbage cans over a fire. No longer do I drive my own jeep but I now have someone to drive me. But ever since I was put in charge of a regimental area with my own CIC team, I had been my own boss and generally speaking, was on equal terms with staff officers, so the change wasn't all that great."

Agent Matteson interviewed many of the German aristocracy who were living in Altsee, Austria, the Alpine redoubt area. He said what they had liked about Hitler was that he had unified the Reich against Bolshevism which they feared more than death, and that he had controlled labor and "put it in its place." He observed that everyone there in Altsee seemed to be a Count or a Prince or a Baron, and there were many cliques vying for influence with our CIC which they called the American Gestapo. "Each of them would pass us clandestine notes condemning the others." Matteson's CIC unit quickly arrested more than 150 Nazi intelligence agents, political leaders, Gestapo police, and war criminals. Adolf Eichmann had just been there but had eluded them, since they had little information about Eichmann at that time.

Security Inside the Building

Major Robert E. Matteson drew up a more complex plan for internal security in the Palace of Justice complex. On November 2, 1945, after the trial had begun, he had received orders from Third Army headquarters to go to Nuremberg and set up a better internal security

Fig 13—The grand hotel in Nuremberg near the Palace of Justice
This had been hit by bombs but was repaired rapidly to accommo-date the staff of the trials. A more modern wing to the right had been built on by the Nazis for their accommodations.

plan. Under this plan, he was to take charge of safety and security for all members of the International Military Tribunal and for all dignitaries, visitors, and ranking personnel at the Nuremberg trial. He took with him Agents Lloyd Roach (fig. 12) and David Marks. The request from the Nuremberg tribunal to CIC head-quarters in the European theater was for "first-class Intelligence Operatives who would be responsible for all dignitaries in Nuremberg." They were to guard especially against Nazi Werewolf assassins.

Lt. Colonel Van Sutherland of the U.S. 1st Infantry Division, of Omaha Beach fame, had been placed in charge of overall military security for the whole Nuremberg area. His division was quartered just north of Nuremberg. At the same time, Colonel Andrus was placed in charge of the security of the 22 major Nazi war criminals in the cellblock itself and in the court-room. This arrangement created a conflict and frag-mentation of ultimate authority which caused unfortu-nate tensions. It led to some bitter exchanges between crusty Colonel Andrus and the officers of the 1st Infantry Division.

Major Matteson was given an office in the Palace of Justice. He visited Justice Robert Jackson's assistant and found that there were only 300 seats in the courtroom, of which 250 were for correspondents. Roach, Marks, and he were given free access to all sessions of the trial. Colonel Sutherland was very cooperative and said Matteson could use any 1st Infantry Division military personnel he needed to establish absolute security. Matteson's living quarters were in the Grand Hotel, the only hotel still standing (fig. 13). It was close to the

courthouse and its few bomb hits were repaired rapid-ly. It was reserved for people connected with the trial and was full of people of all sorts and denominations, including many Russians.

Matteson and Roach were given all three colors of passes, which allowed them discretionary access to examine the buildings they were charged with keeping secure.

Matteson submitted his overall security plan to the G-2 (Security Division Chief) of Third Army in person. After it was approved, Colonel Andrus was ordered to implement it. Andrus had bragged that he had made security so tight, no one could cough in the prison with-out his permission. Suicide would be impossible. On November 9, a week after he had arrived, Matteson decided to test the security of the cellblock itself, an area which was Colonel Andrus's responsibility. He elevated Private Roach to captain simply by buying captains' bars for him at the PX. Together they walked up to guard post Number 1. They were surprised that they were not stopped at all. They were supposed to show an Interrogation pass signed by Colonel John Amen of Justice Jackson's staff. On they went to guard post Number 2. Again their officers' uniforms got them by. Down the wooden corridor they went, past other guard posts, until they arrived at the iron grilled gate leading into the cellblock itself. The guard from inside moved aside a little "Judas window" to see who they were and then slowly opened the heavy iron door. Again they were not challenged. They started to walk down the cellblock when the voice of the Captain of the Guard called out saying, "Sirs, please sign the visitors' book and indicate which prisoner you wish to see." So they signed the book and asked to see Kaltenbrunner.

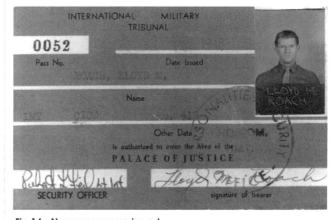

Fig 14—New passes were issued
In an effort to improve our poor security, Major Matteson had photographs added to all passes. This one was for CIC Agent Roach.

Since the suicide of Ley (on October 25th), G.I. guards were now stationed at each cell door, in one-hour shifts, with orders to keep the prisoners under 24 hour observation. But Roach and Matteson could have been anybody at all, dressed in their American officers' uniforms.

Kaltenbrunner, in accordance with procedure, had to stand when an officer entered. Matteson said he was surprised by two things: once again by Kaltenbrunner's size, and second, by his appearance. While he had spent several hours with him in May at the time of his capture, he said he had forgotten how large he was—6'4" in height and (at that time) weighing 220 pounds. One somewhat exaggerated description by Florence Miale and Michael Salzer (experts on psychological testing by Rorschach ink blots) in their book *The Nuremberg Mind*, said, "He was almost 7 feet tall and had a heavily scarred face—Kaltenbrunner looked like what he was, head of the security police (SIPO) the security service (SD) and the Reich's security head office (RSHA)." As such, they pointed out, he had under his authority the Gestapo, the extermination squads that murdered millions of Jews, and the death camps. Miale and Salzer quote another, more vivid description of Kaltenbrunner by one of Hitler's aides: "A tough, callous ox—looks like a big grizzly bear. Small brown eyes that move like a viper's, all glittering. Bad teeth, with some missing, so he hisses."

The second thing that impressed Matteson was the change in Kaltenbrunner's manner. He looked like a man who knew he was going to die. The strain was written on his face and he seemed unsteady and pale. Little did Matteson know that Kaltenbrunner was on the point of having a cerebral hemorrhage. He had been told by one of the British personnel that Kaltenbrunner had been at camp "0-2-0," in England, and had been given the "third degree" treatment. He had been placed under a hot spotlight, was given no rest, and ate only bread and a little water. Later, in 1979, when Matteson was at Oxford, he learned from the author, Hugh Trevor-Roper, that Camp "0-2-0" was under the supervision of "Tin-eye" Stevens, a man with a monocle and riding whip who was known to be a master of psychological "persuasion." During the few minutes Matteson talked with Kaltenbrunner that time, the prisoner's only interest was in his mistress, Giesela, and her young twins by him; not in his wife nor his other three children. It was evident to him that his gambit, on the basis of which he had surrendered without a fight, had not worked. He had hoped to persuade General Eisenhower that he should be accepted as an advisor or even as the leader of an independent Austria. Parlaying his Intelligence Service knowledge of the Soviet Union with the SS troops at his command in the national redoubt area and Skorzeny's sabotage and Werewolf brigades, his plan was to join forces with the United States and the British in a final war against Russia. The contact that Kaltenbrunner's man, Dr. William Hoettl, had obtained with Allen Dulles's OSS people in Switzerland was to be the basis for his contention that he, against Hitler's wishes, had been trying to arrange a secret surrender of the Nazi Alpine Redoubt forces, and thus end the war without a further battle in the redoubt.

After this brief second encounter with Kaltenbrunner, "Captain" Roach and Major Matteson left. Thinking that it was a fluke and that security in the cellblock could not be that bad, they decided to try to repeat their unauthorized entrance though the guard posts an hour later. Again they were successful and this time asked to see Reichmarshal Hermann Göring. Göring stood at attention when they entered his cell. Matteson said he appeared shorter and more trim than he had expected from his photographs. On a shelf by his cot he had many pictures of his wife. Matteson asked Göring how things were going and he said, "Good." He asked if he had seen his wife yet and Göring replied, "No." Both Kaltenbrunner and Göring seemed to be startled by the visit, because all the prisoners except Hess had recently been left alone. Matteson and Roach exchanged a few more words and then left, not wishing to be caught by the prosecution interrogators invading their territory without having shown the proper credentials (i.e., the passes signed by Colonel Amen, which they had not been asked to show).

When Matteson returned to his office, he wrote up a report on their two breaches of security and transmitted it to Lt. Colonel Sutherland of the 1st Infantry Division and also to Colonel Fickett, G-2 of the Third Army. Within a few hours Matteson said, "All hell broke loose." Matteson was sure the security fiasco had not really made Colonel Sutherland unhappy. He and Colonel Andrus were waging a silent jurisdictional war. Colonel Andrus had been given special directives by U.S. Forces European Theatre (USFET) which interfered with Colonel Sutherland's overall authority under the 1st Division of the Third Army for the ultimate security of the entire area. Colonel Andrus had been assigned the security of the cellblock and courthouse which were part of the Palace of Justice, and were the most important security problems of all.

As soon as Matteson's report was read at Third Army Headquarters, the place exploded. Down came Commanding General Lucian Truscott and his G-2 (Intelligence Chief). The result was that six of the officers and twenty enlisted men, including the guards at the guard posts, were relieved. The captain in charge of the cellblock went to the hospital with a nervous breakdown. Matteson quickly became the most unpopular man living at the Grand Hotel, but the fact was that even the internal security had been terrible.

In drawing up a new overall security plan for the Nuremberg area, Matteson and Roach made sixty recommendations. The G-2 had assured them that they would all be carried out and enforced. I.D. cards were now to carry photographs of the owner, and sandbags were placed around machine guns at corridor junctures (figs. 15 & 16). The name of Major Matteson's unit was now changed to War Crimes Trial Personal Security

Fig 17—Badges indicating the occupation of each worker were attempted
This one shows that the wearer was designated as a prison carpenter. It was bright yellow and easily seen. Evan Lattimer Collection.

Office. It included the security for Justice Jackson, "Wild Bill" Donovan of the OSS, Francis Biddle, the U.S. judge, Judge Parker and Lord Justice Geoffrey Laurence of England, who was President of the Court. Also, Sir Hartley Shawcross, the British Chief Prosecutor, Professor Vabres de Menthon, the two French prosecutors and four Russian officers, including General I. T. Nikitchenko, Lt. Colonel A. F. Volchkov, and General Roman A. Rudenko. In addition to these principals at the trial, there was a constant stream of dignitaries coming in for a day or so to view the sessions. Special passes were printed for each session with seat numbers (fig. 17). It was like a theatrical production with multilanguage simultaneous translations at all times. The four-language simultaneous translation system proved to be so good (550 sets were in use) that it was adopted for the United Nations General Assembly.

A week or so later, Matteson and Roach tested the security of the cellblock once again, on orders from the Third Army G-2 officer. He wanted to see whether security had improved. This time Matteson and Roach were stopped at each guard post but instead of showing an Interrogation pass signed by Colonel Amen, as should have been required, they showed only their Counterintelligence Corps badges. These were impressive gold badges in leather cases. Again Roach and Matteson were allowed to pass through. While security had improved, the guards were still not following their strict orders to demand the right card. On entering the inner cellblock illegally for the third time, they asked to see Julius Streicher. Streicher was 60 years old, a short, aggressive bouncy extrovert, publisher of *Der Stürmer* and Hitler's leading Jew-baiter. He was full of energy as always, but preoccupied just then about a hole in his

Fig 15—Sandbagged machine gun emplacements
These were erected inside the Palace of Justice, to defend the critical points, after Matteson demonstrated how vulnerable they were to infiltration.

Fig 16—Visitors gallery passes
These were white, with a session number and a seat number. It was like a theatrical production, with multi-language translations and a strict schedule. Over 250 of the seats were reserved for the press. Competition for the advance scheduling was keen. The sessions where the aggressive, clever British prosecutor matched wits with Göring, were in great demand. Evan Lattimer Collection.

trousers. He said he needed to get a sewing kit from his wife or another pair of trousers. This kind of concern seemed to reflect the level of his I.Q. (106), which was the lowest of the group.

The guards finally caught up with the two agents this third time and quite correctly arrested them for illegal entry into the cellblock. Streicher pleaded with the guards to let the agents stay and talk. One of the prison officers said, "I don't know how you got in, but you have no pass, so here you stay." When word finally reached Colonel Andrus he ordered their release but again there were reverberations up and down the Palace of Justice, for this was the third illegal entry in two weeks. Again it was fuel for Colonel Sutherland's feud against the concept of divided responsibility between himself and Colonel Andrus. It certainly shook our confidence in our own security system.

One of the new guard officers was the aforementioned Lt. Jack Wheelis, who had arrived in November, via the 1st Division, as a replacement. He was furious with Agent Roach, a fellow Texan, when he heard what Roach and Matteson had done.

Security was also a problem for the Soviet soldiers. The Soviet soldiers were frequently being shot at night by lurking Germans who lived in the catacombs beneath the city. The security for the Russians was so poor that they finally flew in an entire company of Russian soldiers to provide their own security around their people. This was a great relief for Matteson and Roach.

The opening of the trial on November 20, 1945, was accompanied by intensified elaborate security precautions because it presented the underground Nazis with an appropriate occasion to make some dramatic move to avenge the imprisonment of their leaders. Unfortunately, because of the shortage of labor necessary to finish the courtroom on time, the SS prisoners were still being used in the construction gangs. They were a distinct security threat since redeployment of our own troops now resulted in a woeful lack of American security guards, especially those with any experience in combat. As a further security measure, special badges for carpenters were developed (fig. 17).

Many times, Roach and Matteson came across groups of unguarded SS prisoners in the Palace of Justice halls, conversing with German civilians who had access to the outside world and who were employed by our office of the Chief Counsel within the Palace of Justice. They estimated that there were at least 1,000 SS men at large and unaccounted for in the Nuremberg area and in the catacombs under the city. In addition, on November 8, 1945, just twelve days before the trial began, 45,000 German civilians were expelled from

Fig 18—A guard peered into every cell, every minute
The grill and spotlight in the small window in each door can be seen, where a sentry kept a continuous lookout, 24 hours a day. Note the small size of the club carried by this sentry.

their jobs by the military government because of previous associations with the Nazi Party.

Ten days before the trial commenced, there were still open, unguarded doors through which German civilians could gain access to the Palace of Justice and the courtroom. They could have easily planted time bombs, booby traps or other similar devices. Also, the guards on the posts that had been established in the Palace of Justice cellblock area were lax and did not know what their orders were. Each time, our reports brought a reshuffling of the guards and enforcement of more stringent security measures, but it was no wonder that those who were responsible for security became increasingly apprehensive about incidents which might mar the opening of the trial. The Russians, who were our guests in the American military zone for the period of the trial, were especially anxious that their security be tightened. The Nazis had a particular hatred for the Soviets and the Soviets were well aware of it. In December, CIC Agent Hodges came down to take over as head of security when Major Matteson went home. Major Matteson did get to hear the beginnings of the prosecution of Kaltenbrunner after his return to the trial from his first cerebral hemorrhage. Statistics, such as the murder by Kaltenbrunner's units of 135,000 persons in the first four months of the Russian campaign, and then in the next months 230,000 more, were startling. Eichmann, Kaltenbrunner's subordinate and friend, had estimated in one report to him that, all-in-all, his Einsatzgruppen alone had killed two million Jews in the Russian campaign. And his was only one of many under Kaltenbrunner, as it came out.

The accounts of witnesses like CIC Agents Matteson

and Roach were fascinating, as the top echelons of the Nazi empire crumbled and fell into our hands.

Security Within the Cellblock Itself

Each cell had a small square access window, with a traylike sill in the middle of the heavy door through which the sentry could inspect the interior and meals could be passed (fig. 18). Colonel Andrus had so few men, at first, that one man had to supervise four cells, peering into each door in rotation for a few minutes. This made it impossible to keep close track of the prisoners and what they were doing. Their main concern was to prevent suicides.

Dr. Leonard Conti—the Nazi minister of health whose agency was accused of permitting all sorts of crimes against sick people such as euthanasia and medical experimentation of the grossest kind—became progressively more and more upset. His self-recrimination became obsessive, and he would pace the floor night and day, obviously in terrible emotional conflict. Dr. Douglas Kelley, our psychiatrist, had warned of his suicidal intent. Despite this warning, Conti was able to hang himself on October 6th by looping a strip of cord around the bars of his cell, standing on his chair, and slumping downward with enough weight to obstruct the arteries to his brain. After that, all bars and projections on the cell walls to which a noose might be fastened were covered over and all chairs were moved outside the cells at 8 P.M. During the day, no chairs could be placed closer than four feet to a wall. Tables were too flimsy to bear a man's weight. Colonel Andrus tried to use the calamity of Conti's suicide as a justification for more guards, but none were forthcoming at that time. Conti's death was kept secret for many days, at Colonel Andrus's suggestion.

Just three weeks later on October 25th, Robert Ley, the Nazi labor minister, strangled himself while sitting on the toilet in his cell (fig. 19). He had torn a strip from the edge of his towel to make a cord which he looped over the water pipe leading to the toilet. He then stuffed rags in his mouth so as not to make noise. This finally brought some action. Colonel Andrus was now assigned 200 more men from the 1st Infantry Division, plus 12 officers. These men made it possible to station a sentry at every door for periods of one half hour so that each prisoner was under continuous surveillance (fig. 20). This brought an end to the suicides until just two hours before the hangings were to start, when Göring killed himself with an obviously well planned maneuver.

Fig 19—The all-important toilet in the end of each cell nearest the door

Using the toilet in the niche beside the door provided the only place where the prisoners were not under the full-time gaze of the guard peering through the window in the middle of the door. Only their feet could be seen. The water pipe supplying the toilet can be seen in this view, running down the back wall of the niche. It came out of the wall near the top of the niche, where the bright reflection is visible. There was a fitting at this point which had a small "cuff." It was on this fitting that Ley was able to hook the partly opened zipper of his jacket. To the jacket he tied strips from the edge of his towel, which he looped around his neck. When he leaned forward, the pressure from the loop occluded the arteries in his neck (to his brain) and he died. It requires relatively little pressure to stop the blood supply to the brain, causing unconsciousness and then death. In the beginning, there was a small curtain across this niche in each cell, but these were removed after Ley's suicide. It was while standing facing the toilet that Göring undoubtedly removed the cyanide ampoule from its protective brass case and placed it in his mouth for his suicide (see p. 105). The table which can be seen in this photograph was deliberately made flimsy, so that it would not bear the weight of a man who might try to stand on it to get at the wiring in the ceiling or hang himself in any way. The chair was the type used by Conti to drape a strip of towel around the bars in the window and then lean down so that the narrowed loop of towel strangled him. After that, the rule was that no chair could be placed closer than 4 feet from any wall, during the day. Chairs were removed during the night. All bars and projections were removed. The bed seen on the right, was attached to the wall and covered with Army blankets. More blankets were available if the weather turned cold. There was a heating pipe along the wall of each cell, which kept it reasonably warm. The barred window in the door through which a spotlight shone on the prisoners all night, can be seen here. A shelf or small table at the bottom of the window accommodated the water vessel and mess kit at meal times. The prisoners passed their eye-glasses out to the sentry before the lights were turned down to a lower level at 9:15 each night. This was an effort to prevent the use of shards of broken glass being used to slash wrists. Later, at Spandau, Hess did exactly that, breaking his eye-glasses and cutting his wrist. He was discovered just in time to be "saved" by his jailors, however.

Fig 20—The main jail corridor

Here the sentries peered in at each prisoner 24 hours a day, in half-hour shifts. At first (until Ley committed suicide,) Colonel Andrus had not been allotted enough men to have one sentry at each door, all the time. One man had to patrol four cells for 2 hours, looking periodically into each. Even the suicide of Dr. Conti, who had time enough to die between the rounds of the sentry to his four cells, did not arouse the bureaucracy quickly enough to assign more guards to the prison. However, when Ley committed suicide 3 weeks later, under much the same circumstances, the authorities finally "moved" and allotted Colonel Andrus enough men to permit a sentry at each door for 24 hours a day, in shifts of 1/2 hour at a time. A grill fit over the small window in the upper part of each door. One of these grills can be seen on the wall next to the doorway in Fig. 18 second from the right. Just below it is the spotlight which the sentry hung on the grill to illuminate the prisoner during the darkest hours. This was kept on brightly until 9:30 p.m., when it was dimmed by 50 per cent in order to permit the prisoners to sleep. A small shelf on the bottom of each window would accommodate a mess kit and a metal cup at mealtimes. The baggage room was adjacent to the last cell on the right, and could be entered by the prisoners if they requested some special item. A supervising officer made sure that they removed only what they needed. The upper tiers of this cellblock were used for the prisoners who were not condemned to death, after the sentences had been pronounced. Exercise walks in the garden were not permitted after the sentences were pronounced, but prisoners could walk up and down in this corridor, shackled to a guard, if they wished. Surprisingly few of them wished to do that, once they were condemned. Wire screening covered the upper walkways because a German officer had jumped or been thrown from one of these upper balconies, in another wing, before the trials really got underway. He was not one of the major defendants. Dr. Pflücker, accompanied by one of the guard officers and occasionally by one of the American medical officers, visited each of these cells twice daily. He kept close track of the condition of the prisoners, quickly detecting any excessive nervousness or loss of weight and prescribing for headaches and minor complaints, as needed. In the evening he distributed sleeping pills to anybody who wanted them. It was surprising that very few of the major defendants wanted sleeping pills, because they did not want their wits dulled by medications, during the time they hoped to formulate their defense or to hear the prosecution allegations read in court. For example, Göring liked one sodium amytal capsule, which was greenish-blue, plus one tablet of phenobarbital which was white. Later he preferred a (red) seconal capsule instead of phenobarbital. Jodl and Dönitz would never take sleeping pills until after the sentences were pronounced. Then they found themselves so upset that they could not sleep. They were appreciative of sleeping pills at that time, from Dr. Pflücker, if approved by the U.S. Army doctor on duty.

Factors That Saved Us from a Prison Break

Clearly our security against a well-planned armed attack was totally inadequate. It was indeed a paper tiger. The tanks and armored cars were window dressing with no experienced fighting men to man them. Skorzeny and his commandos could have overwhelmed us at will.

Fortunately, the vast majority of the German population, including the soldiers, were intensely and demonstrably relieved to have the war over. It is doubtful that they would have helped to hide the top members of the Nazi hierarchy, even if a group of their fanatic followers had liberated them from the prison. (We saw examples of this disillusionment many times.) When Ley was captured in Bavaria, for example, he was masquerading successfully as a schoolteacher, but members of the local populace pointed him out to the paratroopers of my old 501st Parachute Infantry Regiment, even though our soldiers had not been at all suspicious of

him. The same was true of Streicher, who was masquerading as an artist (also in Bavaria) and had let his hair and beard grow and become white. This was so different from his well-known dark "cue-ball" haircut, that it made him unrecognizable. It turned out that he was thoroughly disliked by most of the populace and that his anti-Semitic newspaper, *Der Sturmer*, was not

Fig 21—Ribbentrop talking with lawyer in courtroom

Here at one of the breaks in the middle of the morning, as in the middle of the afternoon, Ribbentrop can be seen talking to his lawyer in the seats just below the prisoners. There was much exchange of documents and envelopes and Göring could easily have obtained his poison from his lawyer at that time, if both had desired to do it. It seems highly unlikely that these top lawyers would have taken such a chance, however. After the sentencing, there were no further opportunities for the lawyers to exchange things with the defendants since they were no longer meeting in court each day. There are many things that point to the fact that Göring did not have the poison until just a few days before his death. Nevertheless, the possibility existed, as you can see from this photograph.

held in high regard even by the Nazis themselves (except for Hitler). Certainly Streicher's fellow prisoners from the top Nazi hierarchy wanted nothing to do with him. They snubbed and avoided him at every possible juncture. He had been shunted out of the top Nazi circles, but since Hitler had relished his newspaper, he continued as its editor, publishing it from his farm. Göring very nearly had him killed for hinting that Göring's child had been conceived by artificial insemination.

It is, of course, possible that some of the more popular figures, like Göring, Speer, the generals and the admirals, might have been respected enough that they would have been sheltered and hidden by the German civilian population. On the other hand, now that the populace knew that Hitler had abandoned them by committing suicide, had ordered the destruction of Germany, and had declared to Speer near the end that the people "did not deserve to survive, since they had lost the war," they had a somewhat different view of the Nazis. The fact that Himmler had also become a traitor to Hitler at the end, and then had abandoned them all by committing suicide, left his SS troops disil-

lusioned, as well. Some of the younger SS troops were still a surly, fanatical lot, as we occasionally found out.

Another factor in our favor was the lack of transportation for the Germans. The railroads were damaged and trains were not running except for Allied military missions on the few repaired tracks; there were no buses and no easily available fuel supplies. It would have been necessary to steal U.S. Army vehicles, Army petrol and American Army uniforms. All of this might possibly have been done, had some expert like Skorzeny been available and convinced he should do it. Skorzeny, fortunately, had surrendered by May 16 and was in prison. His still active, underground organization was gearing up now, primarily to take care of the hardship cases among the demobilized officers. It was always difficult to know how much of an underground communication network was in action in the prison, but since the "help" were German POWs, I was very doubtful about the actual dedication of these people to our side. Many of the prisoners such as Albert Speer, Baldur von Schirach, and Walther Funk later told of their smoothly functioning pipelines to the outside. (Funk could always get cigars and champagne.) Colonel Andrus was ridiculously gullible in his belief that the POW "help" were all trustworthy and loyal to him, but after talking to Skorzeny I did not believe this.

Andrus had carefully selected what he insisted were highly dependable, loyal people to staff his prison. These were cooks, mess attendants, and barbers whom he had interviewed and selected from among a vast number of German prisoners. The presence of these fellow Germans gave a great boost to the morale of our prisoners. The POWS had known the rigors of imprisonment and therefore behaved very helpfully towards our prisoners whenever there were no supervisory personnel around. They managed to whisper to them the news from the papers, as well as good wishes and encouragement. The wives of several of our prisoners reported later that they had been able to arrange communication links with their spouses through the prison help. This belied the absurd boasts of Colonel Andrus that he was "in total control." He repeatedly made the mistake of undermining his own credibility by expressing total confidence in his staff of prison workers in a most naïve way.

There was also the opportunity for the prisoners to exchange papers and envelopes with their lawyers who sat immediately in front of them during the mid-morning and mid-afternoon breaks (fig. 21). On the other hand, there was no opportunity to exchange things in the interview rooms where they met their lawyers and visitors.

Dr. Pflücker, the shy German POW doctor,(Fig. 24)

who was our day-to-day interface with the prisoners, appeared to be very careful not to overstep Colonel Andrus's confidence in him. Nevertheless, the prisoners all wrote notes to him, expressing deep appreciation for the encouragement he had given them (fig. 25). It became obvious that even he, with so much to lose in the way of special privileges for his family, had transmitted a great deal of information to our prisoners. Göring wrote a separate note of thanks to Dr. Pflücker (fig. 26).

I believed the POW "help" was loyal to us only because we controlled the food, the assignment of living quarters, the fuel and practically everything else. The civilians outside were living in holes in the rubble with no heat or electricity and very little food.

I saw the underground network in action one day, for

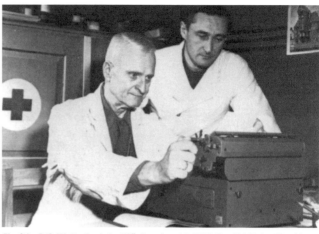

Fig 24—P.O.W. Dr. Ludwig Pflücker (and P.O.W. Dentist Heinz Hoch)
Our timorous 65-year-old cardiac P.O.W. doctor who made rounds twice daily and was a great morale-booster for the prisoners. He wrote me lengthy, perceptive notes about each of our "patients." With him is Dr. Heinz Hoch, the P.O.W. prison dentist.

example, when one of the German news agency officials in Nuremberg, William Stricker, asked if the Nazi suicide capsules were available to the public. Two hours after hearing this question, one of his own German reporters handed him a cyanide capsule of the standard design in its brass case. Declaring he could procure all we wanted, he had purchased it for three packs of cigarettes on the black market at the always-crowded local railroad station.

A major factor in our favor was our control of the food supply. Everyone who worked for or with the occupation forces was fed a great deal better than any other Germans. This was a powerful incentive in controlling the loyalty of the workers who were assigned to us. One day a cranky Göring said he would not feed his dogs the coarse army food we were giving him. The German POW attendant responded, "Then you always fed your dogs better than you fed the German people, for this is far better food than the Germans have been getting."

Another very effective control mechanism was the intervention by our prison officials on behalf of the families of the Germans who were working for us in the prison. We managed to have them assigned to better quarters closer to the prison. They were not only better cared for, but they were more available for visiting by the personnel who were working at the prison. I observed this particularly in the case of Dr. Pflücker. Because of his privileged arrangement, he was in a position to do all manner of unsuspected things, though I doubted that he would take any great risks because of the great personal value he placed on the fact that he was able to manage better quarters and bet-

Fig 22—The prisoners were separated while walking
During any exercise periods the prisoners had to walk far enough apart but they could not communicate. They had their hands in handcuffs.

Fig 23—Final judgement passes
These special passes were issued for the heavily attended "final judgement" session. Evan Lattimer Collection.

Für Dr. Pflücker

Dies wird dich immer unterscheiden
von vielen, die im gleichen Kleid;
auch andre Ärzte lindern Leiden,
du linderst Leid.

Herzliche Glückwünsche von den dankbaren Patienten

Raeder

Dönitz

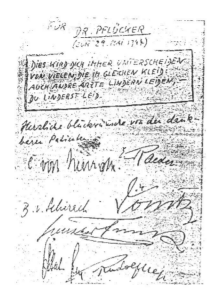

Fig 25—Prisoners thank Dr. Pflücker
This "thank-you" note in rhyme, written by Dönitz, was signed by several of the prisoners, indicating that he was helpful to them, probably much more than Col. Andrus would believe. Evan Lattimer Collection.

In aufrichtiger Dankbarkeit
für Ihre menschliche Güte
und den besten Wünschen
für Ihre Zukunft.

Hermann Göring
Reichsmarschall
Nürnberg 28. Sept. 1946.

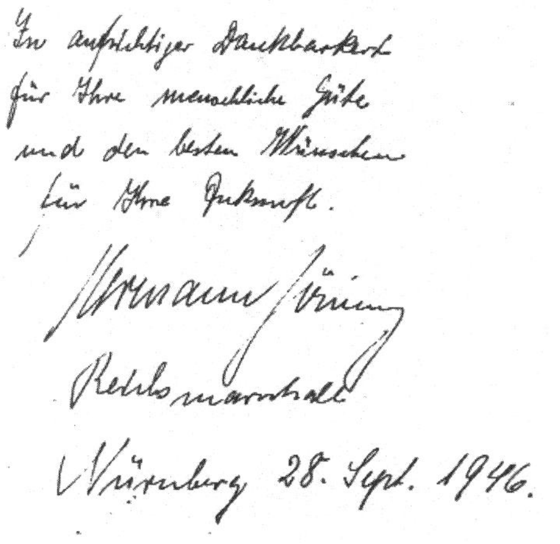

Fig 26—Göring wrote his own grateful note to Dr. Pflücker
This note clearly indicated that the doctor had done Göring many kindnesses. It also raises the question of whether he did Göring one small but important final favor. Göring wrote the following - to Dr. Pflücker: With sincere gratitude for your human kindness and with best wishes for your future. Hermann Göring, Reichsmarshall, Nuremberg 28 Sept. 1946 (the last day of the trial). Evan Lattimer Collection.

ter rations for his family than any of their acquaintances. This privilege was on the authority of an order signed by General Eisenhower himself. It was a matter of great pride for Dr. Pflücker and it gave him a major degree of motivation.

It took a while for such strategies of management to be developed. They did not come naturally to the old cavalryman, Colonel Andrus. It was primarily through the pressure of the American Army staff doctors that he finally acceded to this style of management. He was so crusty that the vast majority of the Allied civilian personnel who worked at the prison disliked him intensely, even though most of his techniques of strict army discipline were fairly effective, especially considering the weakness and untrained nature of his guard detachment personnel. Interestingly, the rank and file Germans reacted well to his authoritarian manner.

Even after the surrender, most of the German soldiers were still hoping that the Americans might unite with them and attack the Soviet Army. One could not talk to a German officer or soldier for very long without his bringing up this possibility. It seemed to them to be eminently logical. For the first several months, this seemed absolutely ludicrous to me because these same Germans, who had been trying to kill us for several years, now wanted us to join them and turn against the Soviet Army which had been fighting and risking its lives to support us throughout the war. During the trial, it came out that Himmler, Kaltenbrunner and even Hitler, had counted on this same ploy in the end.

I must say that later, we all had second thoughts about this whole matter when Stalin quickly began to act like an adversary. General Patton came to this conclusion early on, and when German commanders of troops, even in prison detachments, asked his permission to speak, he would hear them out. He thought their proposals sounded eminently reasonable and told me that he thought they were a "great idea." The fact that our atom bombs were able to hold the Soviets under control during all those aggressive postwar years was a great tribute to our scientists. Whether this optimism on the part of the Germans, that we might eventually join them in a campaign against the Communists, played any part in the willingness of the Germans to cooperate with the American Occupation Army is hard to tell.

Still another factor in our formula for success in dealing with the demobilized German Army was their knowledge that the Soviets had requested that certain Germans be sent to the Soviet zone for prosecution. They had actually seen this occur, and as was frequently the case, they knew it did not matter whether the accusation was correct or not; if the Soviets demanded it, it might be done. Whereupon the prisoner just "disappeared." Certainly during the days when the surrender was being arranged, the Wehrmacht units that were marching toward the Americans to surrender were much happier than the units that were compelled to stand and hold off the Russians, into whose hands they would eventually fall when their ammunition ran out and their defenses finally collapsed. Admiral Dönitz, who had taken over command of the German nation, was well aware of this and deliberately deferred sign-

ing the surrender for a week, during which period hundreds of thousands of German soldiers marched west to surrender to the Americans rather than be gobbled up by the Soviets. The "Russian threat" was a very powerful device for persuading the German populace and the disbanding German Army in the American zone to behave themselves. It also quickly became apparent to the German populace that the Americans were almost eager to help them rebuild their shattered country. The extent, of course, to which this tendency has been carried during the following 50 years has indeed been astonishing.

Luckily for us, the German populace as well as their defeated army also recognized that the Americans were the group to depend upon for the future. They made the right choice and it made our job easier, even as we prosecuted their failed Nazi leaders.

Security on Hanging Day: The Final Worry

We had one final spasm of anxiety on the day the condemned men were to be hanged. All the many efforts to restrict knowledge of the date of the executions were useless. Actually, the date had already been set at the time of the sentencing on October 1st. It was to be on October 15, 1946. Tradition suggested that the hangings would start at dawn, and this was the general assumption. As usual, the rumor market knew all about the date and about the three gallows that had been erected in the prison gymnasium, but *not* about the early hour of the executions. Colonel Andrus had made an effort to conceal the erecting of the gallows by staging a noisy staff basketball game, but this was futile. Word had reached us that German nationalist groups were planning a mass march on the Palace of Justice as a demonstration of protest on the 16th.

The one very effective secret that was not revealed widely was that the hour the hangings were to start would be 1:00 A.M., rather than dawn. Everyone, including the prisoners, were misled by this.

Dr. Pflücker, however, was told by Colonel Andrus's staff at 3:00 P.M.. that the prisoners would be awakened at 11:45 P.M., given their final meal (a choice of sausage and potato salad or pancakes and applesauce) and told to dress in their courtroom clothes, for the execution. The doctor was told to adjust his sleeping pill administration to anticipate the earlier hour and not to sedate them too heavily at the usual bedtime. Almost immediately, he made an additional visit to Göring and had a long conversation with him, in addition to giving him some saccharin for his coffee. As Ben Swearingen speculated, Dr. Pflücker very possibly told Göring at that

time that the commencing of the hangings had been moved up to 1:00 A.M. This enabled Göring to extract the suicide capsule from its brass covering and then to use it to kill himself at the last possible moment, after it had become obvious that any last-minute reprieve (which he had half-expected) was not going to occur. When he was asked if he said anything to Göring about the earlier hour, Dr. Pflücker said Göring had asked him if it was worthwhile getting undressed for bed. He said that he replied that "Under the conditions, a night might seem very short." He denied telling Göring the actual time when the hangings were to begin.

To guard against any demonstration, the garrison was put on full alert in the evening and troops from the 1st Infantry Division, quartered north of the city, were moved into town unobtrusively. The gates around the Palace of Justice were locked and patrolled in an extraordinary manner. The moving up of the hour for the hangings was very effective in defusing the tension, since the executions were a *fait accompli* when the morning newspapers came out. Even the officers at the gates were surprised to learn in the morning that the hangings had finished.

Göring's embarrassing, last minute suicide distracted the press, many of whom were taken by surprise after reporting in haste that he too had been hanged. The fact that three of the defendants—Schacht, von Papen and Fritzsche—were acquitted and were now available for interviews (and more than willing to talk at length) also distracted the attention of the press who had a feeding frenzy in interviewing them. The civilian populace had the newspapers to occupy them and this worked very well. Still another surprise development was the move by the German civilian police to arrest all three of the men who had been exonerated and to try them now in German civilian courts. von Papen refused to leave the prison for several days but was eventually seized by the German police. After lengthy appeals, none of the three received anything more than token sentences and were again released.

The Cremations

After the hangings, a closely guarded convoy of trucks, laden with the bodies in their coffins, completed their high-speed, escorted journey down the autobahn to the outskirts of Munich. They were two hours later than had been anticipated, arriving at the Ostfriedhof (cemetery) crematorium in Munich at 9:00 A.M. instead of the scheduled 7:00 A.M. time, as documented by Ben Swearingen. The crematorium staff guessed of course that the bodies were those of the 11 defendants rather than the alleged bodies of 11

Fig 27—The hangman
The laconic Sergeant John C. Wood, an experienced army hangman, had hanged 375 men. He sent to America for good hemp rope, which he stretched and bent into nooses of his own design. He kept a short segment of each rope as his personal keepsake, foiling Col. Andrus' orders, once again. He said he was proud of hanging the Nazis.

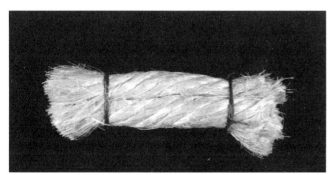

Fig 28—Hangman Wood also defeated Colonel Andrus
He saved a short segment of each prisoner's rope in defiance of Colonel Andrus' guarantee "That no souvenirs would be kept." This one was from Streicher's rope. Evan Lattimer Collection.

American soldiers whose families had decided to have them cremated (the cover story of the men bringing the bodies). We did not fool them one bit. The men at the crematorium had already heard the news about Göring's suicide and guessed immediately that that two-hour delay was caused by the investigation of his death. Nevertheless, in spite of all our worries and precautions, no demonstration or other effort was made to protest this landmark trial or its outcome.

Additional trials of various groups at Nuremberg and Dachau had been arranged. Security measures were greatly reduced for these trials, based on the complaints about Colonel Andrus's excesses and the lessened fear of suicide. The big event was now over without any outside violence. We were all greatly relieved.

Colonel Andrus's security system undoubtedly protected our prisoners from unauthorized visits and harassment, but against an armed military assault we would have been helpless. We all thanked goodness that Skorzeny had given himself up after a couple of weeks and that Colonel Andrus's paper tiger was never put to the ultimate test.

The American Medical Staff for the Prisoners

The American doctors who were known to me had been recruited from the units quartered near Nuremberg. The first overall medical officer was Lt. Colonel Renee Juchli who was in charge at Mondorf. Dr. W.N.J. Miller served under him. Major Douglas M. Kelley was an excellent psychiatrist who was brought in to examine Göring, and who then arranged to be assigned as the prison psychiatrist (fig. 29). He left to go home at the end of 1945, after the transfer to Nuremberg and the beginning of the trial. He had a distinguished academic career at Bowman Gray Medical School in North Carolina and then at the University of California but inexplicably committed suicide on New Year's Day, 1957, at the age of 44. Major Gustav Gilbert, our Columbia-trained prison psychologist arrived in October 1945 as an interpreter and stayed on as our psychologist for the entire trial (fig. 30). He died in 1977 at age 66. Captain Richard Worthington succeeded Major Kelley but suffered a fractured skull in a jeep accident after only a few weeks (fig. 31). Major Leon Goldensohn followed Dr. Worthington, and was with us the longest of the psychiatrists, from January until July of 1946 (fig. 32). He died suddenly in 1962, at age 50, after a distinguished career.

Major Goldensohn was followed in turn by Lt. Colonel William Dunn, (fig. 34) who came over from the States from August to October 1946. Dr. Dunn died in the 1950s. Lieutenants Roy Martin and Charles Roska came early in 1946 and officiated during the hangings. Dr. Martin (now Captain Martin) accompanied the prisoners who were transferred to Berlin for a brief time at Spandau (fig. 33). After being promoted to captain Dr. Roska served at some of the subsequent trials, Captain David Smith was our dentist from October 1945 until he went home in August of 1946 (fig. 35). In general, the prisoners were afforded the same dental care as our own troops. Funk had a lower tooth extracted by Dr. Hoch, under Dr. Smith's supervision. Göring cracked one of his porcelain jackets on an upper incisor, but this was not repaired because it was considered cosmetic rather than a disease or a life-threatening problem. Admiral Francis Braceland, a distinguished

Fig 31—Worthington, Richard, M.D., prison psychiatrist from December 1945 to February 1946

Then he was seriously injured in a motor accident. He graduated from Yale Medical School and trained at the Henry Ford Hospital and at the Foxboro State Hospital in Massachusetts. He was the Chief of Neurology/Psychiatry for several veterans hospitals and has retired to California.

Fig 29—Kelley, Douglas M., M.D. Prison psychiatrist, June 1945 to January 1, 1946

He came first to the Interrogation Center at Mondorf and then moved with the prisoners to Nuremberg. He was born in California, was a graduate of the University of California, was a Rockefeller Fellow and got his psychiatric training at the Columbia Presbyterian Medical Center in New York. He was an expert on the Rorschach method of psychiatric examination and the President of the American Rorschach Association. He was also a magician and President of the American Society of Magicians. After the war he became Professor of Psychiatry of the Bowman Gray Medical School in North Carolina and then at the University of California. He died January 1, 1958 of cyanide poisoning.

Fig 32—Goldensohn, Leon, M.D., prison psychiatrist from January-July 1946

A graduate of George Washington Medical School. he trained at Montefiore Hospital in New York. He was a U.S. Army regimental psychiatrist at the end of the war and was recruited to take care of the prisoners. He later became President of the White Psychiatric Institute. He died in 1962.

(Left) Fig 30—Gilbert, Gustav, Ph.D. prison psychologist, Oct. 1945 to Oct. 1946

Dr. Gilbert was born in New York City in 1911, trained in psychology at Columbia University and was recruited to the Psychology Departments of Bard College and the Connecticut College for Women, before entering the Army. Following his Army experience he was on the faculties of Princeton, and Michigan State Universities. He then became Chairman of the Department of Psychology at Long Island University. He was the President of the Investigative Society of Psychologists, a member of the American Psychological Association and was awarded the Berings Award for the best psychological study of social tensions in 1950. His book - Nuremberg Diary, (Farrar & Straus/New York) is excellent. Dr. Gilbert died in 1977. Here he is shown speaking bluntly to Speer, Funk, Fritzsche and Schacht.

Fig 33—Our general medical officers for most of 1946

Dr. Roy A. Martin (left) was a graduate of the University of Louisville Medical School, and later trained at Tulane. He came in the spring of 1946, officiated at the hangings, and accompanied the group who went to Spandau. He is now an otolaryngologist in Louisville. In the center is our head nurse Cartier, and on the right is Dr. Charles Roska who worked with Dr. Martin and also officiated at the hangings. He served at some of the subsequent trials, as well. He is a graduate of the Case-Western Reserve Medical School and trained in New York and Cleveland and was later on the staff of the University of Illinois Hospitals. He is now retired in California.

Fig 35—Capt. David Smith (DDS) our prison dentist

Dr. Smith served at Nuremberg from October 1945 to August 1946. He supervised the work of Heinz Hoch, our POW dentist.

Fig 34—Dunn, William H., M.D., prison psychiatrist from August to Oct. 1946

Member of the staff of the New York Hospital Cornell Medical Center, New York City. brought over from the states to finish out the main trial.

Fig 36—Braceland, Francis J., M.D., Psychiatric consultant

He was sent to examine Hess, in early 1946. Dr. Braceland was one of the country's outstanding psychiatrists. He was President of the American Board of Psychiatry and Neurology, the American Psychiatric Association and the World Psychiatric Association. He was a graduate of Jefferson Medical College, was the Dean at Loyola Medical School and the head of several large psychiatric institutions. He died in 1985.

Fig 37—Ford, Manley, M.D., Urological consultant
Urological surgeon of the 116th Ganeral Hospital at Nuremberg and a consultant for patients Dönitz and Funk at various times. He trained at Case Western Reserve Medical School and the Cleveland Clinic. Also at Akron hospitals and has been one of the leading practitioners in Akron since the war.

Fig 39—Whisenand, James M.,M.D., Urologist for Funk
Born 1922 in Wyoming. He went to St. Louis University Medical School and trained in San Diego as a urologist. He was the urologist at the 97th General Hospital and called to Spandau to examine Funk who was in chronic urinary retention. Dr. Whisenand did a vary successful transurethral prostatectomy on the 67-year-old Funk, in September, 1954 in Spandau after many months of Foley catheter drainage. Dr. Whisenand returned to La Jolla, California to private practice as the Chief of Staff of the Scripps Memorial Hospital in La Jolla. Deceased in 1995.

Fig 38—Lattimer, John K.,M.D.,Sc.D. Urological consultant and general medical officer to the prison
Educated at Columbia University; 4 diplomas. Trained Columbia Presbyterian Medical Center. Detached from 7th Army Headquarters and the 98th General Hospital in Munich to serve at the trial. Since then Professor and Chairman, Dept. of Urology, Columbia University Medical School and the Presbyterian Hospital, NYC. President of the American Urological Association and International Society of Urologists. Evan Lattimer Collection.

Fig 40—Patton, John, M.D., Dönitz' Urologist
When Doenitz observed the success of the transurethral prostate operation on Funk, he demanded one also. Dr. John Patton, the Senior U.S. Army urologist, came to Berlin and did a highly successful transurethral resection of Dönitz' prostate in 1955. Deceased in 1990.

psychiatrist, Captain Manley Ford, a urological surgeon, and I came in as consultants on detached service when needed (figs. 36-38).

After the transfer to Spandau, Captain James M. Whisenand, a urologist, (fig. 39) was brought in to do a transurethral resection of the prostate on Funk, which was a great success. Admiral Dönitz observed how easily the operation had gone and demanded one for himself. Colonel John Patton, the senior United States Army urologist, (fig. 40) was brought over to perform the operation on Admiral Dönitz which also went very well indeed. Both operations were performed in the British army hospital in Berlin, using the latest American instruments.

Dr. Ludwig Pflücker was our elderly, almost timorous POW doctor who helped us take care of the prisoners. His cardiac status was precarious and he could do no heavy work. He had spent several episodes in the hospitals of our POW camps, during the two months after the surrender.

Dr. Pflücker was a native of Bad Wildungen, born in 1880. He had studied medicine in Goettingen, Marburg, and Erlangen, had worked at various hospitals, and had been a ship's doctor from 1910-1913, traveling to the Orient. In WWI he was a hospital staff physician. After the war he trained to be a urologist with Dr. Carl Kruger and practiced in Bad Wildungen. From 1921 to 1934, and again from 1948-1949, he was president of the Physicians' Association in Bad Wildungen.

During the Second World War, he was physician-in-chief at the Military Reserve Hospital there, and after the surrender was rounded up with all who were in uniform and herded through a series of prison camps. In July 1945, he was selected to help at the U.S. Army Prisoner Interrogation Center at Mondorf, Luxembourg: his ability to speak English as well as his deferential but confident manner made him an excellent choice. He had been accustomed to dealing with famous patients as a urologist at the spa, so he was an easy choice among the candidates interviewed.

When Dr. Pflücker arrived at Mondorf, he was instructed emphatically by Colonel Andrus that he was to speak to the prisoners only briefly and directly with no extra conversation. Colonel Andrus also demanded that he keep track of the prisoners' morale. The American, army staff doctors quickly persuaded Andrus to permit a little more normal conversation with the prisoners who were chafing under the overly severe restrictions placed upon Dr. Pflücker.

At first, Pflücker would come to "attention" in the presence of Göring or the four top military men, but he relaxed as time went on. As he proved his worth, the medical staff arranged for his family to be moved into much better housing closer to the prison. He served us well during the first trial, and stayed in the same capacity at the subsequent trials until 1948. He then returned to his private practice as an office urologist at the spa in Bad Wildungen. He retired in 1950 and died in 1953 at age 73.

Because Göring left him several notes of appreciation at the end, and gave him choice and valuable mementos such as a signed photograph of his wife and child, some thought this signified that he had done many more favors for Göring than we realized. It even stimulated speculation that he did Göring at least one small final "favor" on the night of his suicide, as described in the chapter on Göring.

All things considered, we felt greatly relieved at the end of the trial. Göring had outwitted Colonel Andrus in poisoning himself and two men had hanged themselves, but at least no jailbreak had occurred. The executions came off on schedule and we all heaved a great sigh of relief. But let us look closely at the rest of the prisoners.

CHAPTER SIX

Dr. Leonard Conti

Fig 1—Dr. Leonard Conti

Dr. Conti was a State Health Commisioner, who was to represent the medical profession, even though he had not been directly involved in any atrocities. He was severely agitated and depressed, and hanged himself in his cell, using a strip of towel on October 6, 1945. His suicide was kept a secret until January, 1946.

Dr. Leonard Conti, the national health commissioner, was selected for the initial war crimes trial above the two dozen or more Nazi doctors who had actually been involved in the human experimentation and euthanasia programs. I was puzzled as to why they selected *him*. He was a member of the table of organization of the Nazi government, but it seemed to me that there were much more shocking candidates who could have been tried in this showpiece first trial.

One of them was SS Colonel Karl Brandt, one of Hitler's own doctors, who actively participated in the killing of many victims during the course of the various "tests" conducted by the Nazis on a systematic basis. Brandt was indeed tried in a subsequent trial of all of the remaining doctors and was convicted and hanged. He would have made, in my opinion, a much more dramatic appearance and been clearly guilty, in contrast to Conti who was actually a rather shadowy figure in all of the proceedings.

Conti often sat in the second row at conferences, while other Nazi doctors occupied the front seats and were more obvious in the decision making. His staff had sometimes actually objected to some of the medical experiments that were being done, probably reflecting his views, although he himself had never vigorously objected on the record to any of the proceedings. There were general manifestos issued by Hitler to kill off mentally defective children and persons of various ages and ethnic groups. These rules, spelled out by Hitler, were put into action, undoubtedly, by Conti's organization. But Conti was an administrator and never clearly appeared as a performer of any of these genocidal experiments. Even the decisions were obviously based on Hitler's decrees.

It had apparently not been firmly decided that Conti would be tried with the others in the first trial, since there was consideration of shifting him to the "doctors" trial which came later. Unfortunately for him, none of this had been decided in time. It seemed very possible that he might have received a much lighter sentence had he been tried with the other shockingly guilty doctors. This was the case with several of the other defendants later on, when they were shown to have been plotters against Hitler, as Conti had been, and thus punished less severely.

Certainly his departments did perform experiments on humans, such as those to determine the effects of bacteria and various toxins, and comparisons of the effectiveness of various treatments. It should be remembered that these experiments were done before the days of antibiotics. Furthermore, it was disclosed that concentration camp inmates had been used by other SS doctors in experiments to determine how long humans could be exposed to ice-cold water before they would expire. These ghoulish experiments also determined exactly what the order of lethal effects was, how soon their hearts would stop, and at what point they might or might not be salvageable. Similar experiments were done with high-altitude simulations to determine exactly how the body died, when it could be revived, and after how long a period without oxygen.

The chests of living "patients" were sometimes cut open to watch the heart stop or start beating again. In records of the "freezing" experiments, it was described how the bodies were sometimes warmed by placing them in a bed with a healthy female. It was determined that one female working enthusiastically was more effective than two females, where inhibitions possibly prevented their total devotion to their task. If the patient could be revived and was in condition to perform intercourse, his recovery was even faster, apparently because of the hormonal effects. The final conclusion was that immersion in very hot water was more effective than any other method for re-warming the almost frozen bodies of aviators or sailors who might be trapped in the cold waters. There was no advantage to warming the bodies slowly; rapid warming was the most effective method. There were also comparisons of homeopathic and allopathic (usual) medical dosages, which came out heavily in favor of the allopathic dosages. And bacterial infections were confirmed as being dependably deadly when instilled into damaged tissues surrounding a wound.

After his transfer to Nuremberg, Dr. Conti paced his cell day and night in a fit of despondency. He then penciled a long, twenty-page statement about his political and professional career. He wrote a note about Hitler's last known state of health and wrote a letter to his wife in which he said, "I part from life because I made false statements under oath. I was out of my senses. For months now I have had the gravest moods, depressions, ideas of death, feelings of fear, visions, although I have never been a coward. I wanted so much to see my family one more time."

On October 6, 1945, Conti decided he could face the world no longer. He took his towel, made it into a long slender cord, and tied it around the bars of his cell window. He then took his chair and put it against the wall so that his feet would be clear of the floor and jumped from the chair. This was during the time when the number of guards assigned to the prison was totally inadequate, so that one man had to tour four different cells, looking in each one periodically. Conti timed his action so that the guard would be away for the maximum time. By the time the guard came back, he was dead.

After Conti killed himself, a news blackout was declared and a cover-up was instituted. No word of his suicide came out. It was only in January of 1946 (three months later) that the suicide was reported in the Army newspaper *Stars and Stripes*. They were acting on information supplied by an unnamed source and reported the full story. On January 14th, Colonel Andrus wrote a memorandum to the commanding general in which he reported that he had told the inquiring correspondents that they had to address their questions to the "unnamed" source from which their information was obtained, "since we have no information to give out." Andrus told the General that "as far as the Office of Internal Security is concerned, its records show Conti was transferred to a hospital. At the time of Conti's death, my office was ordered to classify the matter as 'secret.' "It was Colonel Andrus's opinion that nobody still at the prison could have discussed the suicide with the correspondent that had written the story. Possibly the fact that Conti's covered-up suicide could not be kept a secret for very long, influenced future policy. The subsequent suicide of Ley was reported immediately.

CHAPTER SEVEN

Admiral Karl Dönitz

Fig 1—Grand Admiral Karl Dönitz, age 54
Admiral Dönitz, the Head of the German State for 7 days, as the designated successor, by Hitler, was a haughty, intelligent, bad tempered Admiral. He had come up through the ranks, to be a cruiser commander and then a submarine commander and later as the chief of all submarine warfare. He had replaced Raeder as the Commander of the entire Navy in the final 2 years of the war. If Hitler had listened to his pleas for a much larger U-boat fleet early on, the Nazis might have won the war. He was given only 10 years of imprisonment, to everyone's surprise. He signed this photograph for the author. Evan Lattimer Collection.

Karl Dönitz had been commander in chief of U-Boats since 1935 and was promoted to grand admiral and chief of the entire German Navy, after Admiral Raeder "stepped down" in 1943. He was a tall, slender, slightly imperious, tight-lipped admiral of high intelligence (fig. 1). Following the death of Hitler, he became chancellor in May 1945. Hitler had designated Dönitz to follow him in this post.

Dönitz had been born in 1891 in Grünau (near Berlin). He joined the navy in 1910 and in 1914 was transferred to the naval air arm where he became a flight observer, and later a seaplane squadron leader. From 1916 to 1918, he was in the U-Boat Service. He was taken prisoner at the end of the war and in 1919 was taken on by the new German Navy. In 1929 he commanded the cruiser *Emden*, and in 1932 he went "on staff" at the North Sea Naval Station. Three years later he was promoted to Kapitän zur See and then commander of U-Boats; in 1939, he was made Konteradmiral; in 1940, Viceadmiral; in 1942, admiral; and in 1943, Grossadmiral, in command of the entire navy. He was awarded the Knight's Cross, in April 1940; and Oak Leaves to the Knight's Cross, in April 1943.

He had an IQ of 138 which was near the top of the list—the same as Göring and only three points less than Seyss-Inquart. (Hjalmar Schacht had the highest I.Q. of all at 143, only because of an allowance for his age.)

Dönitz surrendered all German forces at midnight, May 8, 1945 (fig. 3).

Despite his situation, Dönitz did not hesitate to complain. He wrote the following note to General Montgomery after the surrender:

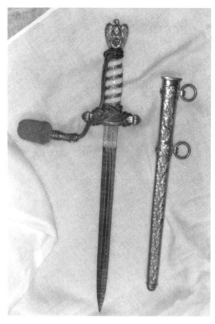

Fig 2—Dönitz' dress dagger
A naval honor dagger U-boot-Sieger.

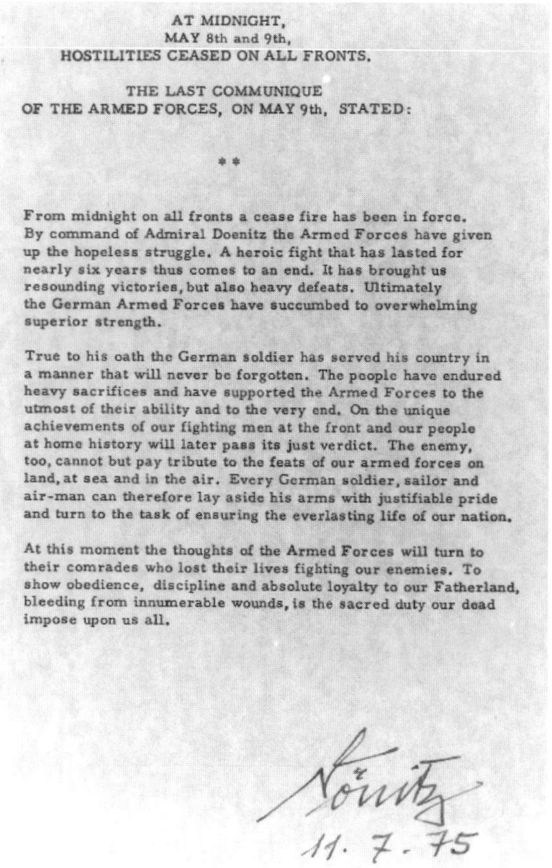

AT MIDNIGHT,
MAY 8th and 9th,
HOSTILITIES CEASED ON ALL FRONTS.

THE LAST COMMUNIQUE
OF THE ARMED FORCES, ON MAY 9th, STATED:

* *

From midnight on all fronts a cease fire has been in force. By command of Admiral Doenitz the Armed Forces have given up the hopeless struggle. A heroic fight that has lasted for nearly six years thus comes to an end. It has brought us resounding victories, but also heavy defeats. Ultimately the German Armed Forces have succumbed to overwhelming superior strength.

True to his oath the German soldier has served his country in a manner that will never be forgotten. The people have endured heavy sacrifices and have supported the Armed Forces to the utmost of their ability and to the very end. On the unique achievements of our fighting men at the front and our people at home history will later pass its just verdict. The enemy, too, cannot but pay tribute to the feats of our armed forces on land, at sea and in the air. Every German soldier, sailor and air-man can therefore lay aside his arms with justifiable pride and turn to the task of ensuring the everlasting life of our nation.

At this moment the thoughts of the Armed Forces will turn to their comrades who lost their lives fighting our enemies. To show obedience, discipline and absolute loyalty to our Fatherland, bleeding from innumerable wounds, is the sacred duty our dead impose upon us all.

11. 7. 75

Fig 3—Dönitz ends the war
A copy of Dönitz' last communication to the German Armed Forces. With this bulletin, he ended the war in Europe. The date is when he signed this copy for the author. Evan Lattimer Collection.

To the High Commander of the 21st English Army group Field Marshal Sir Reg. Montgomery.

Field Marshal:

I feel myself compelled to report to you the following:

After my arrest of May 23rd in Flensburg, by troops under your command, I was subjected to a body check without any regard to my rank.

At the same time my personal belongings were searched. Besides a number of valuables my Marshal's Baton was also taken away, which I had intentionally left in my personal luggage, assuming that this symbol of honor of a soldier of my rank would be respected even by a victorious adversary.

I did not receive any receipt for the removed valuables, nor for my Marshal's Baton, not even for the Interims Baton, which was also taken away during the search.

Inasmuch as I am certain that you, General Field Marshal, will not tolerate violations of honorable conduct and removal of personal belongings, I am reporting these occurrences to you, and I am certain that this will result in the return of my Marshal's Baton as well as the Interims Baton and of the removed personal belongings.

I remain with my highest esteem,
DÖNITZ
Grand Admiral

Dönitz also wrote to Eisenhower, on the same day as Keitel, saying

General, I respectfully submit the following:

On 23 May the representative of the Supreme Commander of the Allied Invasion Forces in Flensburg, General Rooks, informed me and the Second in Command of the OKW [German High Command], General Jodl, as follows: On the basis of your decision, the German Government and the OKW were considered to be dissolved. Grand Admiral Dönitz and General Jodl were to consider themselves "POW" and would on that day be transferred to a POW camp.

Actually, we were transferred to an unmilitary civilian collecting point, which, insofar as conditions were concerned, resembled a detention prison. Here, under orders, the treatment is such that it dishonors a soldier and runs counter to the Geneva Convention. It includes such things as the taking away of military decorations and private property except, in the latter case, for the barest minimum.

I request for myself and in the name of General Jodl, quarters suitable for men of our rank and treatment that does not dishonor our unbesmirched standing as soldiers.

I remain most respectfully,

Dönitz, Grand Admiral

He also demanded the correct shirt to go with his blue suit, as follows (fig. 4):

To

Lt. Carver

Please, when I get my blue suit, I want my blue shirt then too. I have no shirt at all, only underwear, but that does not close at the throat, and the blue suit is open at the chest.

Dönitz

As noted above, Dönitz had been selected by Hitler to follow him as chancellor, after his (Hitler's) suicide. He was surprised by this honor but accepted it, with the following:

Announcement to the German People

May 1, 1945

The Führer has nominated me as his successor. In full consciousness of my responsibilities, I therefore assume the leadership of the German people at this fateful hour. My first task is to save German men and women from destruction by the advancing Bolshevist enemy. It is to serve this purpose alone that the military struggle continues. To impede the accomplishment of this task, we must also continue to fight and defend ourselves against them.

The British and the Americans in that case will not be fighting in the interests of their own peoples, but solely for the expansion of Bolshevism in Europe.

Dönitz

Our psychologists and psychiatrists characterized Dönitz as being imbued with great self-esteem and acting still very much the "Grand Admiral" as he strode about the exercise yard. He treated all the other prisoners with aloofness. He now blamed his old friend Speer for suggesting to Hitler that he should be the new successor as Führer. Dr. Gilbert found him to be an upright character, very intelligent, but politically very naïve: "He feels that he was 'kicked upstairs' to answer for crimes he knew nothing about." Our psychiatrist, Lt. Colonel William H. Dunn, who examined him much later on in the trial, said that he was by then very poised, affable, and pleasant-spoken. He had a better sense of humor than most of the defendants, but at times it became barbed, particularly when speaking of the trial, which he considered dominated by the politicians. He had very little dejection and no suicidal ideas, in Dr. Dunn's view.

Dönitz felt that if he had been tried before a military tribunal, he would have been cleared in three hours. His conscience was clear, he said. Neither he nor his defense counsel intended to make any defense of him personally, but only for the benefit of his officers and men. He felt that he had fought cleanly for his country and for the government in power. He was never a Nazi Party member and was never too sympathetic with that government. He demonstrated rather strikingly the attitude of the "good German" who feels he was discharging his duty to the nation and was not involved in the common guilt and shame of his people.

In the spring, Admiral Dönitz was visited in the prison by a ranking U.S. admiral—Chester Nimitz. The admiral had asked permission of Colonel Andrus to interview Dönitz and also said he would like to see how the prison was run. He was allowed into Dönitz's cell, as would any visiting high-ranking VIP, and with a sentinel standing by, he was allowed to talk privately with Dönitz. Colonel Andrus said he showed Admiral Nimitz the rest of the prison and that, "He thanked my officers and myself and departed."

After this visit, Dönitz became unbearable. He was puffed up and indicated that this U.S. admiral had in fact sympathized wholeheartedly with the former "Grand Admiral's" present plight. He had left a note with Dönitz saying "I want you to know I am on your

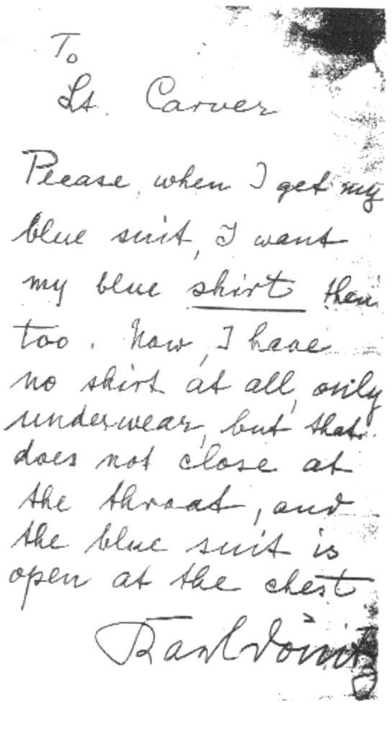
To

Lt. Carver

Please, when I get my blue suit, I want my blue shirt then too. Now, I have no shirt at all, only underwear, but that does not close at the throat, and the blue suit is open at the chest.

Karl Dönitz

Fig 4—Grand Admiral Dönitz begs for a shirt
Hitler's successor had a hard time keeping up a dignified appearance, with his underwear showing, despite his blue suit. In this note he asks Lt. Carver, a guard officer, to help him get a shirt. Evan Lattimer Collection.

side." This appeared in headlines in the American newspapers because Leonard Lyons, a widely syndicated columnist in the United States, had written: "During the Nuremberg trial, a visiting United States admiral, who was still in the service, arrived with three aides. Later that afternoon the lawyer for the Grand Admiral showed the U.S. legal staff a note, which he said the American admiral had given to Dönitz, which said 'I want you to know that I am on your side.'" Mr. Justice Jackson promptly phoned the admiral at Bremerhaven and told him that he would be called as a defense witness, because of this note. The admiral told him in effect to "get lost," that he had no intention of coming back to Nuremberg and was flying back to the United States that night. There was some concern that Dönitz, who now felt he had nothing to worry about, would get a shock when the Tribunal thought differently and gave him a stiff sentence.

Dönitz the Poet

Dönitz wrote thank-you notes on behalf of the group to Dr. Pflücker and others (fig. 5). To my surprise, these were usually in verse, and rhymed cleverly in German (fig. 6).

Fig 6—Dönitz' note of appreciation to Dr. Pflücker
This is in his usual poetic "verse," and is signed even by his enemy Raeder, and the scheming Hess. It rhymes (in German) and translates roughly as follows:
> *Dear Dr. Pflücker (May 29, 1947)*
> *In this you will always differ from others of your kind.*
> *Other physicians alleviate sorrow.*
> *Cordial congratulations from your grateful patients.*

C. von Neurath	E. Raeder
B. v. Schirach	Dönitz
Walther Funk	Rudolf Hess
Albert Speer	

Evan Lattimer Collection.

Fig 5—Dönitz the Poet
He asked the German doctor (Pflücker) in German verse: which translates roughly as follows:
> *Dear Doctor, send me bread and jam*
> *I would be eternally grateful to you*
> *For it would indeed be pity*
> *If I died (exaggeration) of hunger today*
This "gallows humor" rhymes well in German.
Evan Lattimer Collection.

Dönitz's Defense

By coincidence, Dönitz had to start his defense on May 8, 1946, the anniversary of V-E Day. He began by declaring that as an officer he had no concern with deciding whether a war was aggressive or not, he just had to obey orders. He said that the orders for U-Boat warfare had come from Admiral Raeder, and explained how the arming of merchant vessels forced the Germans to issue orders to "attack without warning." Similar orders from the British admiralty were also read to the court to justify the German procedures. The British, Dönitz alleged, had violated the rules of naval warfare, just as much as the Germans had. Dönitz described Germany as surrounded by enemies. He stated that any attempt to overthrow the government in wartime would be a threat to the state and, (with a dig at Schacht) anybody who planned such a "putsch" would be a traitor. Dönitz repeatedly justified his orders to sink ships without notice and not to rescue the survivors. "It is necessary to understand the conditions of military expediency," he declared.

The Judgment on Dönitz

The court concluded that although Dönitz built and trained the German U-Boat arm, the evidence did not show that he was privy to the conspiracy to wage aggressive wars or that he prepared and initiated such wars. The tribunal was of the opinion that the evidence did not establish with the certainty required that Dönitz deliberately ordered the killing of shipwrecked survivors. The evidence further showed that the no-rescue provisions were not carried out and that the defendant ordered that they should not be carried out. Dönitz was also charged with responsibility for Hitler's commando order of October 18, 1942, by which the members of the crew of a captured Allied torpedo boat were turned over to the SD (Sicherheitsdienst) and shot. As a consequence, Dönitz was found guilty on counts two and three, and sentenced to ten years' imprisonment.

Dönitz had an imperious manner that irritated many of the other defendants. He looked down on most of the other prisoners, including Admiral Raeder and particularly patronized Colonel Andrus. He was loud in his assertions that Hitler had lost the war by not paying attention to Dönitz' suggestion to build more U-Boats before he had declared war. Had Hitler built sufficient U-Boats, he argued, Germany could easily have won the war. It's entirely possible that Dönitz was correct in this. His tactics of attacking by "wolf packs" were tremendously successful until much later, when the numbers of Allied ships and warships became overwhelming.

Dönitz approached Speer (who had always been his friend) shortly before his release from Spandau and accused Speer of telling Hitler to appoint him (Dönitz) as his successor. Speer denied this accusation, although he did admit that he had spoken highly of Dönitz to Hitler on various occasions. Dönitz therefore blamed Speer for getting him into the mess of being responsible for Germany after Hitler's suicide. He had been Führer for only seven days, during which time he managed to hold off on the peace negotiations so that hundreds of thousands of his German troops could be disengaged from the Russians and marched west to surrender to the Americans.

As the hour of his release got closer, at the end of his ten years at Spandau, he broke down with dizziness and weeping. However he rallied enough to go home on schedule and live for 24 more years.

One of his notable achievements after his release was to assemble a thick book made up of letters or statements from practically every important and knowledgeable military person in the world including his former adversaries. They indicating that they thought military leaders should not be prosecuted in any subsequent war crimes trials, since they were compelled by the nature of war to do the things they did. (I must say that, as a military officer, I felt that way myself.)

In short, Dönitz was a highly intelligent, very straightforward, rather cold admiral who told everything the way it was. He did not hesitate to criticize his colleagues and was aided by a stroke of luck when Admiral Nimitz confirmed that his actions were entirely normal for his situation. The clever use of a photo-

Fig 7—Submarine towing lifeboats to safety
This shows a German submarine towiing a string of lifeboats filled with survivors from a ship it had torpedoed and sunk. A photograph like this was skillfully shown around by Dönitz' defense lawyers, after he had been criticized for allegedly giving an order to sink lifeboats from torpedoed ships. Actually the towing of lifeboats to the submarine's mother ship was fraught with great danger both to the submarine and to the mother ship. Allied warplanes had strafed several such "tows," thinking that they were survivors from another submarine. It was my personal belief that skillful use of this photograph saved Dönitz from a heavier sentence. This copy was acquired later.

Fig 8—Dönitz' fountain pen
This is the pen he used to write all of his notes in verse. Also his memoirs after his release from Spandau. All the prisoners chewed the ends off their pens. Evan Lattimer Collection.

graph of lifeboats being towed by a U-Boat was very valuable to his defense (fig. 7). All in all, it seemed to me to be wrong to prosecute the man who had been placed as the administrator-leader of the country, against his wishes, and who had done everything in his power to make the surrender details go in favor of our side. He had moved all the German warships to the west out of the reach of the Russians, so we could capture them. He told us about his new submarine that could cruise submerged around the world, and urged us to develop it.

He had been made to officiate at the surrender of his country. Therefore it did not seem to me right that we should be giving him ten years in prison for his straightforward actions and statements. It seemed to me that it would have been much more effective to utilize him in our own strategic war machine and for the rebuilding of Germany just as we should have used Speer in the same way. In fact, we did use their rocket experts, like von Braun, with no compunction. We should have been smarter than we were in using Dönitz, as I saw it.

Admiral Dönitz's Prostate Problem

Dönitz's mildly enlarged prostate was already giving him some trouble with slow urination; he was getting up at night several times, even at Nuremberg. He said any infection, even a cold, always had settled in his prostate. He blamed this on having to sleep in wet clothes, in submarines. At first his condition was tolerable but it got progressively worse during the next nine years in Spandau. He was so impressed with the success of the prostate surgery performed on Funk, however, that he decided he, too, needed such an operation. As usual, the Four-Power Committee took a long time to process his request, but finally in January 1955, the senior urologist of the U.S. Army, the distinguished Dr. John Patton came to Berlin. On January 6, 1955, he did the transurethral prostatic resection on Admiral Dönitz at the British military hospital in Berlin. This went very smoothly and was again a great success. Colonel Patton impressed both the admiral and his wife with his kindliness and consideration, as well as his technical skill. Frau Dönitz wrote him a grateful letter and the admiral wrote to him several times thereafter, expressing his gratitude. Dönitz's other annoying medical problem was his eyesight, which, due to cataracts, was deteriorating progressively. By the time he was 89 years old, his eyesight had deteriorated so badly that he could not even identify books for which he was looking at home, as he said in his letters. He also had a large inguinal hernia which annoyed him but he did not want it operated on.

He died peacefully at home in 1980 at age 89.

Fig 9—Dönitz leads the group going to Spandau
Four of the prisoners to be transferred to Spandau, von Schirach on the left, Funk in the center and von Neurath on the right, starting in the prison door under the watchful eyes of the machine-gun carrying guard. Admiral Dönitz is facing them, urging them to hurry, obviously still "Commanding" the group.

CHAPTER EIGHT

Hans Frank

Fig 1—Frank's Portrait
Attached is his signature verification, signed by him at Nuremberg after imprisonment.

Hans Frank, (fig. 1) the notorious governor-general of Poland from 1939 until the end of the war, was a large, chubby, red-faced, loud-talking lawyer with a high-pitched, inane laugh that came out at inappropriate times when you talked with him. He had been born in 1900.

His father, a barrister, had been struck off the register for corruption. Frank's mother had abandoned her family to live with a German professor in Prague, leaving Frank dependent on his dishonest, womanizing father. Hans enrolled in the university in Munich and was much interested in music and art. He became an accomplished pianist and played classical music by the hour. He viewed Germany's literature and music as superior to all others. During his time at the university, he met his future wife, Brigitte. She was five years older than Frank but after a vigorous courtship, they were married. (Unbeknownst to Frank, she brought along a former lover on their honeymoon.) Frank tried to divorce her during the war, but she wrote letters to all the Nazis, including Hitler, demanding that they defend her. Hitler finally told him to forget about the divorce.

In 1927, after passing the German bar examination, he saw an advertisement in a Nazi newspaper seeking a lawyer to defend Party members. Thereafter, he accepted cases, mostly Nazi storm troopers who had abused other citizens, and got them off with light sentences. At one point he called Hitler as a witness and impressed Hitler with his verbosity, despite his rather high-pitched voice. Hitler then hired him as his own personal attorney and he defended Hitler in hundreds of small actions. He was rewarded by Hitler, as was his custom, with promotion after promotion, to become the head of the Nazi legal department.

In 1933, Frank was made minister of justice in Bavaria and until the sum-

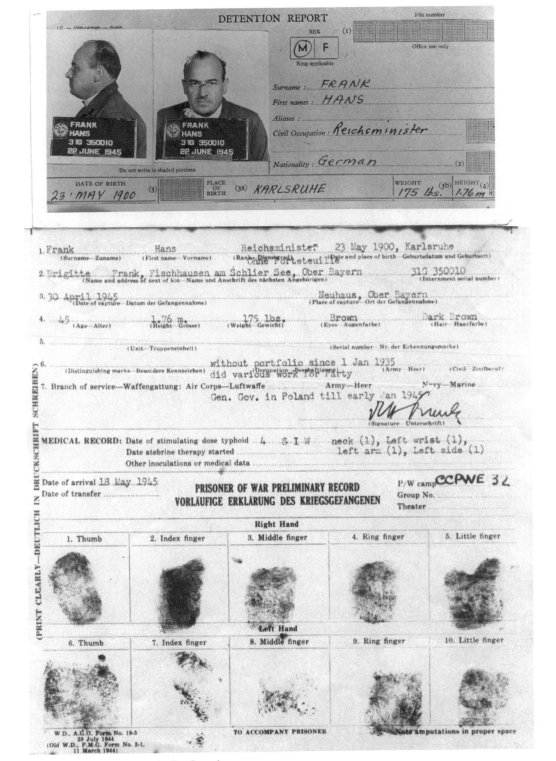

Fig 2—Frank's Prisoner of War Preliminary Detention Report

Along with his "Mug shot," it indicates that he was captured at Neuhaus, Ober Bayarn, on 30 April 1945, the day Hitler died. It gives his birthplace as Karlsruhe, 23 May 1900 and lists his weight as 175 pounds and 5'9" (1.76 meters). It lists his wife's name and address and his occupation as Reichsminister since 1 January 1935. He gives his occupation as Governor General of Poland until early 1945. It shows his fingerprints and lists the scars of his left wrist and left arm and also the left side of his neck from his two suicide attempts, shortly after his capture.

mer of 1942, was the head of the Nazi Party's law division. Naturally his private law practice boomed. With the Party's top lawyer as your counsel, how could you lose? He made millions.

From 1939-1945, he was appointed governor-general of Poland (fig. 3). He often said that Hitler put him in that job to get rid of him, since it was a thankless assignment.

After his capture, he cut his throat in a failed suicide attempt and then slashed his wrists in a second attempt. In doing this, he had cut the tendons to the fingers of his left hand, except for the one to his little finger. He therefore kept a glove on his left hand much of the time. He also had a visible scar on his neck.

The initial interrogators had a difficult time with him because he acted surly and evasive, and would sometimes stomp out of the interrogation room, cursing and calling them swine. By the time he got to us, however, he had decided that he would convert to Catholicism and was acting-out an abject change of heart. He would read his Bible at length, turning the pages with the little finger of his wounded left hand. He decided that Hitler had been his nemesis and cursed him with amazing vigor and great literary facility. He also concluded that the trial was a great demonstration and a spectacle about the fate of the Nazis, and that heavenly justice was indeed being invoked. "Do they get on their knees and pray to God for forgiveness? No, they worry about their own little necks and cast about for all sorts of excuses. Can't they see that this is a horrible tragedy for mankind and that we are all symbols of an evil that God is brushing aside?" His voice would become louder and louder.

When he had heard that others had tried to assassinate Hitler, he said that that was *his* great mistake, that he *himself* didn't shoot him. He said that he had come to his senses in 1942 and realized the evil Hitler represented:

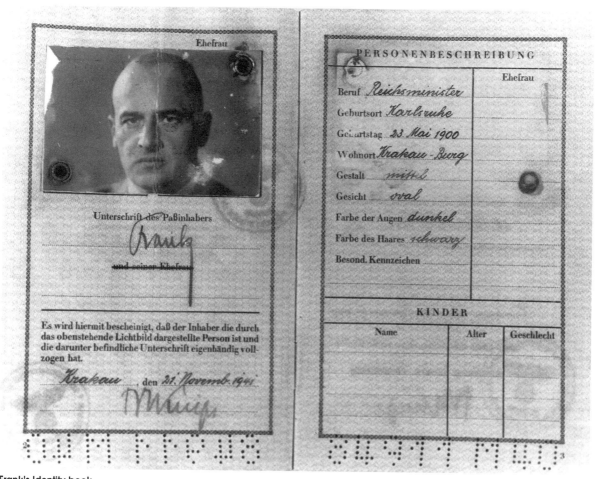

Fig 3—Frank's Identity book
This indicates that his residence at that time was in Krakow, Poland, where he lived in the castle used by the Governor General. The photograph on his identity book shows a cynical, hard-faced lawyer and a Nazi official who was known as "Butcher of Poland." Evan Lattimer Collection.

When I protested against the terror measures, in public at that time, he deprived me of my military rank and all political power. However, he made me sit as the figurehead governor-general of Poland, so that I would go down in history as a symbol of the terrible crimes in that miserable country. So here I am, but it serves me right. I was in league with the devil in the beginning. Only later did I realize what a cold-blooded insensitive psychopath Hitler really was. He hated all legal, diplomatic, and religious institutions, all of the social controls that represented restrictions to his impulsive ego expression. He pretended to be an art and music-lover but he had no conception of art. He liked Wagner, naturally, because he could see himself playing God with dramatic splendor. He loved nudes because nudes represented a protest against convention, which he was able to understand.

Frank declared, "The psychiatric hatred of convention and law was the real keynote of Hitler's personality. That's when he took only diabolical men of action as Himmler and Bormann for confidants. Bormann was a contemptible flatterer and a brutal intriguer, a clear reflection of Hitler's character."

Frank talked at length about his sex dreams, including nocturnal emissions. Some of these involved Hitler. Others involved his daughter and still others, groups of yodelers.

At one point during the trial, Frank's attorney startled everybody who knew Frank, by asking whether the Vatican was helping the prosecution, and saying that, in that case, his client would have to leave the church. Frank said that it would put all German Catholics in a difficult position.

Frank's Diaries

Frank kept detailed diaries, in several volumes, of everything that went on in Poland under his governor-generalship. He recorded his own philosophies as well. The numbers of people killed and all of the atrocities were described in great detail. He turned these diaries over to the prosecution early in the game. They were enough to convict him, even if there had been no other grounds. It was a startling demonstration of how the Nazi mind worked. One of his diaries stated as follows: "Before the German people are to experience starvation, the occupied territories and their people will be exposed to starvation. This territory [meaning Poland] in its entirety, is the booty of the German Reich. I have not been hesitant in declaring that when a German is shot, up to 100 Poles will then be shot. I am pleased to report to you officially, Party Comrade Sauckel that we have up to now supplied 800,000 workers for the Reich."

None of us could resist asking Frank if he were not sorry he ever handed over his diaries to the prosecution. He replied, "No, not at all. God knows what I did, so mankind might just as well know the whole truth too. All of it, the good and the bad." He said, "I have no illusions about my fate, as I've always told you. I know they are going to hang me. Now only the truth will remain."

Our psychologist, Dr. Gilbert, found it quite easy to induce Frank to lapse into a mood of "free association." While he started out with a violent renunciation of Nazism, he said he began to wonder just what he should do during the trial. Should he make a last stand with the other Nazi leaders? "Or renounce them and give them their last kick down the stairs on the way out. It is hard for me to decide."

Frank's basic lack of integrity became more and more evident. It became evident that his religious conversion was essentially a hysterical conversion symptom of the guilt reaction and that even his renunciation of Nazism had to be weighed for its ego value. Gilbert took pleasure in asking him whether the discovery of his partially Jewish ancestry had anything to do with his new animosity toward Hitler. He was always vague on that subject and answered evasively. He finally began to show ambivalence towards Göring. He said he didn't know what to think about Göring: "He could be so charming at times, but how could he steal all those art treasures for himself, in wartime, with the people in such desperate straits? That's what I cannot understand."

As the trial continued, Frank began to interrupt all of his conversations with a high-pitched laugh. It made him sound a little insane. When he was talking about Göring taking responsibility for what he had done, that seemed to please him. He said, "God, the paintings he stole ... I did not send him a single one from Poland. I told him if he had only been the way he is now [off narcotics], he could have led the whole country. I said to Göring, 'It's too bad you weren't thrown into jail a few years ago, Ha! Ha! Ha!'"

Frank was very perceptive about the other defendants. In criticizing Schirach's defense, he said that Schirach was trying to simplify things too much with his grand confession: "Did you notice how all the dirt came out in cross-examination? That's just what I expected. He wanted everybody to think that he was just a misguided innocent boy. Why, he even tried to make it appear like Henry Ford was responsible for Auschwitz and that's not all. I know what his relationship was to Hitler and what the fear of losing influence

with him meant. Why do you think he sent that tele-
type to Bormann proposing the bombing of an English
cultural city? It was because he was afraid he was losing his influence with Hitler. He was being scorned as
a weakling by Bormann, who was always at Hitler's
ear. So Schirach makes this great suggestion to bomb an
English cultural city. That's the sort of thing that burns
me up. I had at least thought that one moral accusation
we could make against the Allies was their unnecessary
bombing of our cultural cities like Rothenburg. But
now this comes out. We don't even have *that* left. I
could sense that there was something a little too theatrical about Von Schirach's confession."

In the summing up, the prosecutors dismissed Frank
as a governor-general of Poland who "Reigned but did
not rule." The statement of the judgment on Frank was
as follows:

> Frank was appointed Chief Civil Administrative
> Officer for occupied Polish territory and on
> October 12, 1939, was made governor-general of
> the occupied Polish territory. On October 3, 1939,
> he described the policy which he intended to put
> into effect by stating: "Poland shall be treated like a
> Colony, the Poles will become slaves of the Greater
> German World Empire." The evidence established
> that this occupation policy was based on the com-
> plete destruction of Poland as a national entity and
> a ruthless exploitation of its human and economic
> resources for the German war effort. Frank was a
> willing and knowing participant in the use of ter-
> rorism in Poland, in the economic exploitation of
> Poland in a way which led to the death by starva-
> tion of a large number of people, and the deporta-
> tion to Germany of slave laborers of over a million
> Poles and in a program involving the murder of at
> least three million Jews.
>
> Verdict: guilty on counts three & four; sentence:
> death by hanging.

When Dr. Gilbert visited him in his cell after, Frank
smiled politely but could not look at him. "Death by
hanging," he said softly, nodding his head in acquies-
cence. "I deserved it and I expected it, as I have always
told you. I am glad I have had the chance to defend
myself and to think things over in the last few months."

Niklas Frank, the second son of the Reichsminister,
had been taken to see his father at age seven, just before
Frank was hanged. As time went on, Niklas found himself carrying around an intolerable burden of shame,
guilt, and anger that could only be expunged by a
headlong dive into his family's history. His vitupera-
tion was extraordinary. He wrote, "You throttler of justice, you slime, you lachrymose supplicant for divine

Archiv für das Recht der internationalen Organisationen

Archivio per il diritto di organizzazione internazionale
Archives du droit des organisations internationales

Herausgegeben
vom

Präsidenten der Internationalen Rechtskammer

Reichsminister Dr. Frank

unter Mitwirkung des komm. Verwalters
der Union des Associations Internationales

Band II / 1941

ARTHUR GEIST VERLAG / BREMEN

Fig 4—Frank inscribed this book for Dr. Goldensohn
*Frank, like the rest was delighted to be asked to sign one of his
books, purged by the Nuremberg Public Library and brought to
the prison by Dr. Goldensohn. Evan Lattimer Collection.*

mercy you cliché-mongering windbag, you man who
turned your heart into a spider's nest for murderers."
He described his father's meteoric rise in the Nazi hierarchy, mainly as a demagogic, bigoted toady but hardly ever as a leader with power and authority of his own.
He further described his father's story as a sordid one
of petty ambition, greed, and corruption; and named
him as an accessory, many times over, to murder and
genocide.

As a senior editor of *Der Stern*, Niklas was upset to
observe how many of his father's former colleagues
(Nazi jurists and sympathizers) worked their way back
into positions of power in Germany. He complained to
his long dead father that Germany is "getting to be
more and more a state created in your own spirit....
Once again a choking, suffocating putrid mantle of
political self-glorification has settled down over
Germany. The arrogance of power is on the march, just
as you were then."

Frank's older son Norman was actually much closer

to his father and was treated very well by him. He was inducted into the Hitler Jugend, but the family moved around so much that he was never assigned any duties.

He said he felt none of his brother's bitterness towards his father, but only sadness for him.

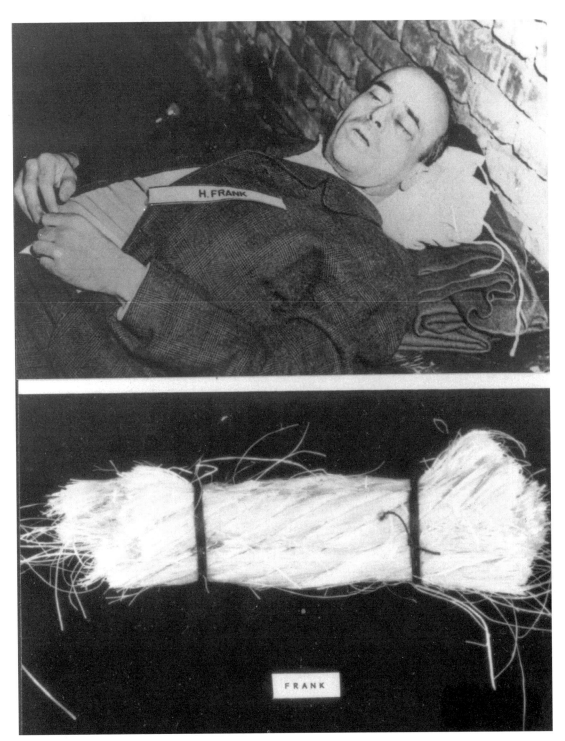

Fig 5—After the hanging
Frank's dead body lying on the coffin in which he was cremated some hours later. He went to his death serene in the conviction that his conversion to Catholicism would save his soul. The rope segment is from Evan Lattimer Collection.

CHAPTER NINE

Wilhelm Frick

Fig 1—Frick's Official Portrait

Here he poses as a Reichsminister and Protector. This is a good image of this cruel policeman-lawyer who drew up all the laws which Hitler imposed. He was a big, 5'10", tough-appearing man with a "butch" haircut, but a surprisingly soft voice. He had lost weight by the time we got him, and was down to 130 pounds. He was resigned to his fate and did not even respond to the charges in court.

Wilhelm Frick (fig. 1) was a frightening combination of a vicious lawyer and a brutal policeman. He was born in 1877 in Alsenz, Pfalz. He studied law at Göttingen, Berlin, and Heidelberg universities. After 1900, he was in the State Administrative Service. From 1904-1924, he was with the Munich Police. He had no war service. An early admirer of the Nazis, he helped the "Feme" murderers (Freikorps members) escape capture and took part in the infamous 1923 putsch. From 1930-1931 he was a minister in the Thuringian (the first German Nazi) government, in charge of education. In 1933 he was made Reichsminister of the interior, and in 1939, a member of the ministerial defense council (succeeded by Himmler in 1943). Since then, he had been the Reich protector of Bohemia and Moravia. He was a Reichsleiter, and was head of the Nazi parliamentary group in the Reichstag (fig. 2).

Frick stated from the beginning that he knew he was going to be hanged and did not wish to bother testifying in his own defense. The court judged him thus: Frick was an avid Nazi, largely responsible for bringing the German nation under the complete control of Hitler's organization. The numerous laws he had drafted, signed, and administered abolished all opposition parties and prepared the way for the Gestapo and the concentration camps. He was largely responsible for the legislation that suppressed the trade unions, the church, and the Jews. He performed his tasks with ruthless efficiency. Always rabidly anti-Semitic, Frick drafted, signed, and administered many laws destined to eliminate Jews from German life and the economy. His drew up the Nuremberg decrees (which persecuted the Jews) and he actively enforced them. He knew that insane, sick, and aged people were systematically being put to death. Complaints about

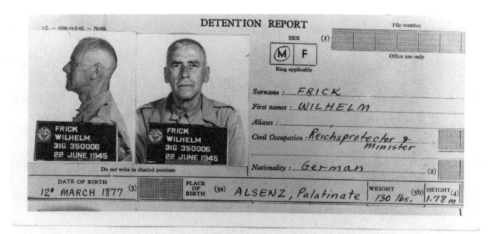

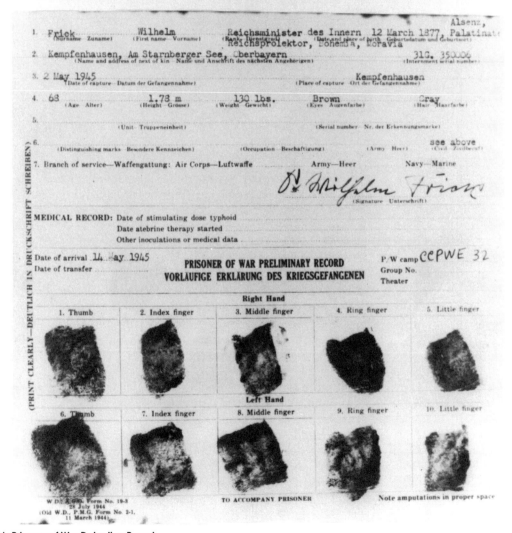

Fig 2—Frick's Prisoner of War Detention Report

It shows that he was born in 1877, in Alsenz, Palatinate. He was captured on May 2, 1945 at Kempfenhausen on the Starnberger Sea, Oberbayern. He listed himself as the Reichsprotektor of Bohemia and Moravia and Reichsminister of the Interior.

Fig 3—The plaque on the radio set
This indicates that it was a gift from Dr. Goebbels in March of 1937.
(Middle) A powerful radio set given to Frick by Dr. Goebbels
With this, he could keep in touch with everything going on, as it might affect the "Party".
(Bottom) An impressive list of the cities
These could be received by this set.
Evan Lattimer Collection.

these murders reached him, but he did nothing to stop them.

He was declared guilty on counts 2, 3, and 4, namely: crimes against peace, war crimes, and crimes against humanity; and was sentenced to be hanged. In prison he spoke very softly and in very short sentences, as if not wanting to be trapped by anything he might say. It reflected his experience as a policeman in interrogating other people, it seemed to me. Everyone thought him callous and indifferent, never displaying any emotions or imagination. Under these conditions, it was surprising to me that he tested at 125 on the IQ test.

The only thing that he ever could be made to com-

ment about was his pleasure in outdoor activity and his desire that the prisoners be permitted to walk in the sunshine. He did mention how beautiful it had been in Nuremberg at the time of the old festivals. He had no psychiatric problems, but Dr. Dunn thought he might feel heavily burdened and his depression might deepen. It was almost impossible for our psychiatrists or our psychologist to get through to him and elicit any details of his makeup. It was interesting that he had relatively gaudy uniform jackets made up, not as flashy as Göring, but noticeably more ornate than those of Hitler (fig. 4).

During the brief times together at the lunch table, Frick was hard to involve in any conversation. When the testimony indicated that the Reichstag fire had been started by Goebbels and Göring, however, this was news to the group. Frick was the *only* one who refused to believe that testimony, or even to give it any plausibility. He claimed that the Nazis did not need a Reichstag fire for propaganda purposes because they already had a majority; so the whole idea was silly that Göring would have started the fire. Frick very rarely commented on the goings-on in court, except on occasions where witnesses were brought in who had just the opposite effect on the credibility of the prisoners, as had been hoped. When that happened, Frick merely said, "It was stupid of them to bring those witnesses when they should have known that the prosecution would get hold of their own books and 'kill' them with them." While Frick refused to testify in his own defense, he did prepare notes for his lawyers. He asked to have one witness, Mr. Gisevius, a one-time Gestapo official whose testimony was devastating against Göring. At this time, Dr. Gilbert was able to elicit a brief response as Frick was preparing his last-minute notes for his defense counsel.

Frick didn't have much to say about the proceedings except that he had not even *seen* Hitler after 1937 and he had *never* approved of the atrocities. Gilbert asked him whether he didn't realize that the Nuremberg Laws, which he drew up, were the beginnings of a state-sponsored racial discrimination and hatred whose outcome was all too obvious. To this he shrugged his shoulders and said, "Every race has the right to protect itself, just as the Jewish race has done for thousands of years." Dr. Gilbert asked him if he didn't think it was madness to try to revive this racial-clan rivalry concept from the dark ages, now that people cannot avoid living together in modern society: "Can you justify that as a lawyer?" "Well, you will have the same problem in America," Frick responded. "The Whites don't want to intermarry with the Negroes. And mass murders were certainly not anticipated as an effect of our Nuremberg

Fig 4—Frick's Uniform Jacket
This was of magnificent quality doeskin with a gold aigulette and a gold-bullion embroidered wreath on the sleeve, indicating his rank. He had a very low-numbered Party Badge, also shown in this picture. It is notable that the quality of this doeskin was far superior to that of Hitler's jackets, but not quite as good as that of Göring. Raymond Zyla Collection.

Laws. It may have turned out that way, but it certainly wasn't realized that they might have that effect."

The witness, Gisevius, whom Frick brought in, was devastating in his condemnation of Göring's actions, which Frick did not seem to mind a bit. Frick simply said that the witness was telling the truth as he knew it, and that the background of Himmler's rise to power was now coming out into the open. "I could have broken Himmler's neck myself," he said, "but Hitler always supported him. Besides, Hitler didn't want to do things my way. I wanted things done legally and after all, I *am* a lawyer." Frick's attitude clearly betrayed a malicious satisfaction in getting back at Göring for helping Himmler to get power at Frick's expense, just as Göring had conjectured.

In the summation by Justice Robert Jackson, Frick

was characterized as the ruthless organizer who helped the Party to seize power, supervised the police agencies to insure that the Nazis stayed in power, and chained the economy of Bohemia and Moravia to the German war machine.

Frick sat pouting until his name was mentioned in connection with the murder of the ill, aged, and insane. He reddened a little and lowered his head. Sir Hartley Shawcross then asked, "What special dispensation of Providence kept these men ignorant of all these things?" He quoted Goethe as saying that some day fate would strike the German people. They would ingenuously submit to some mad scoundrel who appealed to their lowest instincts, who confirmed them in their vices, and taught them to conceive nationalism as isolation and brutality. Goethe spoke with a voice of prophesy, Sir Hartley added, for these were the mad scoundrels who did these very things.

In short, Frick, the brutal policeman with the mind and abilities of a lawyer, was a ruthless administrator. He solidified the Nazi machine of government, giving it a foundation in legality which made it very difficult to break down. I feared and hated this man. It seemed to me that he was the most brutal of the Nazis we were able to bring to trial: cold, ruthless, and heartless. No one regretted his being hanged. He went without a whimper (fig. 6). His last words were: "Let live the eternal Germany."

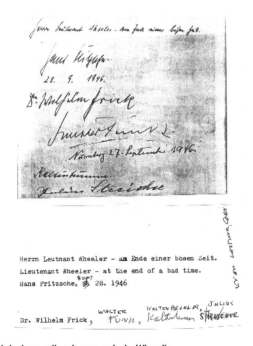

Fig 5—Frick signs a thank-you note to Wheelis
He joined Funk, Kaltenbrunner and Streicher in signing a "goodwill" note to Lt. Wheelis, at the end of the trial. Evan Lattimer Collection.

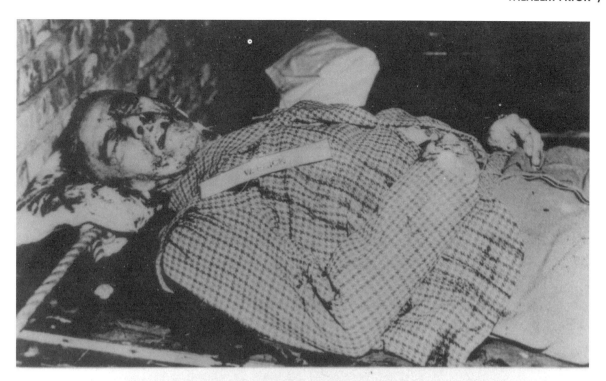

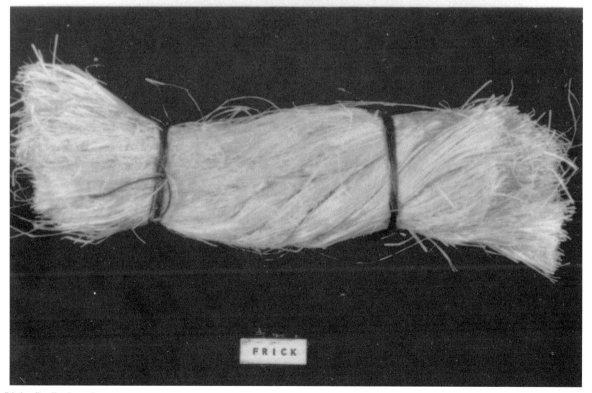

Fig 6—Frick after the hanging
Frick lying dead on his coffin after the hanging. Below is a segment of the rope used to hang Frick. It was removed ahead of time by Sgt. Woods, the hangman, as his personal souvenir. Evan Lattimer Collection.

CHAPTER TEN

Hans Fritzsche

Hans Fritzsche (fig. 1) had been the director of the Reich Ministry of Propaganda. His other title was Plenipotentiary for the Political Supervision of Broadcasting in Greater Germany. He was a tall, thin, tense man who was so glib that he seemed more intelligent than his IQ of 130 would indicate. He tried hard to be friendly and his manner of speaking reminded one of a sportscaster; he did wonderful imitations of broadcasters describing tense situations in court, to the delight of his fellow prisoners.

Aged 45 at the start of the trial, Fritzsche was merely a cog in Goebbels's propaganda machine, a man who read the broadcast scripts over the state radio as they were handed to him. He had exhibited unsatisfactory enthusiasm for the Nazi philosophy and, recognized as opposing Hitler's regime, had been thrown into the Dachau concentration camp. He had just been released at the time of the surrender and was captured by the Russians in their zone. Since they had practically no major Nazi figures, except Raeder, to contribute to the trial, Fritzsche was included. He was dumbfounded at this and stated his innocence so well that he was acquitted and discharged by our tribunal. He was a very pliable, naïve man, chiefly worried about his family. He was arrested and convicted by the Germans after his release by our tribunal, and served four years of a five-year sentence in a denazification program.

Dr. Gilbert considered him to be sincere in his patriotism and in his conventional morality. He declared that he had made the mistake of believing the Nazi leaders and their propaganda line, which he had then "pushed" over the radio. Now he was depressed and bitter over the betrayal of his ideals by the leaders.

Date 16. 11. 45.

This is to certify that the following is my proper signature.
(Ich bestätige hiermit, dass dieses meine richtige Unterschrift ist.)

Hans Fritsche, acquitted. Held
not guilty of conspiracy, war crimes
and crimes against humanity.

Fig 1—Hans Fritsche

Hans Fritzsche was a tense, anxious, 45-year-old who had become the chief radio announcer for Goebbels' Propaganda Ministry. He had become disillusioned with the Nazis, and had been thrown into the Dachau Concentration Camp. He had just been released but made the mistake of traveling east, where the advancing Russians captured him. Since they had only Admiral Raeder to offer for trial, they included Fritzsche, much to everyone's surprise.
Evan Lattimer Collection.

Dr. Dunn found Fritzsche to be very tense. He was frequently seen pacing in his cell and only felt better when he was permitted the optimum amount of exercise possible under the circumstances. He tended to be dejected but not too depressed. There was considerable anxiety, but no suicidal ideas were presented to Dr. Dunn; Fritzsche had no psychiatric disorder. "He may very well develop a reactive depression following the sentencing and be a suicidal risk, particularly if he is turned over to the Russian authorities, who want him back." There were many, even among the other defendants, who could not understand why he was on trial. I certainly could not understand it. It was pointed out that he had no power whatsoever under Goebbels, his superior. Indeed he had been imprisoned in the Dachau concentration camp after being deemed disloyal, shortly before the trials began, as Dr. Dunn pointed out, once again.

Fritzsche had been educated in a Bochum public school and was barely old enough to enlist at age seventeen in the First World War. After the war, he had attended the university in Berlin where he studied history and political economy. In 1924, he entered the political arena and later journalism. Through his work as a writer, he met Goebbels who was impressed with him and found his talents useful as a broadcaster. In 1933, Goebbels brought him into the propaganda ministry. He rose quickly to become chief of the German press section and finally, in 1942, Reichsminister for radio propaganda. In this capacity he supervised all broadcasts in greater Germany. He made regular broadcasts which were looked upon as setting the tone for German propaganda. His broadcasts were clearly anti-Semitic, venting a personal dislike which he had developed at the university. He claimed that the Jewish students remained aloof from the non-Jewish students and he had learned to hate them then. He had developed this dislike further as he grew older. In jail at Nuremberg, he sought to excuse the vigor of his broadcasts by pointing out that he had always objected to the violence and pornographic obscenity in Streicher's anti-Jewish publications.

Fritzsche was a sharp and clear thinker and realized that the crimes against humanity were the most serious charges brought against the Nazis at Nuremberg. He also concluded that incitement to such crimes might be the grounds for his own conviction. It was clear that this was the basis of the charge against Streicher, which resulted, incidentally, in his being hanged.

Fritzsche spoke long and loudly about his bitter resentment towards his superiors—namely Hitler, Himmler, Goebbels, and Ribbentrop—whom he believed had misled him and lied to him all the way. He told us that Goebbels had been a genius at assimilating information and at manipulating people. He could make the situation sound like the truth, regardless of how false it was. He had an uncanny knack for interpreting things in a way that his audience would appreciate.

I was astonished that Fritzsche did not make more of the fact that Hitler had turned on him and had thrown him into Dachau shortly before the end of the war. In the summation by the court, the official statement of the court read as follows:

The Radio Division, of which Fritzsche became the head in November of 1942, was one of the twelve divisions of the propaganda ministry. It appears that Fritzsche sometimes made strong statements of a propagandistic nature in his broadcasts, but the tribunal is not prepared to hold that they were intended to incite the German people to commit atrocities on conquered people, and he cannot be said to have been a participant in the crimes charged. The verdict: Not guilty.

Fritzsche's ecstatic reaction, along with those of Schacht and von Papen, was short lived. He was told that the German civilian police would arrest him the minute he stepped outside the courthouse. He stayed for four more days, and, at night, was spirited out to the home of his chief defense lawyer. Here the German police found him, nevertheless. He was taken to court and after some argument by his lawyer and an American officer, he was allowed the freedom of Nuremberg, as long as he did not leave town and would check in periodically on his own recognizance. After several months, he was tried by a denazification court, which had reviewed all of his propaganda broadcasts. Again, the fact that Hitler had thrown him into Dachau was ignored, and Fritzsche was sentenced to five years of hard labor and stripped of the right to hold any public office, receive any public pension, or be able to vote. During this time he wrote his memoirs, titled *Hans Fritzsche Speaking*, and was finally par-doned in 1950. He died in 1953, of cancer of the testicle. He had shown no testicular abnormality in 1945-1946. It was surprising to me that anyone as intelligent as he, would have missed the significance of a hard mass in the testis, but apparently that is exactly what happened.

My own impression of Fritzsche was that he was a simple, glib radio announcer used by his mentor Goebbels, and who appeared to me to be now genuinely repentant over his mistakes. The fact that he did not make more of the circumstance that Hitler had thrown him into Dachau as evidence of his deviation from Nazism was something that I found hard to understand. Whether the German court had more insight into his true value to the Nazis, through their detailed reviews of all his broadcasts, is something I could not judge. But it seemed to me that they were overreacting in punishing him the way they did. It reminded me of Lyndon Johnson's old saying that if you get into the pen with pigs, you're going to get some of it on you. It certainly contaminated Fritzsche, and got him four more years in prison at the hands of the German court.

CHAPTER ELEVEN

Dr. Walther Funk

Fig 1—Funk's Portrait and Signature Card
He signs as President of the Reichsbank and Minister of Finance. Evan Lattimer Collection.

Funk, (fig. 1) the president of the Reichsbank, was a thick-lipped, fat little man, so devoid of any self-assurance and adult male attributes that it seemed a mystery that he had ever been allowed any responsibility. He was always whimpering and whining. Göring expressed contempt for him and could not imagine why this "cypher" had been categorized as a "top Nazi."

Funk was born in 1890, in East Prussia. He had studied law, economics, philosophy, literature and music in Berlin and Leipzig, and in 1912, journalism. In 1916, he joined the staff of the *Berliner Börsenzeitung*, and became chief editor in 1922. After joining the Nazis he became economic adviser to Hitler, and in 1932 and 1933 was press chief for the Reich government and the secretary of state in the Ministry of Propaganda. He helped Goebbels in creating the Chamber of Culture and in 1937 succeeded Schacht as Reich minister of economics, when Schacht was fired by Hitler. In 1939, he also succeeded Schacht in the presidency of the Reichsbank (fig. 2).

Unlike most other Nazi leaders, he was not a failure before starting his Party career. He apparently had no economic philosophy of his own, but was largely an opportunist. Most of the war-related responsibilities of his ministry were given to Speer in 1944 and after that, he had lost his seat in the cabinet. His directorships had included several banks. It was a mystery to all of us how he could possibly have been vice president of the Reich Chamber of Culture, secretary of state for the propaganda ministry, the Reich minister of economics, and president of the Reichsbank. Nevertheless, he bragged about his titles. It was surprising to me that when Dr. Gilbert tested his IQ, he was above the average at 124. Gilbert found his complaints were far out of proportion to any physical findings. While he had been a one-time cheerful Bavarian businessman, gourmet gadabout,

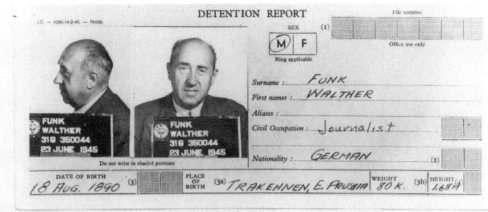

Fig 2—Funk's Detention Report

Mug-shot and POW record of Walther Funk states that he was captured 13th of May, 1945 in Gastein and that was President of the Reichsbank. He weighed 80 kilos and was 1.68 (5 feet, 6 inches) meters tall. It has his fingerprints, and "captured on May 15th," one week after Hitler committed suicide. He listed his occupation as a journalist, saying nothing about his role as President of the Reichsbank.

and playboy, he was now a dismayed, fat, little diabetic hypochondriac and *very* forlorn. He felt he had been "roped" in by Hitler, betrayed, and was very depressed.

At first Funk discussed his Party activities and his opportunistic transition into Party affairs from his "editorial" position. He looked and acted so much like a little neighborhood storekeeper, with his fat lips and his habit of spreading his palms outward toward you as he shrugged his shoulders in disbelief at anything that came up, that it was hard to imagine him as a true member of this group of world-class criminals. Yet he could always manage to get champagne smuggled into the prison to celebrate any event, much to the amazement of the other prisoners.

When Dr. Gilbert asked each of the men to write down their reactions to the indictments, Funk was verbose and emotional in his protestations of innocence. He said, "I have never in my life consciously done anything that could contribute to such an indictment. If I have been guilty of the acts which stand in the indictment, through error or ignorance, then my guilt is a human tragedy and not a crime." After hearing Schacht's skillful manipulation of the language, it was hard to understand that Funk could ever follow him as president of the Reichsbank.

During the showing of the atrocity motion pictures, Funk mumbled something under his breath, then broke into tears. He blew his nose, wiped his eyes, looked down, and then cried throughout the remainder of the motion picture, saying things like, "horrible ... the dirty swine." He cried bitterly and clapped his hand over his mouth as thousands of women's naked corpses were bulldozed into a pit. Watching the bulldozer blade on a tractor push dozens of bodies, tumbling over and over into the pit, was a real shock. When Gilbert tried to interview him after this motion picture, Funk was deeply depressed and burst into tears as soon as he was asked how he was affected by the film. "Horrible, horrible," he repeated in a choking voice. When asked whether he would need a sleeping pill, he sobbed, "What's the use, what's the use?"

As the evidence accumulated, Funk became more and more depressed, declaring that it was, "hardly bearable. Germany is disgraced for all time. Believe me, that is worse than any consequences of the trial." He blubbered while saying all this. "But do you think I had the slightest notion about gas wagons and such horrors? I swear I heard about such things for the first time at Mondorf. I only did what I could to prevent illegal acts. I prevented the surrender of the Belgian gold [in French custody] to Germany because its ownership wasn't clear. I also prevented the devaluation of the

franc during the occupation. By that act alone, I saved France more money than all the confiscated property was worth. The only accusation I can make to myself is that I should have resigned in 1938 when I saw how they stole and smashed Jewish property. But even then, I understood that the Jews were supposed to collect damages, according to law, for the destruction of their property."

Dividing the prisoners into separate lunchrooms in order to make Göring eat alone, and thus lose the opportunity to browbeat the others, was a stroke of genius. It was proposed by Speer after watching what went on, and was put into action by Dr. Gilbert who saw the merit of it immediately. Funk was assigned to what we called the "youth" lunchroom with Speer,

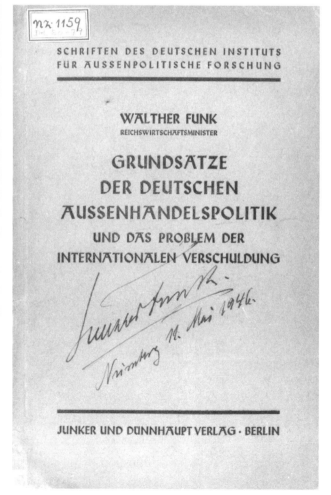

Fig 3—A book by Funk autographed for Dr. Goldensohn
A book by Walther Funk entitled Grundsätze der Deutschen Aussenhandelspolitik (Principles of German Foreign Trade Policy). This is one of the books Dr. Goldensohn got out of the Nuremberg library which was being purged of Nazi books. He brought this and others to Funk for his signature. Evan Lattimer Collection.

A dedication to Major Goldensohn by Walter Funk dated 31 May 1946. In the front of another book by Funk entitled "Ein Leben für die Wirtschaft" (A Life for the Economy). Evan Lattimer Collection.

Fig 6—Funk's picture on the cover of another one of his books.
Book entitled Walther Funk Ein Leben für die Wirtschaft *(A Life for the Economy). Evan Lattimer Collection.*

(left) Fig 5—Another book by Funk Inscribed to Major Goldensohn
The title page of still another book written by Funk and with a dedication to Major Goldensohn once again. The title of this book is "Wirtschaftliche Neuordnung Europas" (The Economic Reorganization of Europe). This one bears the stamp of a Munich library from which Dr. Goldensohn got it. The inscription reads as follows - For Major Goldensohn in gratitude for his kind medical and humanitarian assistance during difficult times in prison in Nuremberg. On May 11 1946. Evan Lattimer Collection.

Seiner Exzellenz, dem Herrn Reichsminister

Walther Funk

Durch die großzügige Förderung meines Schaffens
zu tiefst verpflichtet, bitte ich die Widmung dieser Partitur
und beiliegende Platte als Zeichen aufrichtiger Dankbarkeit
und Verehrung entgegenzunehmen.

Lehár

Im Kriegsjahr 1940.

Fig 7—Franz Lehar honors Funk
The composer, Franz Lehár, presented Funk with the full orchestral score, in a gold tooled Morocco folder, of his famous operetta "The Merry Widow." He asked that the Reichminister accept this score as a sign of his thanks and his reverence because of his generous promotion of Lehár's creations. Evan Lattimer Collection.

Endlich einmal Menschlichkeit!

Walter Funk   **Dr. Whisenand**

fe. BERLIN, 15. Sept. (Eig. Ber.)
Die Menschlichkeit hat sich
jetzt endlich auch einmal im
Spandauer Kriegsverbrecher-
Gefängnis durchgesetzt. Die
Sowjets haben zugestimmt,
daß der seit langem schwer
kranke ehemalige Reichswirt-
schaftsminister Walther Funk
in einem britischen Militär-
krankenhaus in Berlin-Spandau
operiert wird. Funk ist bereits
gestern aus dem Gefängnis in
das Krankenhaus überführt
worden.

Die Operation führt der ameri-
kanische Militärchirurg Dr. J. M.
Whisenand aus Frankfurt durch,
der Funk bereits vor einigen
Wochen untersucht hat. Funk hat
ein schweres, schmerzhaftes Pro-
stataleiden.

Der 64jährige Funk ist der erste
der Spandauer Häftlinge, der für
kurze Zeit das Gefängnis verlas-
sen darf. Er verbüßt eine lebens-
längliche Haftstrafe. Der Zeit-
punkt der Operation liegt noch
nicht fest.

Der Zustand des ehemaligen
Reichsaußenministers von Neurath soll sich in den letzten Tagen
etwas gebessert haben. Es besteht
keine Lebensgefahr mehr.

Fritzsche, and Von Schirach. The purpose was to let Speer and Fritzsche wean the other two away from Göring's influence. Funk was easily persuaded that Göring had intimidated and manipulated him. Göring was furious with this new arrangement, recognizing that it greatly diminished his ability to influence the group.

Funk's concern over the legality of organizing Jewish property for the state became understandable as prosecutor Jackson continued to present documentary proof that Funk as well as Heydrich was involved in Hitler's plan for the elimination of Jews from economic and public life and their segregation in ghettos. Funk was frank to concede that Göring and Schacht were strong personalities, in contrast to the rest of them. "I assure you I do not have the stuff for heroism. I did not then and I don't now. Maybe that is the trouble, but I often wonder what I would have done if I had known these things before. I don't think I would have lived through it." Then he began to blubber. "But those atrocities, that remains a permanent shame no matter what Göring or anybody else says, no matter what sentences are pronounced, this systematic mass murder of the Jews remains a disgrace for the German people that they will not live down for generations."

In the prosecution's summation about Funk, they said that as minister of economics, Funk accelerated the pace of rearmament. As Reichsbank president, he banked for the SS the gold teeth and fillings from concentration camps victims, probably the most ghoulish collateral in banking history. At the end of the trials, when Funk received his sentence of life imprisonment, he staggered around the cell with a bowed head, mumbling as if he couldn't quite grasp what had happened. "Life imprisonment! What does that mean? They won't keep me in prison all my life, will they? They don't mean that do they?" Then he grumbled that he was not surprised at Fritzsche's acquittal but was surprised that they let Schacht and von Papen off.

Funk's diabetes and cardiac status became gradually worse in Spandau. He was therefore released in 1957,

Fig 8—Funk has prostate operation
In Spandau, Funk's giant prostate and overtaxed bladder finally blocked up. He was placed on Foley catheter drainage for many weeks until the Russians finally relented and permitted him to have a transurethral resection by Dr. Whisenand, from the U.S. 97th General Hospital. It had to be done in the British Hospital in Berlin. This technique was new to all of the Europeans who marveled at how successful it was. This is a newspaper account of the operation and Funk's very rapid recovery. The other prisoners had all expected him to be in the hospital 3 weeks and he was back in 5 days. "The Americans did the operation with a little electric wire," he said. Dr. Whisenand Collection.

after serving only 11 years of his life sentence. He died, unheralded, three years later.

Funk's Prostatism

Funk talked at length about his various physical ailments, including his hypertrophy of the prostate and his urethral stricture. Dr. Pflücker, the German POW doctor who worked with us, had been an "office" urologist and I finally got him some dilators with which to dilate Funk's stricture. The problem was that each time he did that, Funk would spike a raging fever for a few days, as was common in the days before antibiotics. His bladder was gradually becoming decompensated and after his transfer to Spandau, it required several months of indwelling catheter drainage before he was in any condition to have a transurethral resection of the prostate. This was finally done by Dr. James M. Whisenand of the U.S. Army at the British army hospital in Berlin, using an American resectoscope from the 97th U.S. Army General Hospital at Frankfurt. All of the other prisoners expected him to be away in the hospital for at least three weeks and were amazed that he was back among them after five days, urinating well. The Russian doctors had never heard of a resectoscope and were also amazed. This created an interesting situation in that several of the others, who had varying degrees of prostatism, now thought about a transurethral resection for themselves.

CHAPTER TWELVE

General Alfred Jodl

Fig 1—Alfred Jodl, age 55 was the operational Chief of Staff of the Wehrmacht

Here General Jodl is seen conferring with Hitler over a plan. He was the actual Operational Commander of that superb "killing machine," the German Army. He had no specific links to any of the criminal actions, but was convicted because of his nominal leadership in any excess committed by the Army. It was obvious to all of us who were officers in the Allied Armies that we too would hang, if we lost any future wars. National Archives and Evan Lattimer Collection.

General Jodl was a highly intelligent, old-line administrative army officer. Though rather small in stature and not very assertive, he was calm, courteous, and always helpful. He had originally been a Bavarian artillery officer, but in 1938 became head of the operations section of what the Germans called the OKW, *Oberkommando der Wehrmacht* the organization that replaced both the War Ministry and the High Command. In 1939, he became chief of staff to General Keitel who was head of the OKW. In this position Jodl organized and directed all of the army campaigns, except the Soviet invasion. Keitel, himself, was a poor administrator and an ineffective leader, thus all of the policy decisions were left to Jodl.

Jodl attended the twice-daily conferences over which Hitler presided and tried to turn Hitler's wild strategies into concrete tactical operations. In 1944 he was promoted to colonel general. On May 7, 1945, only one week after Hitler's suicide, Jodl signed the surrender of the German armies at Rheims, France. He was stripped of his insignia and thrown into jail with everyone else. In preparing his statements for the court, he quickly perceived that when someone else provided a typed summary statement in advance for the translators, the five-language translations were far smoother and more accurate. He therefore had the intelligence to ask if he too could do that. This was granted to him. In his statement he made the point that the tribunal might possibly establish a reversal of the traditional role of military officers wherein everyone assumed that when they entered the military service and then went to war, they did this under the impression that loyalty to one's nation and to one's leader was the highest loyalty demanded of anyone. There had been no obligation to any "higher authority" or to any higher set of values in the past. He made the point that this trial might indicate that this conclusion was in error and that there *was* a higher morality to which he and all other military persons would now be compelled to owe allegiance, rather than to the leader of their country. He said that if the trial established this precedent, he was willing to accept whatever punishment the court meted out to him.

Everyone at the trial admired his statement and there were many who said, "Now *there* is a man." He was the only one of the defendants who had anything constructive to say. All the others just complained and made wild accusations. Jodl was a man who looked the facts straight in the face and made a logical philosophical statement, despite the fact that it involved his own death.

Dr. Pflücker, who got to know all of the defendants very well, admired Jodl's calm manner and remarked that even after his sentencing, Jodl had sent out for classical authors to read. He admitted to Dr. Pflücker that he now saw that Hitler had lied to him about such matters as the Austrian government's welcoming the annexation of Austria by the German Army. Dr. Pflücker told him that he took his sentence like an "old Roman." Jodl replied, "What, me an old Roman? No, they could have done it much better."

Quite frankly, a great many of the personnel, particularly the military people, were greatly opposed to Jodl being tried at all and certainly did not think that he should be hanged. In the postwar years, when Admiral Dönitz gathered his huge book made up of letters and ideas of the top military people of the world, all of them were of the same opinion.

Nevertheless, the enormous number of atrocities committed by the Germans during the war was turned against Jodl with fatal effect. Again, it seemed to me in retrospect, that a great many of the criminal actions were committed by SS troops under Himmler rather than by the regular army's (Wehrmacht) troops under Jodl's command. Jodl went to his death without a complaint, exactly as everyone knew he would.

In spite of Jodl's favorable image with most of the personnel at the trial, Dr. Gilbert who could not do much with him, found him to be "a rigid, impassive militarist." The war, said Gilbert, "did not violate his sense of values, although the atrocities did." Psychiatrist Dr. Dunn said General Jodl was a rather rigid, well-controlled, strongly disciplined German officer, very correct in his social manner. He was astute, alert and interested. He talked very little about the war except to address his feelings that he had conducted himself as a soldier should, carrying out the duties of his country and government. He obviously had possessed the strength of character to try to resist Hitler's wild impulses at times. This was admitted by many people. He had no inner discomfort about the war, but was obviously disturbed about the evidence of the atrocities. His code as a German officer, as well as his strong character, enabled him to face his final disposition very well. Some of our soldiers tended to joke about his red nose, his beady eyes, and his huge ears and nicknamed him "Happy Hooligan" because of his vague likeness to the cartoon strip character of that name. He had an IQ of 127 which was right up with the best of the group. His wife, a very attractive

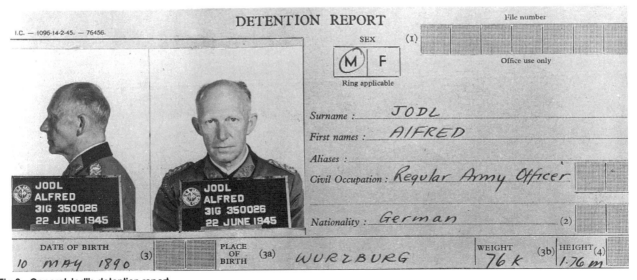

Fig 2—General Jodl's detention report
General Jodl was photographed for the record, at Mondorf (Ash Can) on 22 June 1945. He was 55 years of age at that time, weighed 76 kilos and was 1.76 meters tall. National Archives

Fig 3—Jodl signs the surrender
General Jodl is here signing the surrender of the German Armed Forces to the Allies at Rheims on May 7, 1945. National Archives

lawyer, came to the court as an assistant to his regular lawyer. She was of considerable help in organizing his defense and put together a petition to Field Marshal Montgomery, on the outside, in an effort to plead for a milder sentence. This was abruptly rejected. She continued to write about the situation and to correspond with various historians who agreed with her for the most part.

In short, it seemed to me that Jodl was a highly competent technician, caught in the tremendous avalanche of atrocities, even though he personally and his branch of the service were not responsible for them. I asked some of the prosecutors later why they thought he was hanged and the admirals were not. It was their opinion that atrocities were much easier to trace on land than at sea. Certainly the momentum gathered by the mass of horrifying scenes paraded before us at the trial was almost overwhelming. It was said that Jodl was irritating Hitler by resisting him to the point that Jodl was

about to be replaced by someone else.

When he was interrogated about the concept of a military "aristocracy" he replied that he had been brought up in a military family and had married into the aristocracy. He said he accommodated to both very easily.

Jodl, referring to Göring who had framed two of the top German generals, told Dr. Pflücker that Göring was "a contemptible, conceited, ambitious and arrogant cur in those days. The way he took advantage of von Blomberg's embarrassment just made our blood boil. We despised him too, for his uncouth vanity." (In 1938, Field Marshal Werner von Blomberg, then commanding officer of the entire German Army, was relieved of his command by Hitler when Göring was said to have shown Hitler a police report on von Blomberg's new bride, which described her as a prostitute.)

Jodl was exonerated posthumously by a German denazification court in 1953. This confirmed my own opinion of the general.

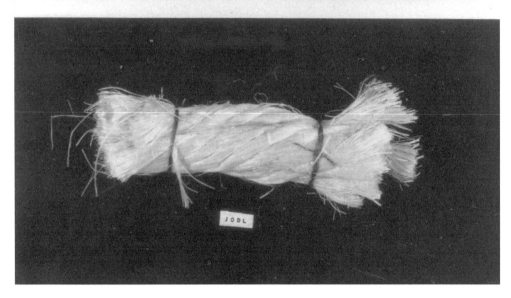

Fig 4—Jodl's rope
General Jodl lying dead on his coffin after the hanging, with a segment of the rope used to hang him, which was kept by the hangman as a souvenir despite strict orders to the contrary.
National Archives
Evan Lattimer Collection.

CHAPTER THIRTEEN

Ernst Kaltenbrunner

Fig 1—Kaltenbrunner's Official Portrait
Here he is wearing his 1944 war merit cross with swords. The scars on his face were from an automobile accident, but were widely thought to be from saber duels as a student. He permitted the rumor to continue.

Kaltenbrunner, second youngest of all the prisoners, was a tall, tough-looking man of low intelligence, with a scarred face and a lantern jaw (fig. 1). He was 6'4" but down to 170 pounds when he was finally brought to us—he *had* weighed 225 pounds. He was the hatchet man of the group.

Born in 1903 in Ried (Austria), he went to elementary school in Graz. As an impoverished student he did odd jobs and studied without much direction for some time before taking up law at his father's urging. He got his degree of doctor of jurisprudence in 1926. He was certainly not outstanding as a lawyer though in 1928 he entered politics and eventually became an undersecretary in the Austrian government. While he had been interested in the illegal Austrian Nazi Party, he did not actually join until 1933 when Hitler took over Germany, and not until 1939, when the party was legalized in Austria, did he openly become a Nazi.

This was the behavior of a timid man: a great, hulking, tough-looking murderer, who at heart was a sniveling coward. He had large bones and gross features marred by scars that resembled the scars of dueling students, but actually were due to an automobile accident. He was a typical bully, tough and arrogant when in power, but a craven coward in defeat, unable to withstand even the pressures of prison life.

In 1933, he had become legal adviser to the SS in Austria and then became commander of one of the SS-Standarte groups. Still later he rose to be head of the entire SS in Austria (fig. 2). In 1934, he took part in the Dollfuss putsch and was imprisoned for four months at first, and later for a year. When the Nazis took over, he became commander of still another SS unit and State Secretary for Security in the government, after the Nazis put in Seyss-Inquart as governor. He was then made an SS Brigadeführer, in 1941

Fig 2—Kaltenbrunner's SS Cuff Links
He was an SS Brigadeführer, an honorary post. Evan Lattimer Collection.

lieutenant-general of police, and in 1943 chief of the internal security mechanism of the entire Reich. In 1944, he was awarded the War Merit Cross with Swords. In January of 1945, he was made head of all police, concentration camp, and punitive activities in the Reich, including the Gestapo.

After he had been in our jail about six months, and just shortly before the trial was to begin, Kaltenbrunner became extremely depressed. Dr. Kelley visited him frequently and each time Kaltenbrunner broke down and cried. He was frightened and wanted to be comforted: he was sure he would not receive a fair trial. All the toughness had melted away. The hardness of character that had marked him when he was the executioner of all of the condemned German generals and officials after the attempt on Hitler's life, had now been replaced by this soft, sobbing personality who eagerly sought reassurance as to his future. He complained that he had been only a tool of Himmler and an unimportant one at that.

His IQ was among the lowest at 113. One of the psychiatrists remarked that just on the basis of his hard looking appearance, he would have been cast in his present role in the movies. Kaltenbrunner was sure he would be executed and his general attitude was one of bitterness. He felt completely justified by the fact that he was fighting Bolshevism. Some day, he said, the world will recognize this. He also said the main charge against him was killing Jews, but declared he would be absolved of that completely, even though he was frank about his anti-Semitism. There was considerable worry among the psychiatrists that he might attempt suicide. On November 17, 1945, he suddenly developed a spontaneous subarachnoid hemorrhage. A tiny blood vessel had ruptured in the membranes covering his brain and there was

bleeding into his spinal canal and the fluid around the brain. He was rushed to a U.S. Army hospital near Nuremberg with great secrecy. While such a hemorrhage can be fatal, Kaltenbrunner suffered only severe headaches and an inability to move around. When he was returned to the courtroom, he was met with coldness by the other prisoners, who by that time had seen a great deal of evidence of the brutality of his organizations. He subsequently suffered another subarachnoid hemorrhage and was again hospitalized for some time. After that he sat in court as an unemotional observer.

I must say that I had never heard of Kaltenbrunner before the trial and was astonished to learn that he had succeeded to all the posts occupied by Heydrich, who was known as the butcher of the Nazi Party. (Heydrich had been assassinated by Czechoslovakian partisans. A village called Lidice, in retaliation, was completely flattened by the Nazis, and all the male inhabitants were put to death and the women either killed or put in concentration camps.) Kaltenbrunner took over the management of everything that required murder and all of the various types of secret police, military police, and civilian police of Germany. This gave him total power over everyone. After the attempt on Hitler's life on July 20, 1944, he was the one assigned to kill all of the officers and officials who were even *suspected* of having knowledge of the plot. Several hundred people were killed, including several of the top German generals. This crippled the German Army far more than we ever realized. Kaltenbrunner was the master of this entire slaughter, which included suspending people by steel

```
ICH BESTAETIGE DEN EMPFANG VON 3950 REICHSMARK UND
HABE GLEICHZEITIG HERRN LEUTNANT WHEELERS GEBETEN,DIESEN
BETRAG WIE FOLGT ZU VERSENDEN:

  RM  2.950 AN MRS.GISELA WESTARP,OTTOBRUNN BEI MUENCHEN,
                  SEEBAUERSTRASSE 7  BAVARIA

      AND

  RM 1.000.- TO DR.STEINBAUER,LAWYER IN THE DEFENSE COUNCIL
       HIER IN NUERNBERG.
```

Kaltenbrunner.
3. X. 46.

Fig 3—Kaltenbrunner's note to send money to his mistress and his lawyer
Here he requests the transfer of 3,950 Reichs Marks by Lt. Wheelis (which he has misspelled as Wheelers). 2,950 of these were to go to his mistress Mrs. Gisela Westrap (although he sent no money to his wife or his children by her,) He also asked that 1,000 Reichs Marks be sent to Dr. Steinbauer, lawyer in the defense council in Nuremberg. He signed it "Kaltenbrunner," October 3, 1946. This was less than 2 weeks before he was hanged. Evan Lattimer Collection.

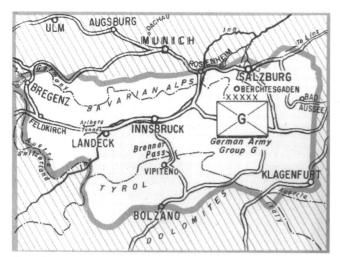

Fig 4—The proposed Alpine Redoubt
The white area on this map shows the highly defensible mountain range region around the Austrian city of Innsbruck which the Nazis had contemplated using for a final last ditch stand by the German Army. The German Army Group G was headquartered there near the city of Salzburg which in turn was near Berchtesgaden. Tons of office records, documents and office equipment from the German army headquarters had been sent to this area in anticipation of this possible move. Kaltenbrunner had offered to not defend this area against the Americans, if the Americans would join the Germans in attacking the oncoming Russian Army. The Americans approached this area very slowly and cautiously because of the rumor that it would be strongly defended. Luckily the German Army collapsed before this was attempted.

Fig 5—CIC Agent Matteson captured Kaltenbrunner
Here he shows Kaltenbrunner's Minox camera and gold party badge after single handedly capturing him and his heavily armed body guards in their mountain hide-out shown above.

Fig 6—The other prisoners detested Kaltenbrunner
Here Keitel and Ribbentrop are talking over Kaltenbrunner as if he was not there. They all disliked and despised him after he had slaughtered so many of their friends following the bomb plot against Hitler. He became very depressed by this ostracism and suffered two cerebral hemorrhages.

wires from meat hooks, at Hitler's instructions. (Hitler enjoyed watching motion pictures of these victims writhing in pain.) When he was accused of being responsible for the mass murders, he denied having anything to do with them, claiming he neither gave orders nor executed them. He said the court had no idea how secret these things were kept, even from him. It seemed patently ridiculous that the chief of the security apparatus for the whole country had nothing to do with concentration camps and knew nothing about the whole mass murder program.

On cross-examination, Colonel Amen produced documents, inconsistent statements, and direct accusations that called forth a constant series of flat denials from Kaltenbrunner—even that it was his own signature on the documents. He maintained that even as the head of the intelligence service under Himmler, he knew nothing about the atrocities in his own organization. Our other prisoners frequently muttered, "You devil, you swine." At lunch, the other defendants expressed their contempt and skepticism about the entire cross-examination and said that it was stupid of him to try to deny everything. It stood to reason that he must have known something about something, since he was the admitted chief of the organizations. They were all shocked that he would deny his own signature on documents.

It came out that Kaltenbrunner had been trying to deal with Allen Dulles through intermediaries in Switzerland, to surrender all of the German troops in Austria. It was then proposed that he, Kaltenbrunner, would be the commander of those German troops in the proposed alpine redoubt, in joining the Americans to fight against the Russians. This was done behind Hitler's back and was a surprise to the other prisoners.

In the summation at the end of the trial, Justice Jackson observed, "Kaltenbrunner, the grand inquisitor, took up the bloody mantle of Heydrich, to stifle opposition and terrorize compliance, and buttressed the power of national socialism on a foundation of guiltless corpses." The verdict rendered on Kalten-

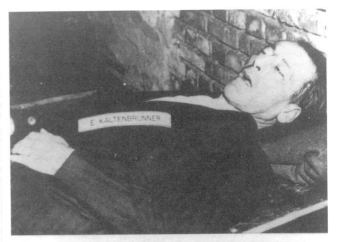

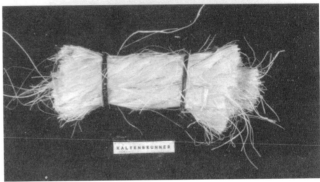

Fig 7—Kaltenbrunner dead on his coffin
He was the only one who sustained a cut on his scalp from the edge of the trap door, probably due to his greater height of 6'4". A segment of the rope used to hang him (below) was saved by the hangman Sgt. Wood in defiance of orders that no souvenirs be saved. Evan Lattimer Collection.

brunner was as follows: guilty on counts three and four. Sentence: death by hanging.

The other prisoners treated Kaltenbrunner coldly and contemptuously, talking over or around him as if he were not there (fig. 6). His role in murdering so many of their friends after the Hitler bomb plot was very much in their minds. They obviously detested Kaltenbrunner. He went to the gallows quietly.

CHAPTER FOURTEEN

Field Marshal Wilhelm Keitel

Fig 1—Fieldmarshal Wilhelm Keitel
Keitel was a tall, handsome Prussian officer of the classic type. He was totally subservient to Hitler's wishes and would carry out any command, no matter how brutal. He was not nearly as intelligent as Jodl but was exactly the type of leader Hitler wanted for the German army.
Evan Lattimer Collection.

When they first arrived at Mondorf the contrast between the sloppy manners of Ribbentrop and the upright, handsome, Prussian Field Marshal Keitel was striking (fig. 1). It was noticed, however, that Keitel had been sitting up awake in his bed for two successive nights. He did not wish to complain about a nasty carbuncle on the back of his neck, which was so huge and sore that it prevented his lying down (fig. 2). He refused to mention the matter to his guards, who were enlisted men. It was immediately incised and corrected, and Keitel was given pillows so he could lie down and rest. Keitel would have endured sleepless nights for a week before he would have asked a favor from an enlisted man. And in keeping with his training as an officer, he demanded a pencil and paper to write a letter to General Eisenhower as soon as he arrived at Mondorf. He wrote as follows:

To the Supreme Commander of the Allied Expeditionary Forces, General Eisenhower:

Your Excellency, you showed no hesitation and even demanded that I as chief of the OKW [*Oberkommando der Wehrmacht*] sign the papers of capitulation and thus assume this responsibility towards the German nation and history. A few days later you ordered my immediate resignation as chief of the OKW and internment as a prisoner of war. The head of the American commission for capitulation sent to Flensburg, to the German armed forces high command, gave me expressly, and in your name, the opportunity to select from my staff an officer who was to be my permanent personal adjutant. I was further allowed a batman and 500 pounds of luggage, all of these to accompany me into imprisonment, as is international custom and in line with

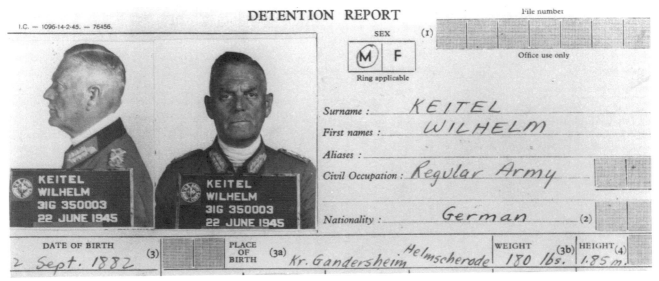

Fig 2—General Wilhelm Keitel's POW Detention Report
This shows that the painful boils on the back of his neck had to be covered with a bandage even as early as this mug shot of 22 June 1945.

the Geneva Convention for POW officers of my rank. Instead of this, I am treated here in Mondorf camp as if I were in a camp for ordinary criminals, in a jail without windows.

In addition it is made clear to me in every respect that I am to be expressly denied the treatment generally accorded an officer POW. The commandant of the camp, or his second in command, declares that they can give no explanation for the cause nor make any change. On the contrary, recently the most extreme measures have been applied. Clothing was taken away, except for a certain limited amount and almost all toilet articles were withdrawn. Not even military decorations of this war and the past one were left in my possession. Even spectacles were taken away. I realize fully that I must bow to your orders and measures, even if they do run counter to internationally recognized custom and the treatment of highest ranking officers. I nevertheless believe I have a right to request an answer to the following questions:

General:

1. Am I a prisoner of war according to international law as expressed in the Geneva Convention and as it was explained to me, for you, on 13 May 1945, or am I not? If not, why not?
2. If I am a prisoner of war, why am I denied the treatment and the accommodations befitting the position of a field marshal?
3. Shall I be allowed for my continued assistance and comfort, the aide expressly offered to me?

(3a) What limitations affect this officer who was simply attached, as to his treatment here and his association with me? (3b) Can I immediately return this officer to the OKW, thus relinquishing the assistance he was intended to give me. Can he be relieved by another officer? (3c) How can this officer correspond with the OKW by way of the German commission at your headquarters?

4. In your name, General, your representative offered me, before I left Flensburg the opportunity of bringing along 500 pounds of baggage. We limited ourselves to one third of this. I am therefore more than amazed that I am now deprived as a field marshal of even such essentials as razors, mouthwash, etc., and I am left with only a few things.
5. I cannot hide the fact that my honor as a soldier has been grievously damaged when my marshal's baton and decorations from two wars were taken from me.

Keitel, Field Marshal

He received no answer to this letter.

Wilhelm Keitel was a Prussian, born and bred, and a typical Prussian general. His father was wealthy, the scion of an old Hanoverian agricultural family, and Wilhelm had been educated by private tutors. His ancestors had been Prussian military men and/or agricultural leaders for more than a hundred years.

Keitel had married in 1904 and had five children. One daughter died of tuberculosis and one son was killed on the Russian front. The whereabouts of his other sons he did not know. They were presumed dead.

He was a traditional Prussian gentleman: intelligent, but lacking overall ability. He was much more emotional than Jodl and consequently talked much more readily. He professed to be concerned over the fate of the German people, but maintained that as a leader of the German Army he was of course responsible only for the military activities of the Reich. Although he had served on the general staff in the First World War, he won promotions relatively slowly until after the Nazis came to power. He had been top man of the German military ever since Hitler's dismissal of von Blomberg and von Fritsch in 1938.

Keitel was an ideal assistant for Hitler. His conditioning to unquestioning obedience was absolute. For him there was no such thing as objecting to an order from the Führer. When I asked him how officers and gentlemen could have carried out the outrageous orders of Hitler, he said again and again, "We can only receive orders and obey. It is hard for Americans to understand the Prussian code of discipline." In jail he worked hard at trying to understand the non-Prussian code and by the time the trial ended he said in open court, "I did not see the limit which is being set here, for even our soldiers' performance of his duty." Keitel endeavored to be shot to save his neck from the noose, as did Jodl, and with equal failure. But what truly seemed to worry him more than death was preserving the honor of the army leaders. He admitted to the psychiatrist that these crimes and atrocities described to them represented a blot which, if established, could never be removed. He became profoundly emotional when discussing his German honor. I was sure that he would have much preferred suicide to hanging, if he could have accomplished it.

Keitel was always cooperative in interviews and was particularly impressed with our psychological tests. He was loyal not only to his family but to Hitler. He was enthusiastic about Hitler as a military man, declaring that he was easily a genius. Hitler excelled particularly in broad strategy, Keitel insisted, being far superior to Göring, Ribbentrop, and even to Jodl and himself. He attributed the atrocities to the SS, maintaining that he, personally, knew nothing about any of that; if he had learned of them, he declared, he would have left the party. Hitler, he said, had limited his knowledge to what he needed to know for the planning of military actions.

Actually, with the examples always in mind of Blomberg, Fritsch and other generals who offended Hitler, it seemed that Keitel had never had the courage to be anything but a yes-man. He once ascribed his lack

of opposition to the fact that he did not like to go on record even as being tentatively opposed. Hitler had a technique of bringing a secretary into every conference and making a stenographic record, and Keitel complained that this completely eliminated free expression of opinion. Keitel was just as intelligent as Jodl on the IQ tests, but he lacked the latter's planning ability. In the overall setup, it appeared to me that Keitel was the army's front man and pacifier of Hitler, while Jodl did the real work. In jail, both officers were meticulously neat and kept their cells in perfect order. They were the only ones who ever complained about a shortage of scrubbing equipment, no doubt a reflection in both of them of the training of the Prussian military system.

While Keitel maintained his dignity, he did not hesitate to write many notes to the guard officers, asking for what he considered to be his due. For instance, he repeatedly requested of the medical officers that he be

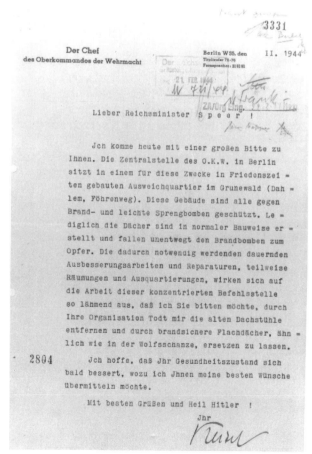

Fig 3—A letter from Keitel to Reichsminister Speer
Asking that a thicker concrete roof be supplied for the office of the Chief of the high command of the German army. Bomb damage in Berlin was getting to be so severe that he felt this was required. Evan Lattimer Collection.

permitted to take a shower bath. This technique got him what he wanted most of the time, without necessitating lowering his dignity to deal with underlings.

Keitel perceived that the attack on Russia was a desperate ploy, but he did not understand that it was Hitler's fear of an early death that made him so desperate as to take this fatal risk. Keitel stated:

The decision to attack Russia was a confession of weakness and the Polish invasion was unnecessary. When we couldn't get across the Channel because we didn't have enough ships, Hitler just had to do something. He wanted to take Gibraltar but Franco was afraid to risk it. If he sat tight, England would starve him out sooner or later. And all the time the lifeblood of our army and air force came from the Romanian oil fields. That was the key to the whole situation. Without Romanian oil we couldn't last a week, and Russia could have cut that off at any time. I think Hitler must have seen that. We were actually in a desperate position and he was getting so much of our oil from Romania that if he lost that, we were finished. The attack on Russia was actually an act of desperation, because he saw that our victory was only temporary. Rommel's little shooting expedition in North Africa was of no consequence. Hitler talked about the Russian campaign like it was a sure thing and our manifest destiny, and our solemn obligation, but when I look back at it, I am sure it was just a desperate gamble.

We heard nothing about the attempts of Chamberlain and Roosevelt to prevent the war. Hitler persuaded us that it was inevitable ... An American just simply cannot understand our desperation under the Treaty of Versailles. Just think, unemployment was our national disgrace ... Every decent German said over and over "Down with the Treaty of Versailles, by any means, fair or foul." They rallied behind Hitler with enthusiasm.

When Dr. Gilbert, to gauge Keitel's reaction, commented that Hitler was certainly a destructive demon, he said:

Yes, and a lucky one, in the beginning. It would have been much better if Hitler hadn't gotten away with so much. Just imagine, we reoccupied Ruhr with only three battalions of troops. The gigantic

French army could have brushed us out of there like a flea, but then when Hitler saw how easy it was, and then when he got away with the Anschluss of all of Austria, without firing a shot, well then one thing led to another.

Keitel was totally malleable to Hitler's wishes and countersigned all his brutal directives. He was exactly what Hitler wanted. The tribunal sentenced him to death by hanging (fig. 4).

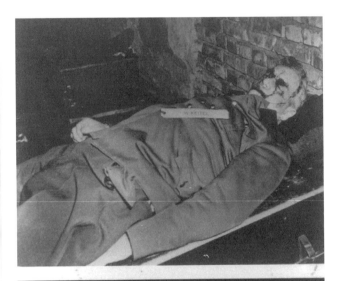

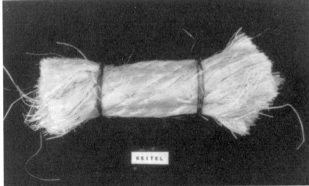

Fig 4—Keitel lying dead on his coffin after the hanging
The blood from his nose is most likely the result of his hypertension, rather than trauma. If his nose had struck the edge of the trap door, as alleged by reporters, it would have been obviosly deformed by the blow, and it is not. Dr. Roska who examined all the bodies confirmed this. Below is a small segment of the rope used to hang Keitel. It was saved by Sgt. Woods, the hangman, as a personal souvenir. Evan Lattimer Collection.

CHAPTER FIFTEEN

Robert Ley

Fig 1—A signed photograph of Robert Ley
Ley is looking cheerful and agreeable in his labor leader uniform. In his days of glory, he exemplified the type of vigorous, totally dedicated workers Hitler used so successfully in reorganizing his depressed country. Ley's brain damage permitted him to make the most absurd uninhibited promises to the labor groups. He hanged himself in his cell October 24, 1945 before the trial started. Evan Lattimer Collection.

Robert Ley was a stocky, bald, loud-talking labor leader who drank heavily. He looked and acted much like Streicher (fig. 1). He had been a flier in World War I and had sustained a head injury in a crash. As a result, he stammered, but surprisingly, he gave rousing labor speeches promising the world, with no intention of delivering. This suited Hitler, who could blame Ley for any failures to deliver. Ley revered Hitler as a godlike person. At one time he wrote a book that was so crass in eulogizing Hitler that even Hitler was embarrassed. Hitler had the entire print run destroyed with the exception of one copy, which he kept for his own library. Ley's secretary described him as seeing the world through rose-colored glasses, assisted by alcohol. He appeared to his associates as if he literally had no judgment, but only spontaneous emotional responses. They thought of him as a vital, tough, excitable, intellectually gifted individual. However, he was generally disliked because of his tendency to express his opinions frankly and bluntly. This made him a social outcast. His lack of tact, his lack of concern for the opinions of others, his uninhibited reactions to any situation, his subsequent dismissal of the unpleasant repercussions of his actions, and his totally bad judgment, are all typical findings in individuals suffering frontal lobe brain damage.

Ley had been commissioned by Hitler to organize groups of guerrillas like the "Werewolves," and the "Hitler Free Corps." They were to carry on guerrilla warfare against the advancing Allies. After Ley was captured by the 101st Airborne Division near Berchtesgaden, he made three half-hearted suicide attempts. He considered himself a patriot and said he would die a patriot. He could not bear the thought of being called a criminal. He wrote out for Dr. Kelley a long document about how to rehabilitate Germany, advocating a German-American conspiracy (as many of them did) in which our military government would join the Germans and afford a camouflage for Nazi rebirth—beginning there, at the Nuremberg jail, where it would be directed by Ley and his colleagues.

He had been highly intelligent as a youth and was extremely well-read. He had joined the Air Force and was wounded and decorated three different times. He received severe burns and a head injury in 1917 in an airplane crash, and was unable to speak for at least a week. After this injury, he developed a stammer that characterized his speech for most of his life and made his capability to give long and impassioned harangues even more impressive. He received his Ph.D. in chemistry, *summa cum laude*, in 1920 and joined the university faculty in Westphalia. From there he joined I.G. Farben but was happy to quit, because of political differences with his superiors. Thereafter he joined the Nazi movement and worked very hard for them. His job was to speak for the Führer at times and places where Hitler could not be present.

Ley gave long, vigorous, political speeches almost every day, always making exaggerated promises. By the time of his imprisonment, he was totally unable to carry on a coherent conversation, turning every topic into a ranting speech. In this he resembled Hitler. At first he would talk in an ordinary manner, but as he became interested, he would jump to his feet, pace the floor, throw out his arms, wave them more and more violently, and begin to shout.

A priest in the village of Schleching in Bavaria, near Berchtesgaden, reported to the 101st Airborne Division headquarters that Ley had been seen going into a house in that village. The 502nd Parachute Infantry Regiment's Intelligence Section detailed Lt. Sweeney with Sgt. Odum, PFC Rosenfelder, and Pvt. Meenan to go and get him, (fig. 2). They found him asleep on the third floor of a cobbler's shop. When they awakened him he tried to drink from a vial on the table, which was knocked away. He subsequently made two other attempts at suicide, all of which were immediately foiled.

Fig 2—Ley captured by 101st Airborne Division troopers
He was pretending to be a painter and a food chemist, but was "turned in" by German civilians, who disliked him.

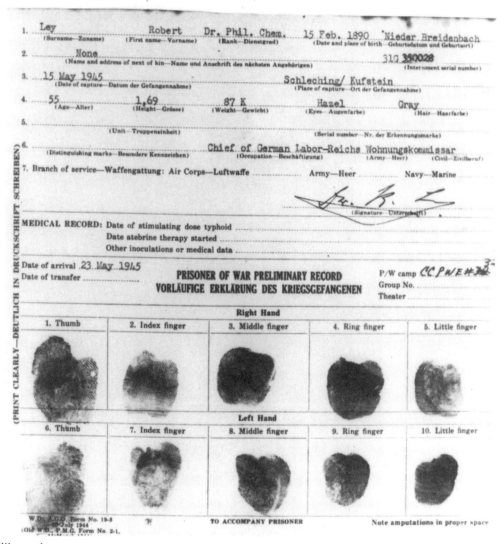

Fig 3—Ley's POW record

This indicated that he was captured at Kufstein on the 15th of May in 1945. It also stated that he avoided capture for about a week after the surrender, masquerading as a painter in the Bavarian mountains. He listed himself as a Doctor of Philosophy and Chemistry and also as the Cheif German Labor Commissioner for the entire Reich. He weighed 87 kilos (192 lbs.) and was 1.69 meters (5 feet, 7 inches) tall. His date of birth was February 15, 1890 which made him 55 years old at the time of his capture.

Ley claimed to be "Dr. Distelmeyer," a chemist dealing with dehydrated foods. He said he had escaped from the Russians and was returning to his home in Düsseldorf, and that he had burned his identification so the Russians could not identify him. Our officers dragged him out of bed in his pajamas and gave him his own German Army boots and an old overcoat, plus a soft hat. He had several days growth of beard and made a very slovenly and disheveled appearance. When the burgomaster of the town identified him without any hesitation, Ley screamed at him that he was a traitor for identifying him. A German army officer, when asked if Distelmeyer was Ley, said he did not recognize him. When interrogated later as to why he did that, the army officer said that he thought he would be a traitor to identify someone else under those circumstances. Ley was then transferred through Seventh Army, Third Army, and eventually to "Ashcan" at Mondorf, where he was selected to be one of the defendants at the major trial (fig. 3).

Immediately after reading the indictments, wherein he was charged with being a criminal, he became violently disturbed, ranting and raving, maintaining his innocence and swearing he would never face trial against such charges. He refused to prepare any defense, saying that he was not required to defend himself against the crimes that Hitler had committed and which he knew nothing about. He paced his cell and brooded over his fate, the whole rest of that day and night. Then at 8:15 P.M. on October 25, 1945, he strangled himself in his cell while sitting on the toilet, out of the sight of the guard. He had taken the zipper out of his jacket and put the partly open zipper over the protruding water pipes where they came out of the wall, about six feet above the floor. He then took a strip of the hem from a bath towel, formed a noose and soaked the knots in water so they would not slip. He tied this improvised cord to the zipper on the projecting water pipe. He sat down on the toilet, put his head through the loop, and stuffed his mouth with rags torn from his undershorts, so he would make no sound during the hanging. He then leaned forward against the noose and strangled himself by deliberate sustained pressure of his own body's weight against the blood vessels in his neck.

At our psychiatrist's request, his brain was removed and taken for post mortem examination to an army medical laboratory. There was distinct atrophy of the anterior lobes; which appeared to be a spontaneous atrophy rather than due to syphilis. His head injury might have started it, and alcohol may have helped. The German undertakers took the body away to a cemetery and dumped it, nude, into an open grave, with no show of respect.

Ley left a suicide note in which he said:

Farewell, I can't stand the shame any longer. Physically, nothing is lacking. The food is good, it's warm in my cell. The Americans are correct and partially friendly. Spiritually I have reading matter and can write whatever I want. I receive paper and pencil. They do more for my health than is necessary. I smoke and receive tobacco and coffee. I may walk at least 20 minutes every day. Up to this point

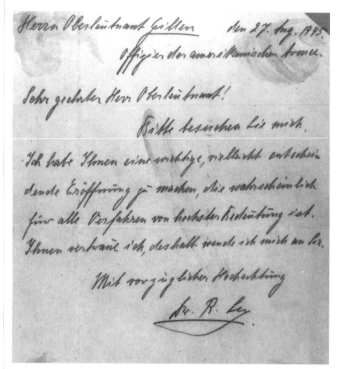

(Left) Fig 4—An "Important Request" by Dr. Ley
This handwritten note by Ley is addressed to First Lt. Gillen, American Army officer, and dated 27 August 1945 and reads as follows:
My Dear First Lt:

Please come to visit me. I have an important, perhaps a decisive revelation that most probably is very significant for all of the trial proceedings. I trust you, therefore I am contacting you about this.

Respectfully,

Dr. R. Ley

This extravagant style reflected Ley's pathological optimism, probably related to his brain disease. His "message" was trivial. Lt Gillen was actually an Intelligence Officer who later became U.S. Ambassador to his native Luxembourg. Evan Lattimer Collection.

everything is in order except for the fact that I would be a criminal; that is what I cannot stand ....

I have always been one of the responsible men. I was with Hitler in the good days, during the fulfillment of our plans and hopes. And I wanted to be with him in the black days. God led me in whatever I did. He led me up and now he lets me fall. I am torturing myself to find the reasons for my downfall and this is the result of my contemplations:

We have forsaken God and therefore we were forsaken by God. Anti- Semitism distorted our outlook and we made grave errors. It is hard to admit mistakes but the whole existence of our people is in question. We Nazis must have the courage to rid ourselves of anti-Semitism. We have to declare to the youth that it was a mistake. The youth will not believe our opponents. We have to go all the way. We have to meet the Jews with open hearts. German people, reconcile yourselves with the Jew. Invite him into your home (with you). We cannot stop the excited sea at once but must let her calm down gradually, otherwise terrible repercussions would result. A complete reconciliation with the Jews has priority over economic or cultural reconstruction. We outspoken anti-Semites have to become the first fighters for the new ideas. We have to show our people the way.

Göring's comment about the news that Ley had committed suicide was "It's just as well that he is dead, because I had my doubts about how he would behave at the trial."

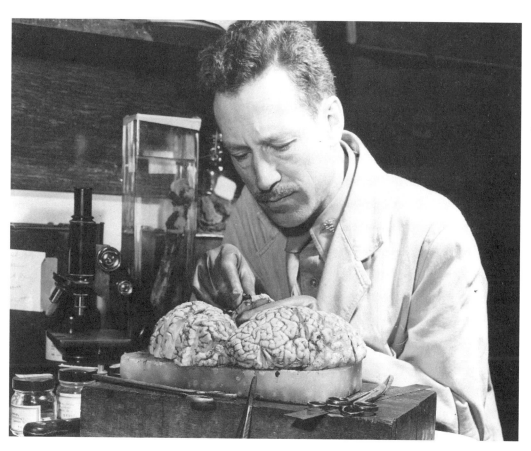

Fig 5—Ley's Brain
This was dissected by Major Haymaker at the Armed Forces Institute of Pathology, Washington. It revealed the reason for his lack of judgement, in the atrophy of his frontal lobes.

CHAPTER SIXTEEN

Konstantin von Neurath

Fig 1—Von Neurath's official portrait
This portrait of the aristocratic old diplomat was taken when he was a favorite with the British Queen Mother. She was the daughter of the German Royal House of "Teck" and enabled Von Neurath to serve Germany very well from 1932 to 1938. His appearance in prison deteriorated as his hypertensive cardiovascular disease progressed.

By the time of the trial Konstantin von Neurath was a fragile old man (the oldest of the prisoners, at age 72) who was obviously suffering from hypertensive cardiovascular disease but tried to conceal it. He took the ordeal of the trial with surprising calm. He had been out of the top echelons of the Nazi government for so long that it surprised me he was even considered as a candidate for this major trial.

However, while he was gauleiter of Bohemia and Moravia in Czechoslovakia, he had aided and abetted the brutality which later filled the horror films we saw in court. Our psychologist, Dr. Gilbert, called him "a bewildered conservative of the von Hindenberg school, who found consolation in the fact that he had resigned when things began to get too bad. He was generally apathetic, with an IQ of only 125." Later on, Dr. Dunn's psychiatric examination characterized him as a quiet, soft-spoken professional diplomat whose manner was most correct and polished. He made no complaints in spite of his age and his severe hypertension. He gracefully evaded discussing his periods of deadly assignment in Bohemia and Moravia and betrayed very little evidence of feeling guilt. He did not impress our psychiatrists as a serious suicidal risk or as being potentially psychotic in reaction to sentencing, which turned out to be correct.

It came out that he and von Papen were Hitler's two carryovers from the old aristocracy, which had formerly dominated the government. Von Neurath was a baron who had been brought up in a family of diplomats and who was educated from the beginning to assume a high post in the government. He had been one of Hindenburg's people in the foreign office, and Hindenburg had wanted to keep him on there so that he could control diplomatic affairs, even after Hitler was appointed prime minister (fig. 2).

Fig 2—Von Neurath signs with Hitler
In this "Letter of State" of November 1934 to the President of the Dominican Republic, Hitler revealed that he had now taken over the total leadership of Germany, by abolishing the Presidency and the Chancellorship and combining them into his new position as "Führer." In this letter, he announced his "New Order." Von Neurath's signature on the lower right blessed the new arrangement. Note that the German eagle had not yet been displaced by the Swastika, as it would be later. Evan Lattimer Collection.

He was appointed foreign minister in 1932 and held the post until 1938 when he was pushed out by the aggressive Ribbentrop. There was a rumor that he had been associated with the group who had tried to kill Hitler, but he would not permit this to be brought out during the trials. It might have lightened his sentence but the scorn of his fellow prisoners would have made him miserable.

Von Neurath had gotten along famously with the British, since he was very close to the King of Württenberg, who was a "Teck." The British Queen Mother (the widow of George V) was "Mary of Teck." She treated von Neurath very well and he was able to encourage Hitler's wishful thinking that the British might be induced to collaborate with the Germans in planning for the future. He was completely at ease with royalty and with the top diplomatic officials from all over the world. He was fond of telling a story about how he was selected for an important post by the King of Württenberg, because the King noticed that instead of standing nervously at attention during the interview, he settled himself into a chair very deliberately and comfortably and *then* listened to the proposition. He often recounted that it was his method of settling into the chair that had gotten him the job.

By 1938, Hitler had begun to do enough illegal things on the diplomatic scene that von Neurath felt called upon to object loudly and publicly. This induced Hitler to ease him out and replace him with Ribbentrop who immediately offended the British, undoing whatever good relations von Neurath had built up with them. Von Neurath was outspokenly critical of Ribbentrop on any and all occasions.

It turned out during the trial that von Neurath had been present and a party to the "Hoszsbach Conference" where Hitler declared that he was going to use force to pursue his agenda in ruling the German state. It was further brought out by the prosecution, to von Neurath's disadvantage, that he did not object to this plan. He did object to making a secret pact with the Russians, however, and this added to Hitler's dislike of him. Rather than fire him completely, Hitler made him the "Reich protector" of Moravia and Bohemia from 1939 to 1941. During this time it fell to his lot to pretend to the Czech government that Germany would "adopt" the Czechs and let them maintain their own government. Instead, the German Army moved in, forcibly annexed the area, and occupied it permanently. There were some small uprisings which were suppressed brutally.

It was due to his actions during this period that he was convicted on all four counts by the court. Since his crimes were relatively minor compared to those of the others, his sentence was only 15 years in prison. It was obvious that his health was failing rapidly as the trial went on, with many cardiac episodes due to his high blood pressure. In spite of the prospect that he might never leave the prison alive, Dr. Kelley admired his spirit and correctly predicted that he would never break down mentally or emotionally.

During the cross examination of Ribbentrop, it came out that von Neurath had refused to sign the nonaggression pact between Germany and Russia because he knew it was a very dangerous matter. Instead, Hitler got Ribbentrop to sign it and shortly thereafter made him foreign minister, displacing von Neurath. Von Neurath complained bitterly that Ribbentrop was sticking his nose into things that were none of his business and in fact had gone out of his way to give the British a deliberate slap in the face by signing this Russian pact while he was still Ambassador to Britain. In the discus-

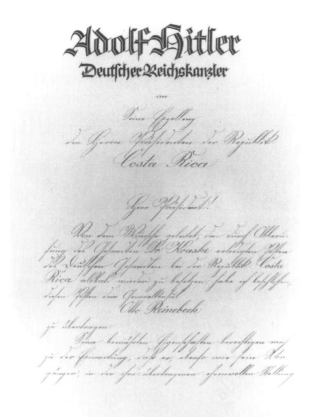

sions triggered by Ribbentrop's testimony, von Neurath observed that Ribbentrop's reputation among the German people was very poor. "You will not find another official who is held in lower esteem than that man Ribbentrop," he commented one night as he was washing his clothes in his cell. "Some of the people were surprised at the extent of his stupidity and the shallowness he was showing in court, but to me it was an old story. I had to put up with that nonsense for years—just a lot of gab and no sense. He still lies. He said he was my state secretary before he became foreign minister, but he wasn't. Not for a single minute. Hitler wanted it, but I flatly refused. He actually did more harm than is evident, with his stupid meddling."

It was apparent to everybody that von Neurath would never leave prison alive because of his fragile health, if his sentence was fully carried out. He was released after serving only eight of the fifteen years of his sentence. He died at home two years later of a heart attack at age eighty-one, unheralded and unnoticed.

Fig 3—A German Letter of State from 1937
The swastika now appears on Letters of State. Von Neurath and Hitler have signed this Letter of State. It appoints Otto Rheinbeck as Envoy to Costa Rica on behalf of the Third Reich. This is a demonstration of Von Neurath's still high position among the top Nazis of the hierarchy of the Third Reich, as of 1937 when this one was signed. He fell from grace the next year. Evan Lattimer Collection.

Fig 4—Von Neurath irritating Hitler
The crusty, arrogant old diplomat, is shown being condescending to Hitler, who was obviously displeased and unhappy, in his "white-tie and tails." This attitude got von Neurath fired and replaced with Ribbentrop.

CHAPTER SEVENTEEN

Franz von Papen

Fig 1—Von Papen as Chancellor
Here we see him wearing his bowler and pin-striped jacket. He was the Chancellor of all Germany, under Von Hindenburg in 1932, in his days of glory. He surrendered this post to Hitler after Hitler's victory at the polls.

Von Papen was one of the old line diplomats who had been forced out by Hitler. He was an appealing little man with white hair, black eyebrows, and an English accent. He was always much better dressed than the rest and refused to have his picture taken with "those criminals" as he referred to his fellow prisoners. If he saw a camera pointed his way he would turn his face away deliberately.

While he had risen to the rank of prime minister under Hindenburg, he had been forced to become vice premier when Hitler came to power. Perceiving the excesses of the Nazis, he tried repeatedly to resign from the Party and was almost killed in the purge. He was thrown into prison and several of his aides were killed. Göring had him released after three days and Hitler then insisted that he take a position with the government as a minister without portfolio. He eventually went to Austria and then to Turkey as an ambassador, hoping, he said, that he could still do some good for Germany by keeping Turkey out of the war, but he would no longer be responsible for the Nazi excesses at home. At the trial, however, the prosecutors insisted that he had still done useful work for Hitler and had turned the German embassy in Turkey into a spy nest.

If the 1944 bomb plotters had succeeded in killing Hitler, von Papen would have had a prominent part in the foreign ministry of the new government. When Göring attacked him after this revelation in court, he said to Göring that they had installed Göring in the government with great faith that as a German patriot and a war hero he would keep Hitler under control. If Hitler got out of control they had expected Göring to grab him by the scruff of the neck and throw him out. Von Papen stated forcefully that Göring had disappointed them grievously in this regard.

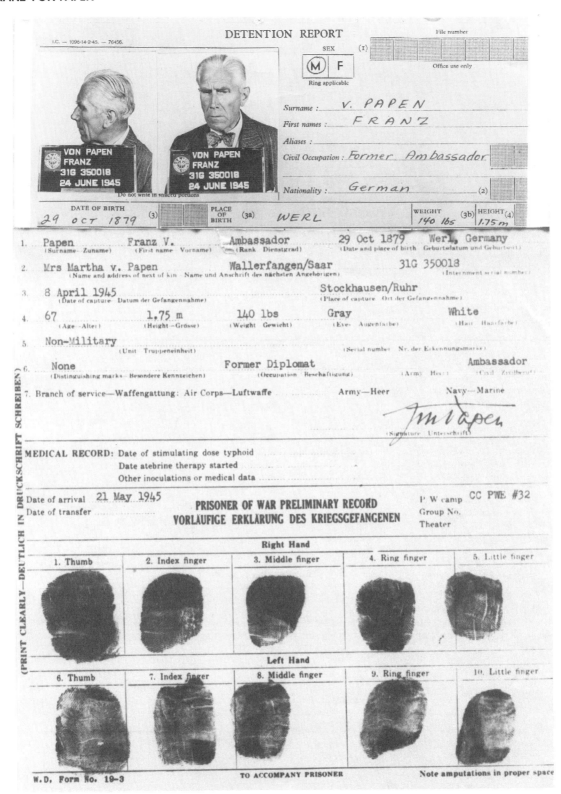

Fig 2—Von Papen's capture sheet
This shows that he was captured at Stockhausen on the Ruhr on April 8, 1945, well before the surrender. He was 67 years old then, weighed 140 pounds and gave his wife's name and address. It said he was 5'9" which I am sure was a mistake since he clearly was not that tall. He listed his occupation as "former" ambassador, trying to distance himself from Hitler.

I must admit that in my mind, his involvement in the conspiracy to murder Hitler, plus his deliberate campaign to distance himself from Hitler's excesses by becoming ambassador to Turkey, should have earned him another prompt acquittal. Apparently the German view of his role in bringing Hitler to power was perceived as more damning than it appeared in the court record. Most of all, I was impressed with his skill at bending the language to suit his own needs during the trial. He was a lawyer and a "diplomat" *par excellence.*

Fig 3—Von Papen walking in step with Hitler at the Berghof
In the early days, von Papen was included in the "inner circle." He was a small man and here you can see that he was distinctly shorter than Hitler. He became disenchanted with Hitler and asked to be permitted to resign. He was continued in various peripheral posts, however, but tried to distance himself from the Nazi government. He ended up as an Ambassador to Turkey, where he could serve his country yet not be involved in Nazi politics.

Fig 4—Von Papen caught off gaurd
Von Papen was irritated whenever anyone tried to take his photograph at the trial. He said he did not want his picture taken with who he repeatedly called "those criminals." He would turn his head away from the photographers whenever he saw them point a camera at him. His suits were elegant, and in court he made a much better appearance than the rest of the defendants.

Von Papen was acquitted of all the charges by our court at Nuremberg but was promptly rearrested and condemned to ten years of hard labor by a German civilian court of denazification. His health had failed so severely that he spent most of the next three years in prison camp hospitals. Finally acquitted on appeal, he then lived quietly with his wife and family in their old home where he completed his autobiography, *Der Warheit eine Gasse,* in 1953. It appeared in English translation in 1954. He died without fanfare in 1969 at age 90.

Franz von Papen, acquitted. Held not guilty of conspiracy and crimes against the peace.

Fig 5—Von Papen's portrait
Here he is wearing his overcoat with his Alpine hat. Von Papen selected this as his favorite photograph after the trial because he said he had especially missed the Alpine outdoors during the trial. He intended to spend much of his time as possible in the crisp but cold countryside. But first he had to suffer through 3 years of de-nazification trials and imprisonment. He was acquitted (again) on appeal. The signature is part of the Evan Lattimer Collection.

CHAPTER EIGHTEEN

Grand Admiral Erich Raeder

Fig 1—Raeder's portrait
Here we see him as "Grand Admiral" of the entire German Navy, having built it up mightily, during his tenure. Hitler had removed him from this post in 1943, replacing him with Dönitz. He is now a stern-faced older man. His signature verification is under the portrait. Evan Lattimer Collection.

Admiral Raeder (fig. 1) had been born in 1876, making him 69 years old when the trial began. He had risen to overall command of the German Navy in 1935 and had helped to build it up, in violation of the Versailles Treaty. He persuaded Hitler to introduce many innovations such as the "pocket" battleship. It was over Hitler's protest that he developed the super-dreadnaught battleship *Tirpitz* which was more effective in tying up the British Navy as a threat than it was in actual combat. He fell into disfavor by 1943, however, and was removed from his command by Hitler and sent into forced retirement. He was replaced by Dönitz, whom he resented.

Raeder's home life, according to Dr. Kelley, had been spartan and unhappy. In his boyhood he had decided to study to be a military doctor but abandoned that course and in 1904 enlisted as a naval cadet. He prided himself on his physical and intellectual ruggedness, which he attributed to his early training. He once told Dr. Kelley that as a cadet, "I noticed the development of an inner firmness and I became hard, even against myself." As a junior naval officer, Raeder edited several papers on navy research. During the First World War he was the commander of a light cruiser. He also was chief of staff of the reconnaissance forces, and in 1928 he became a full admiral. Seven years later he was commander of the entire navy.

Though he initially had little connection with the Nazis, when Hitler came to power in 1933 he became very friendly with him, eventually selling Hitler on the idea of a strong naval organization, particularly with the technical innovations he introduced. It was interesting that some of his early friends described him as a swashbuckling type with heavily padded uniforms, fancy hats, and flamboyant manners (fig. 3). By the time of the trial, it was obvious that he had become a cold, hard, quiet man with very

Fig 2—Raeder's calling card
This indicates that he was a Doctor of Philosophy (in research) as well as the commander of entire German Navy. He was highly intelligent but grumpy. Evan Lattimer Collection.

little to say spontaneously. Intellectually, Dr. Kelley found him to be merely average, nowhere near as brilliant as Dönitz. He was fussy in nature and aloof. During interviews he maintained a wall of formality against any conversational overtures of an intimate nature, although he willingly answered Dr. Kelley's direct questions. It appeared that he got embroiled in politics primarily as a method of developing the strength of the navy: he had been a schemer who planned to use Hitler for the benefit of the navy, in contrast to Dönitz who was a disciple of Hitler.

Raeder's chief medical complaint was a large hernia which was kept in place to some extent by a truss which appeared to annoy him greatly. He kept asking, in vain, for an operation on his hernia and it appeared almost as though he hoped he would die during the anesthesia. The Russians blocked any suggestion of an operation to relieve him. He was one of the few prominent prisoners the Russians had in their zone and they insisted on trying him, even though he had been forced out of the high command of the navy and into complete retirement in 1943.

He clearly resented the fact that Admiral Dönitz had replaced him and now outranked him. He continued to treat Dönitz as an underling much to the latter's annoyance. It appeared to me that the only reason Raeder was tried was that he was one of the few people the Russians could contribute to the trial group. I was amazed at the fact that he was given life imprisonment. It was interesting that Colonel Andrus had a sympathetic view of him and described him as having an air of quiet resignation. Andrus said it was difficult for him as a jailer to have even mild sympathy for prisoners who had committed serious and horrible crimes, but he

could not help but have sympathy for Raeder. By contrast, Dr. Gilbert found him to be an irritable old man with a practical, unimaginative mentality, but who was academically quite intelligent with an IQ of 134. Psychiatrist Dunn said that he saw in him a short, alert man with a rather tense expression. He had much to say to all the doctors, regarding his bad teeth (fig. 5), his hernia, and his concern about his improperly fitting truss.

Raeder gave the impression that he felt deep distress over his present position, and that he was keenly ashamed of being tried with this group and especially of the kind of death which he might possibly face. Dr. Dunn thought that he had no psychiatric disorder but had a reactive depression which might be considered a potential hazard for suicide, because of his aversion to the shame of being hanged.

During the trial Raeder made many interesting statements, such as the fact that Hitler did not want to compete with England in naval rearmament and made a

Fig 3—Raeder in his "Swashbuckling" days
He sported a padded, wide-lapeled uniform, set off by a gold dagger of ornate design. Evan Lattimer Collection.

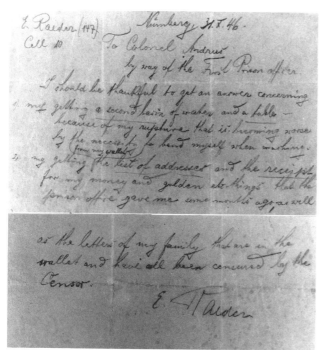

Fig 4—Admiral Raeder asks for a second wash-basin, plus his personal items

A letter to Colonel Andrus dated 31, Oct. 1946, after his sentencing. In it he requests as follows: "I should be thankful to get an answer concerning my getting a second wash basin of water and a table, because of my rupture that is becoming worse by the necessity to bend myself when washing. "That's item number 1. He says "I would be thankful to get an answer concerning (1) my getting a second basin. Also 2) my getting from my wallet the list of addresses and the receipt for my money and golden things that the prison office gave me some months ago, as well as the letters of my family that are in the wallet and have all been censored by the censor." Evan Lattimer Collection.

because they merely beat England to the punch. Raeder said that Hitler had deceived him about his peaceful intentions, permitting Raeder to circumvent and breach the Versailles Treaty through deliberate forms of deceit.

At the end of this session, Schacht summarized his reaction to Raeder's testimony by saying, "He disapproved of aggressive war and was deceived by Hitler, but he planned and began the aggressive war just the same. That's a militarist for you."

Raeder also testified that he and Hitler had advised Japan to attack Singapore to frighten America out of the

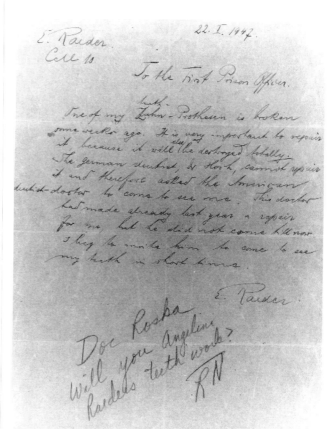

Fig 5—Raeder's false teeth need repairs

While still at Nuremberg, on January 22, 1947, awaiting transfer to Spandau, he writes a letter directed to the "First Prison Officer" (which is what he called Colonel Andrus) as follows: "One of my teeth prostheses is broken some weeks ago. It is very important to repair it, because it will else be destroyed totally. The German dentist, Dr. Hoch, cannot repair it and therefore asked the American dentist-doctor to come to see me. This doctor had made already last year a repair for me, but he did not come back til now. I beg you to write to him to come to see my teeth in short time."
E. Raeder (Cell No. 10)
(On the bottom of this handwritten note somebody with initials R.N. has written, "Doc Roska, will you Angelini Raeder's teeth work?" Evan Lattimer Collection.

naval pact with England in 1935 which preserved a 3 to 1 ratio of British and German naval tonnage. That was a breach of the Versailles Treaty for both sides. He described the plans for the attacks on Czechoslovakia and Poland as simply security measures to protect Germany's borders. He said the sinking of the ship *Athenia* was an accident that irritated the Americans unnecessarily. He claimed that Hitler had ordered that they completely deny that it had happened, and say that Churchill had sunk one of his own ships for propaganda purposes. Raeder implicated Fritzsche as having told him that Hitler himself had ordered the blaming of Churchill. Raeder therefore concluded that Hitler had deliberately lied about it. The prosecution made a big point that Raeder was involved in the planning to invade Norway, but Raeder indicated only that he thought it was justified as a preventive measure war, but that Pearl Harbor was a complete surprise to the Germans. He indicated that he had a hard time getting along with Hitler and finally had to insist on handing in his resignation. He gave the impression that although he managed to have his way in a few little things, he considered Hitler unreasonable and impossible to get along with.

At the end of the trial Admiral Raeder was declared guilty of three of the four indictments: conspiracy to commit crimes alleged in the other counts, crimes against peace, and war crimes. His sentence was life imprisonment.

The cranky old admiral's health deteriorated very rapidly and he was released from Spandau Prison in 1955 after serving only nine years. He finished his autobiography, *My Life*, in 1957, and died at home in 1960 at age 74. His death went practically unnoticed by the press.

CHAPTER NINETEEN

Joachim von Ribbentrop

Fig 1—Joachim Von Ribbentrop
The arrogant and testy German Foreign Minister, who only had one kidney (he had a nephrectomy for TB at age 18). Evan Lattimer Collection.

Hitler's foreign minister was a pitiable creature when I first saw him at Nuremberg (fig. 1). He looked like a crumpled piece of parchment. The pursed lips and the haughty frown of disapproval which we had been accustomed to seeing in the newsreels, and with which he had greeted practically every world leader, were now gone. The "high-society clothes-horse" of the Hitler entourage now looked terrible in his rumpled, baggy prison trousers. The elegant gestures of this one-time actor were now replaced with the stooped, uncertain, mumbling demeanor of someone in total disarray. His personal hygiene was bad and his cell was littered with crumpled scraps of paper from half-completed notes which he threw on the floor and then walked on as he trudged back and forth, night and day. He claimed he had always been a night person and needed only three or four hours of sleep each night.

Ribbentrop had been a tuberculosis victim as a youth, having caught it from his mother who had died from it when he was young. It infected his kidneys, and one of them was removed at age 18. He recovered, but his pulmonary reserve appeared to be limited and he frequently asked to be excused from appearing in court, saying merely that he was sick. While he claimed to be getting only three hours of sleep each night, he refused sleeping pills for fear they would dull his mind for the next day's court sessions. An occasional capsule of inert soda bicarb would make him sleep like a baby on weekends.

At one point he claimed that his right arm and leg had become weak and almost paralyzed. He said he had difficulty in finding the correct words. His symptoms did suggest that he was starting to have a stroke. He was, however, only slightly hypertensive. All his symptoms gradually cleared

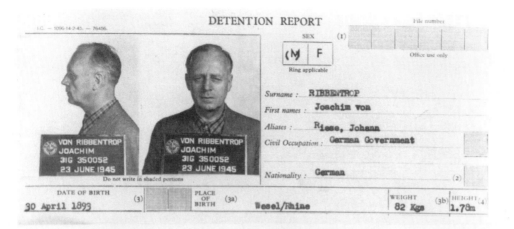

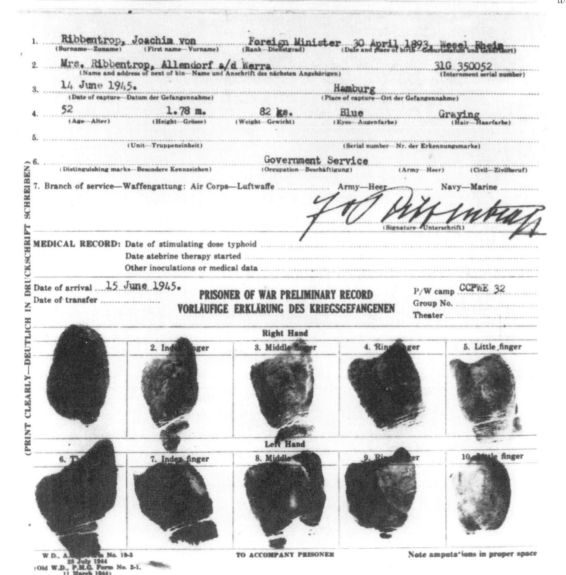

Fig 2—Ribbentrop's detention report and prisoner of war preliminary record
It is dated 15 June 1945, showing that he had avoided capture for 6 weeks after the surrender. It also bears his fingerprints and "mug shot." He could not believe that he had not been awarded any post in the new government by Hitler, in his final will and testament.

up over the course of another day. Testing of his vocabulary and cerebral status indicated that he had no impairment of these functions. On another occasion he said he was sure he had organic brain disease, but again, extensive clinical testing by our doctors could find no evidence of it. These symptoms of Ribbentrop's also eventually cleared up. He was frightened and dejected and looked 20 years older than his stated age of 52.

He was given all manner of neurological tests and all manner of psychological support to try to reassure him that his functions were not impaired. Chaplain Gerecke made a special effort to encourage him, to which he responded well. It was obvious that physically he was not only weak but was indeed worn down by the pressures of the war and now the additional pressures of the trial. He commented that he had become exhausted in 1943 and should have quit the government at that time because it had been apparent to him that his strength was ebbing, even then.

Ribbentrop had also suffered intermittently for several years from a functional weakness of the left facial nerve, with an accompanying neurologic pain in the left side of his face and occasional drooping of the left eyelid. He had called in the leading physicians, requested their advice, obtained their medicine, and then paid no further attention to them whatsoever. He claimed that he knew more about his affliction than they did. He repeated this behavior in prison and gave long, garbled opinions about himself to the American medical officers.

His own doctors described the manner in which his moods had changed according to whether Hitler had smiled on him or turned his face away. If any considerable time had elapsed during which he was not ordered into the presence of Hitler, his mood turned ugly. As soon as he was "called," his mood rapidly underwent a change for the better. After his return from an "inner circle" meeting, he was jovial and extremely talkative. Ribbentrop's tactlessness was also commented on by his German physicians, as well as his tyrannical and intolerant attitudes towards opinions other than his own.

His secretaries said that he had taken a delight in making people wait for him for excessively long periods. It was said that he would frequently require foreign diplomats to sit in his anteroom daily, for periods of weeks, before he would "find time" to see them. In his cell at Nuremberg, however, he was entirely different. He was depressed, uncontrolled and helpless; he had been cut off from his emotional dependence on Hitler. In addition, he could no longer communicate with his wife who had been his greatest source of support. His father, who had taught him well, had died in 1941.

Ribbentrop's cell was by far the most untidy of any in the jail, and he seemed unable to make up his mind on any point whatsoever. He was badly disorganized mentally, according to our psychiatrists. Each day he could be seen pacing up and down through the crumpled papers on his floor, wringing his hands. His greeting was always "Doctor, what shall I do? What shall I do?" He would ask questions and pay no attention to the replies, but he would continually flatter "the Colonel Doktor" in an attempt to find out what others *really* thought about him. He was clever and wily at this. He had slightly above average intellectual ability (an IQ of 129) and in conversation he was able to feel you out and frequently showed himself adept in gaining small additional tidbits of information that you did not intend to reveal. After watching how Göring flattered the guard officers, Ribbentrop also started on Lt. Wheelis, giving him signed photographs with friendly salutations. Wheelis accepted these, however, with less enthusiasm than he had shown for Göring's extravagant gifts.

Whenever the conversation turned to Hitler, Ribbentrop became positively fanatical. Over and over he would say emphatically, "I have always stood behind Hitler, and I always will." Then he would add quickly that while he had stood with Hitler on everything, he had nothing to do with policy and was not guilty of any of the crimes.

One day during the trial, motion pictures were shown, including several scenes of Hitler. Afterwards in his cell, Ribbentrop, whose eyes were literally aglow with remembered glory, according to Dr. Kelley, gripped one of the psychiatrist's arms and said breathlessly, "Couldn't you *feel* his personality?" The doctor was silent and Ribbentrop then lamented, "Perhaps it was not conveyed through the screen, but I could feel his vitality myself. Even though I am in jail because of him, if Hitler was to walk in here I would immediately do anything he said, without any thought of the consequences." He reported that he had even telegraphed Hitler in Berlin at the end, asking his permission to return to the capital to die beside his leader. Hitler had ignored his request.

The severest blow of all for Ribbentrop was that he had not been mentioned at all in Hitler's last will and testament. The position of foreign minister was given instead to Seyss-Inquart, a cold, calculating, highly intelligent lawyer (and fellow prisoner). Ribbentrop became hysterical when he heard this. At first he refused to believe it, thinking that something better must have been assigned to him by Hitler. When it

Fig 3—Ribbentrop's medals
Here is Ribbentrop's bar of medal's and a photograph of him wearing them on his uniform as a "General" of the SS at a military reception. The only medal he really "won" was his iron cross, reflecting satisfactory duty as an officer in the Imperial German Army in World War I. He later worked in Army Headquarters for a year, after the end of WWI. Evan Lattimer Collection. National Archives (photo).

became obvious that his name was not even mentioned, he was sure that Bormann and Goebbels had prepared a false will or perhaps Hitler had become insane and signed the will without knowing its contents. He was totally devastated by this news. It was only after this that he openly questioned the thesis that Hitler was the ideal man. He then finally began to place upon Hitler the blame for the failure of the Third Reich.

Surprisingly, Ribbentrop did not actually deteriorate mentally in prison. He just couldn't make up his mind about anything. He was babbling at all times, depressed and vacillating, but he stayed the same. He was, as Dr. Kelley said, an individual, who, without outstanding ability, had achieved a high position. He maintained his status by freezing out anybody who might challenge him, and at the end, he descended into the depths of despair. Trapped in a cell with only the gallows to look forward to, unable to find a solution

within himself and not knowing which way to turn, Ribbentrop, at the conclusion of the trial, was like a terribly frightened rat in a trap, as Dr. Kelley put it.

Background

Joachim von Ribbentrop was born in 1893 in the German Army garrison town of Wesel. His overbearing, army-officer father pressured him to excel. The family moved to Switzerland when he was ten years old.

Ribbentrop's formal education was carried only up to elementary school, whereupon he was sent to Grenoble in France to study languages at which he became quite adept. He was offered a chance to live with a family in England which delighted him; he learned English both in London and in Canada. In 1910, he was an aspiring actor, but his British accent was so exaggerated that even his fellow actors mocked him. Years later, his propensity to act out roles was quite apparent in his skill at making an entrance and in his apparently effortless and quite unique way of raising his arm when he said "Heil Hitler." His rivals were sure that this was the result of many hours of practicing before a mirror.

In Canada he worked as a bank clerk and for the railroads, in addition to acting. In New York he was a newspaper reporter. When World War I became imminent, he sailed for home, lest he be interned.

In World War I, Ribbentrop served as an officer with modest distinction. He charmed his way into an exclusive cavalry regiment and was awarded the Iron Cross, First Class, The Order of the White Falcon, The Oldenburg War Cross, and The Hamburg War Merit Cross (fig. 3). Toward the end of World War I, he again came down with active tuberculosis. He was hospitalized briefly, but after a short tour of duty in Turkey he stayed on as a lieutenant at the war ministry (fig. 4). He was there until 1919 when he met Anneliese Henckel of the champagne producing family, at a tennis tournament. (Ribbentrop was not only an excellent tennis player, he also played the violin well enough to be in several concerts. He was also a bobsled champion at Arosa, in the Swiss Alps.)

Anneliese was a wealthy, rebellious girl who was chic but not a real beauty. Moody, irritable, and prone to sinus headaches, she was well aware of her family's contempt for Hitler and her outspoken mother's contempt for Ribbentrop. His monocle and his "trick title" were particularly detested. Despite her family's objections to Ribbentrop, Anneliese married him in 1920 and he was taken into the firm, but only as a champagne salesman, never as a partner. His good tailoring and his fluency in French and English were great assets in this

Fig 4—Ribbentrop's I.D. card to enter the War Ministry in 1919
Ribbentrop as a First Lieutenant working in the War Ministry in 1919 after being "invalided" out of first the Infantry and then the Air Force with tuberculosis. Evan Lattimer Collection.

Fig 5—The Ribbentrop family
The Ribentrops and three of their children relaxing at home. Frau Ribbentrop did not hesitate to coach Herr Hitler in the niceties of life. Hitler acquired a surprisingly formal manner and learned to kiss the ladies' hands and conceal his ignorance of the fine points of society life.

field, and his job took him to other countries. Ribbentrop prospered wonderfully in the international champagne business: it was not only profitable, but he quickly discovered that gifts of liquor were an entrée to politically powerful people. He used this approach liberally and skillfully at home and abroad, encouraged by Hitler.

Ribbentrop as Foreign Minister

The other Nazis were openly contemptuous in their remarks about him and were especially critical of his capability to be the foreign minister for their country, a job for which he had no real qualifications. The veteran diplomats, like von Neurath whom Ribbentrop had displaced, were critical of one incident after another, such as when the nonaggression treaty had been proposed but von Neurath had refused to sign it. On this occasion, to please Hitler, Ribbentrop stepped right up and signed it (fig. 7), even though his post was only that of minister-at-large. Two years later, however, he was elevated by Hitler to the exalted position of foreign minister. Schacht, von Papen, and Dönitz were abundantly critical of practically everything he had done, but recognized that Hitler had used him to accomplish his goals: Ribbentrop acted as the front for maneuvers that Hitler knew he was going to repudiate very shortly, such as the Munich Pact (figs. 9-11). This was a travesty that Hitler intended to violate and quickly did. The 1939 nonaggression pact with Stalin and the Russians was also set up by Ribbentrop, under Hitler's direction.

Hitler was bored and uncomfortable with entertaining, and happy to have Ribbentrop entertain foreign dignitaries and please them with gifts of fine liquors. He therefore encouraged Ribbentrop's liquor business to grow, even during the war. Ribbentrop became wealthy enough that he could buy his way into positions of power in the diplomatic arena, without worrying about the expense. During his business trips abroad, he became cognizant of his ability to sell the German government's viewpoint. Ribbentrop had only joined the Nazi Party in 1932. He was first introduced to Hitler by Count von Bülow, as an interpreter of the French and British newspapers. Touted as a member of a wealthy, worldly family, he greatly pleased Hitler in this role. (It seemed obvious to Dr. Kelley that Hitler was a "father" figure in Ribbentrop's psyche and that Hitler had "played him" to the limit for his own purposes. Ribbentrop's egocentric displays were so repulsive that Dr. Kelley was sure they were a psychiatric manifestation of his insecurity. He completely fell apart in prison, acting like a child who had lost all his anchors to stability.)

Hitler was happy to have Ribbentrop join the movement in 1932. With von Papen now the Chancellor under Hindenburg, he used Ribbentrop to try to get himself named vice-chancellor but Hindenburg refused. Then, upon Hindenburg's death, Hitler not only became chancellor but declared himself Führer.

He was so impressed with Ribbentrop that he called on him for advice on foreign relations to a surprising extent. Very early, he gave him an office for his "Ribbentrop Bureau" across the street from the foreign office. He was asked to prepare a daily summary of foreign news from the newspapers. On this basis he

Fig 6—Ribbentrop's Reichstag pass, for 1933
Evan Lattimer Collection.

Fig 8—Ribbentrop's "personal" Nazi party I.D. card for 1938
Carries his signature, colorful stamps and a stern-looking photograph.

Fig 7—The non-agression pact with Stalin
Another of Ribbentrop's grandest moments was the signing of the non-aggression pact with Stalin which also contained a secret clause directing the division of Poland. This was still another agreement which Hitler and he had no intention of honoring, in the long run. At the time, it seemed to protect Hitler's eastern front from attack by the Russians, if he opened a western front (as he then did).

Fig 9—Hitler and Chamberlain
Ribbentrop (left) brokers the first "agreement" between Chamberlain of England, and Hitler.

Fig 10—Ribbentrop supervises treaty signing
Ribbentrop (foreground) having Hitler affix his signature to the pact with the British Prime Minister Neville Chamberlain in the presence of Mussolini (background) and the French Ambassador Daladier to Hitler's left.

Fig 12—The Ribbentrop crest
A silver spoon from Ribbentrop's silver service with the coat of arms designed by his wife in a pattern which is elegant but not ostentatious. Evan Lattimer Collection.

Fig 11—The agreement which Hitler and Chamberlain signed
Here the British almost innocently declared that war between the two countries was unthinkable. Hitler pressured them into all manner of concessions with no intention of honoring the sense of this document.

Fig 13—Ribbentrop talking to Hitler in Ribbentrop's apartment
The elegance of the wallpaper, the furniture and the furnishings was not lost on Hitler, who learned from Frau Ribbentrop the finer points of manners, of elegance in furnishings, and for that matter, in clothing. The difference between Ribbentrop's elegantly tailored, very expensive suit and Hitler's less stylish suit is noticeable. Even the difference in the neatness of their collars and ties is clearly visible, as is the difference in the relaxed manner of Ribbentrop. It was this type of education which Hitler enjoyed from the Ribbentrops, even though it was quite obvious at various points that he had no respect for Ribbentrop's ability, but only for his slavish devotion, which Hitler used to the hilt.

became Hitler's foreign policy advisor, much to the annoyance of the diplomatic corps. He was then appointed to the foreign office in a minor official post, about 1934, but Hitler then amazed everyone by naming him ambassador to Great Britain in 1936.

Another big surprise to me was the very powerful role that Ribbentrop's wife played, not only in his life but in the gentrification of the entire Hitler inner circle. It was she who had urged Ribbentrop to expand his use of gifts of rare vintages to attract the attention of influential people in the new government. Frau Ribbentrop volunteered to give several, very dignified, small dinner parties for Hitler so he could entertain notables. Hitler loved the expensive furnishings (fig. 13), the well-run house, and the perfect servants. (Hitler referred to the Ribbentrops as his "upper-crust" representatives, even though the Ribbentrops were never really in the top drawer of Berlin society, according to Frau Ribbentrop's mother.)

Anneliese impressed Hitler with her skill and knowledge about the finer things of life. It seemed quite obvious that she coached Hitler in matters of decor and dress, and conduct during elegant social events. These were areas where Hitler was ignorant (and realized it). As with Speer, he was surprisingly amenable to being educated by someone he recognized as being more knowledgeable, such as Frau Ribbentrop. This was quite in contrast to his intolerance of advice from anyone on political or military matters. Hitler welcomed her offer to help out, just as he did with Göring.

It seems undeniable that Anneliese's influence caused Ribbentrop to rise so rapidly in the diplomatic service. He had absolutely no qualifications or experience in the field, aside from knowing some champagne dealers (and their titled clients) in other countries, especially England. It was his name-dropping to Hitler that gained him the ambassadorship. He and his wife cut handsome figures at official functions where they were seen with royalty.

Eventually Hitler recalled him to Germany and used him as a diplomat-at-large to negotiate treaties and agreements (that Hitler had no intention of honoring). Hitler came to realize that in Ribbentrop he had a follower who was completely devoted to him, and began to use him to the hilt. This is what led eventually to his being appointed foreign minister in 1938. It was said that Ribbentrop quickly learned Göring's trick of finding out Hitler's own views on any issue and then presenting them to him, as his own. Frau Ribbentrop was a tremendous help to Joachim in all ways. She was his tower of strength in all of his interactions. She realized she could mold his career into a grand success with Hitler. She also recognized Ribbentrop's weaknesses,

revelling in the fact that he depended on her and was succeeding primarily as a result of her machinations. They were very devoted, appreciating each other's mutually valuable points.

They had five nice-looking children: two girls and three boys who always looked a little skeptical when they were summoned to have their picture taken with Hitler. There was no doubt that Frau Ribbentrop's mother recognized her son-in-law's weakness. She frequently made caustic remarks to her friends to the effect that of all her sons-in-law, the one that was the stupidest had risen to the greatest heights. Ribbentrop's wife's devotion was also manifested during the trial. When she was denied any opportunity to see him for over a year, she nevertheless came frequently to the prison, waiting patiently for any word or information about him. Frau Ribbentrop also wrote books about her husband's career, publishing them privately, and kept up a brisk correspondence with anyone who wished to know more about him. She had persuaded him to negotiate for a noble title so he could use the word "von" before his name, and had designed a coat of arms which appeared on their stationery and silverware (fig. 12). It is tasteful and delicate and does not compete with Hitler's silverware; a deliberate precaution, I am sure. Ribbentrop was always mindful not to irritate Hitler by outdoing him in any area. In photographs of the two men, Ribbentrop is always the relaxed courtier, leaving Hitler looking stiff and uncertain (fig. 17).

Von Neurath said that he had learned about the "purchase" of Ribbentrop's title, from a lawyer friend who was having trouble collecting his fee for literally having Ribbentrop adopted by the titled wife of his father's brother, when Ribbentrop was thirty-two years old. (A pension of 450 marks was settled on the woman—Ribbentrop's new "mother.")

Göring , von Neurath, Schacht, and von Papen were scathing in their criticism of Ribbentrop and would quote one blunder after another that he had made. For example, when he was presented to the King of England as the incoming ambassador from Germany, he approached him and then put out his arm in the Nazi salute. This enraged the British who disliked him bitterly from then on. At a luncheon to introduce the new ambassador to London's upper crust, Ribbentrop launched into a Hitlerlike harangue for forty minutes. Winston Churchill, out of his sight, began to mimic him, to the great amusement of the audience. Frau Ribbentrop could see Churchill and was furious.

Because of his insecurity and the knowledge that the other members of Hitler's hierarchy were a hard-driving group of backstabbers, Ribbentrop surrounded himself with loyal "flaks." He became so arrogant and

Fig 14—Ribbentrop's peaked hat, with his diplomatic corps eagle

Fig 16—Ribbentrop's vest buttons
The small buttons bear the insignia of the SS, in which von Ribbentrop was made an honorary General. Evan Lattimer Collection.

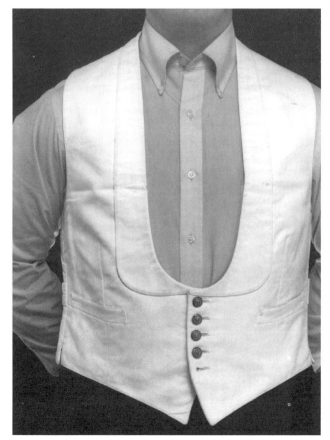

Fig 15—Ribbentrop's white pique vest
One of Ribbentrop's white pique vests for wearing with his white tie and tails. It is from the top tailor in Berlin. Evan Lattimer Collection.

Fig 17—Trying to keep up with Hitler
Ribbentrop demonstrating his relaxed and slightly superior appearing manner with Hitler. Here they are conferring alongside Hitler's mobile command train during the war, where he was trying to "keep up with the crowd" of competing courtiers.

disdainful that it was difficult for anyone to approach him. Speer commented to me about that. Even his employees pointed out that he would come into a room and act as if no one else were there, making an appearance of suddenly realizing their presence. After that, he treated them like dogs. One of their greatest complaints was that he would require his entire staff to line up at the airport and wait for hours until his plane arrived. If his wife was with him they would all have to bring their wives. Sometimes they would wait in a pouring rain for Ribbentrop to arrive, after which he would simply march off to his car, with a wave to the rain-soaked staff.

Everyone acknowledged his theatrical style: his uniforms and his gestures (figs. 14-16). He had special uniforms designed for his staff, adorned with medals. He even got Hitler to help him design them. Any official function was preceded by lengthy memorandums indicating how to attend to every tiny detail. Göring described him as a boundless egotist, a wine salesman who was successful in business but had neither the background nor the tact for diplomacy. Göring tried to advise Hitler to remove Ribbentrop for two reasons: First, Ribbentrop was hated by the British after his insulting introduction to the King; second, he also started advising them on how to compete with Russia, not realizing that the British considered themselves the experts in that area. They were actually trying to give the Germans advice about how to protect Germany from the Russians.

Hitler was greatly appreciative of Frau Ribbentrop, however, and was also well aware of Joachim's slavish devotion to him. Ribbentrop usually carried out *any* order from Hitler. However, in 1941 Ribbentrop argued with Hitler about one of his orders. (This was one of Ribbentrop's favorite stories.) Hitler then put his foot down and Ribbentrop, surprisingly, lost his temper and said that if his opinion wasn't good enough, he would resign. Hitler looked at him, walked up and down, grew pale, sat down in a chair, held his head in his hands and muttered that Ribbentrop was killing him. Hitler's eyeballs turned upwards and stayed that way for several minutes. The "dying" Führer then held forth for an hour, apparently looking very ill, recapitulating all their previous disagreements and any arguments they had had over treaties or problems in occupied countries. With Ribbentrop's sins recounted in detail, he said that his ungrateful foreign minister could then leave but that he (Hitler) was going to lie down and have a stroke. He said his ears were ringing, he felt faint, and that he was going to die and that Ribbentrop must be considered the direct cause of his death. This would be followed by the total collapse of the German nation.

Ribbentrop said he became very upset. Hitler looked like death. He seemed unable to breathe, was very pale, and the veins were standing out on his forehead. Ribbentrop surely thought he would die. He seized Hitler's hands and swore he would never do this again. He said he would always stand behind Hitler, no matter what he planned to do. Hitler then "rallied" and thanked Ribbentrop for sparing Germany's leader. (This ability to fly into a rage and then recover abruptly is often demonstrated by patients with Parkinson's disease, and Hitler was famous for his rages.) At any rate, Hitler's dramatics worked like magic on Ribbentrop and he never crossed Hitler again. Ribbentrop said in all earnestness, that whenever he thought of objecting, the vision of Hitler's face came before him and he would back away. Even when he was going to his death, due to Hitler, he still maintained his loyalty.

According to his secretary, Ribbentrop was extremely demanding of his staff. Any order had to be executed immediately. He denied himself any extended private life, had a reckless disregard for his own health, and expected the same from his subordinates. He said that his work meant more to him than anything else, and he demanded a similar attitude from his staff. Whenever great things were in the making, his "drive" inspired everybody. Everybody happily did the jobs assigned to them. During that time, you couldn't tell if it was day or night, but when the job was finished, he always showed his appreciation. Even in normal times, however, his schedule was unusual. He was indeed a natural "night worker," apparently suffering from insomnia. He could not get to sleep before 3:00 A.M., so he seldom went to bed before 2:00 A.M. He did not like to awaken before 9:30 A.M. Presentations by his advisors started his day and often delayed midday dinner until three or four o'clock. Meal times were no relaxation either since he monopolized the conversation and discussed only his official and political matters. If one of his sons had just returned from a vacation, he might be asked to tell about it briefly, but this happened very seldom. Occasionally he would have a movie shown in the offices at night. He preferred pleasant, humorous films. This left him no time for reading or the cultivation of hobbies. He had a very good memory and could converse intelligently on many topics about which he had had no formal education. He loved to astound experts with bits and pieces of inside information.

He loved music, having been an excellent "concert" violinist as a youth. Before the war he had attended concerts and plays occasionally, but ceased doing so during the war. He preferred Wagner and Beethoven. He was also interested in painting and in hunting. Any time he went on a hunting trip, however, he took the staff with him and everybody stood ready for work at any moment.

He had had no severe illnesses between the two world wars, until 1943, when he came down with pneumonia. This raised the specter of tuberculosis again, but it subsided with rest and a "sulfa" drug. He had his staff bring reports to his sickroom and he dictated and telephoned his instructions from his bed—even while he was still somewhat ill. Hitler demanded that he move his headquarters to East Prussia, and he did so at great risk, according to his doctors. He would follow his doctors' instructions for a few days but then gradually begin to get back to his routine of overwork. He ate, drank, and smoked very little. His secretary considered him to be an extremely clever man with complete idealistic devotion to his mission to improve the foreign policy of Germany. He had been an absolute outsider when he started in the foreign service and he had all the disadvantages of an amateur. His temper did not tolerate any obstructions or difficulties, which made things difficult for everybody.

Still, he completely reorganized the deteriorated foreign office, according to his secretary. She said he improved the existing civil service system, but became personally dependent on a small but absolutely trustworthy staff of workers, though he retained a few advisors among the old professional diplomats. All decisions were to be made by him. No one was to take any steps unless they had express authority from the Reichsminister himself. Instructions were in great detail and seemed to spring from a deeply rooted mistrust of the ability and even the loyalty of his coworkers. He felt himself personally responsible to Hitler for even the smallest detail. This led to a tremendous amount of work on trivia, about which he said, "I just have to do everything myself." His staff was well taken care of financially and he rewarded them generously after some especially well-done job and at Christmas, according to his secretary. If an injury or illness was suffered by a staff member, as from the bombings, he would send the best doctors, would expect a daily report, and would pay all the expenses. He sent fine presents and granted generous vacations. On the other hand, faithlessness or disloyalty constituted the biggest crimes of all, in his thinking. He would fire loyal, long-time staff members under humiliating conditions, if they violated his trust even in minor ways.

As the end neared in April of 1945, several of the top Nazis, including Ribbentrop, made efforts to negotiate with the Western Allies. Hitler was obviously fading away, but would not admit it. The military men were trying to figure out how they could induce the Americans and British to stop the advancing Russians. Kaltenbrunner had contacted Allen Dulles's men in Switzerland; Himmler also tried to arrange a surrender to the British in April.

Ribbentrop tried to get the Japanese ambassador to pressure Sweden to negotiate a capitulation. The ambassador referred Ribbentrop to the Swedish Count Bernadotte. Bernadotte received Ribbentrop but was subjected to an hour-long, arrogant monologue and withdrew in disgust. Thus Ribbentrop had attempted to join several others in trying to desert the sinking ship.

He hung around Dönitz's headquarters, dodging the British and Americans until June 14 when an acquaintance turned him in to the British authorities in Hamburg. From there he went directly to our Mondorf Detention Center. He had hidden out the longest of all the defendants.

The Hanging

What surprised us all was Ribbentrop's acceptance of the leadership role, for the final parade of the Nazi hierarchy who were sent to the gallows. As a result of Göring having killed himself, Ribbentrop came into his own, if only for a couple of hours, as the "top dog" in the Nazi parade.

He recovered his poise and marched bravely to the gallows. Andrus had come to Ribbentrop's cell at 1:00 A.M. and read him the death sentence again. Then he called, "Follow me." Ribbentrop rose, had his hands tied behind him, and walked behind Andrus to the new door to the courtyard. They crossed in the misty rain to the door of the gymnasium, with the chaplain following and a guard on either side of him. As they got inside the gymnasium door, Andrus said he stepped to one side and took off his burnished helmet in a form of salute as the prisoner passed by. Inside the door stood a major and MP's ready to take over the escort to the gallows. Ribbentrop's eyes narrowed as he saw the gallows. Slowly and deliberately, led by Chaplain Gerecke, he walked toward them. Gruffly, a colonel called to the official interpreter, "Ask the man his name" and in a clear voice came the response, "Joachim von Ribbentrop." He glanced up at the gallows once more and started to climb the thirteen steps. From the crossbar overhead hung the metal ring with the heavy rope dangling from it. Sergeant Wood, the hangman, placed the noose with its thick hangman's knot of eight coils around the prisoner's neck. An assistant executioner bent down and bound his knees with a G.I. belt.

Chaplain Gerecke, standing at Ribbentrop's left, then spoke a brief prayer. The condemned man was then asked if he had any final statement. He nodded and in a loud voice said, "God protect Germany. My last wish is that Germany's unity shall be preserved and that an understanding shall be reached between East and West!" The black hood was then pulled down over Ribbentrop's face.

At 1:16 A.M. Sergeant Wood reached forward, tugged the lever, and the prisoner plunged to his death. After a few minutes, a Russian army doctor and a U.S. army doctor with stethoscopes around their necks and flashlights in their hands, stepped under the black curtain that was draped around the bottom of the scaffold. Nineteen minutes after the body had been dropped, they emerged and announced, "The man is dead." His body was then cut down and carried to a box behind the screen, which was to be his coffin. Both segments of the rope were placed in the coffin with the body. The hangman, however, had saved his souvenir segment of the rope (fig. 18).

Thus ended the life of Hitler's high-society clothes-horse, society tutor and sycophant, who had been dropped by Hitler from the new cabinet he had designated before he had committed suicide.

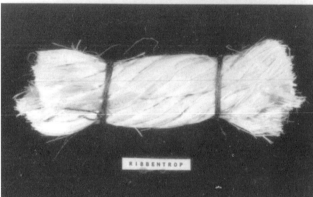

Fig 18—Ribbentrop dead, and a segment of rope used to hang him
National Archives and Evan Lattimer Collection.

CHAPTER TWENTY

Alfred Rosenberg

Fig 1—Rosenberg's portrait
This makes him look like a handsome effeminate young "thinker." His mug shot is not quite so flattering.

Alfred Rosenberg was the so-called philosopher of the Nazi group (fig. 1). Born in 1893 in Reval, Estonia of German Baltic extraction, he studied architecture and did not participate in any fighting in World War I. In 1918 in Paris, he permitted it to be rumored that he was a spy. Thereafter, he continued his studies in Munich, joined the Nazi Party, and was the first editor of the Nazi newspaper, *Völkischer Beobachter,* in 1923. He participated in the 1923 Putsch, and from then on was one of the most voluble, if not very effective, of the Nazi leaders.

In 1933, he briefly was Hitler's private envoy in London. In 1941, he was made Reichsminister for the Occupied Eastern Territories, because of his birth in the Baltics. He was also designated as the official Party philosopher: his book, *Mythus der XX Jahrhunderts* (The *Myth of the Twentieth Century*), ranked second only to *Mein Kampf* in Party literature sales. He was also an honorary SS general who was responsible for the introduction of the crudest form of anti-Semitism into Germany and into Nazi Party policy.

Rosenberg was a *very* dull conversationalist, and when Dr. Gilbert probed him, he found him to be a bigoted, philosophic dilettante who distorted history to justify the Nazi aggression. Rosenberg did, however, admit nervously during the first Gilbert interview that "Maybe we went a little too far." His tests showed a fair intelligence but a tendency to generalize, without deep understanding of anything. Dr. Dunn, our psychiatrist toward the end of the trial, characterized him as aloof and reserved. Rosenberg told Dr. Dunn that from the first he had linked Bolshevism and Jewish strivings rather closely together. He gave detailed accounts of the development of National Socialism and of his own anti-Semitic attitudes. He gave the impression of clinging to his own theories in a fanatical and unyielding

DETENTION REPORT

File number

Office use only

SEX (1)

(M) F

Ring applicable

Surname : *ROSENBERG*

First names : *ALFRED*

Aliases : _____

Civil Occupation : *Author, Architect*

Nationality : *GERMAN* (2)

DATE OF BIRTH (3)	PLACE OF BIRTH (3a)	WEIGHT (3b)	HEIGHT (4)
12 JAN 1893	*REVAL, ESTONIA*	*170 LBS*	*1.80m*

I.C. — 1096-14-2-45. — 76456.

ROSENBERG ALFRED 316 350042 23 JUNE 1945

ROSENBERG ALFRED 316 350042 23 JUNE 1945

Do not write in shaded portions

Fig 2—Roseberg's capture record

Rosenberg's prisoner photograph and fingerprints on his POW registration card. On Rosenberg's preliminary prisoner of war record it stated that he was captured in Flensburg on April 18, 1945, indicating that he permitted himself to be captured 2 weeks before Hitler committed suicide and well before the war ended. He weighed 170 pounds and was 5 feet 11 inches. He listed himself as an author and architect. He also admitted to being a Reichminister. He was born in Reval, Estonia on January 12, 1893 making him 52 years old at the time of his capture.

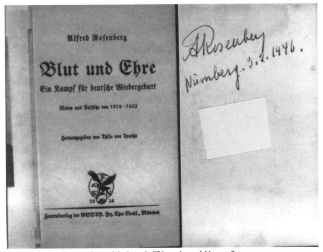

Fig 3—Rosenberg signs his book "Blood and Honor"

Dr. Goldensohn found one of Rosenberg's books in a local library, which was being "purged" of Nazi books. Rosenberg signed it with enthusiasm. Evan Lattimer Collection.

fashion. It came out that none of the top Nazis had ever read his book, *Blood and Honor*, which was alleged to be the basis for the Nazi philosophy (fig. 3).

Rosenberg's reaction to the indictments was one of shocked innocence. He argued that he had rejected the indictments of conspiracy because the anti-Semitic movement was only protective. Because of his characterization as the Nazi Party philosopher, one expected an intellectual giant, but this he was not. He was a tall, slender, flaccid creature, whose soft appearance concealed his fanaticism and cruelty. His conversation, however, did not hide it. As Dr. Kelley described him, he would begin a discussion on any subject, whether history, horticulture, or a paratrooper's high boots, and Rosenberg's quick switch of the subject to blood and race was so certain that you could almost predict it to the second. He gave a remarkable demonstration of the single-track mind in action and he proved a sore trial to the men who questioned him.

Göring coached him further on how to avoid answering hard questions. Dr. Kelley found him of constant interest since his characterization as a philosopher had not prepared us for the dull and very confused man he actually was. A large part of his confusion lay in the fact that he was completely oblivious to his own intellectual limitations. Many persons were surprised by the results of our intelligence tests which showed that this famous Nazi philosopher was of low average intelligence with an IQ of 127, below the mean for the group. However, as a result of his close contact with Adolf Hitler, his influence on the Nazi Party was probably greater than any other single subordinate of Hitler.

Judgment

The court's verdict was guilty on all four counts; the sentence was death by hanging. On October 16, 1946, Rosenberg was hanged. He was the only one of the two top Nazis to make no final statement on the gallows (Seyss-Inquart was the other), to our amazement. He had astonished us for the last time (fig. 5).

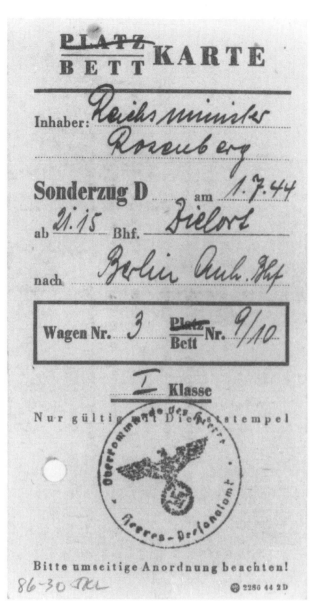

Fig 4—Rosenberg's railroad pass for July 1, 1944
It is interesting that the railroads did not consider him of suffi-cient importance to give him any special treatment. He was given an ordinary berth in car No. 3. This was true, even though he was listed on this ticket as "Reichminister Rosenberg." He still had to get a ticket like everybody else. Towards the end, he was shunted off as Minister to the Conquered Eastern Territories. Hitler always continued to reward his old cronies who had helped him with the initial Putsch in Munich, and Rosenberg was one of them. Evan Lattimer Collection.

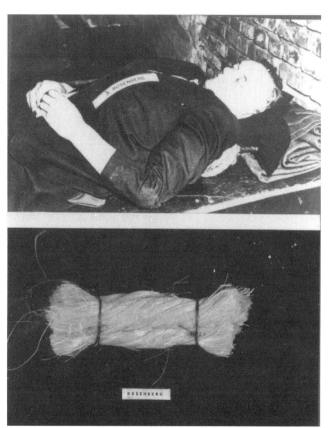

Fig 5—Rosenberg after the hanging. He lies dead on his coffin.
Below is a 2" segment of the rope used to hang Rosenberg. This was cut off by the hangman Sgt. Wood prior to the actual hang-ings and kept as a souvenir. Evan Lattimer Collection and National Archives (photo).

Fritz Sauckel

**Fig 1—Fritz Saukel -
The inadequate little businessman**
Hitler installed him as Gauleiter of Thuringia and later Brunswick and Anhalt, as well. Still later he was also put in charge of labor recruitment and "mobilized" more than five million workers from the occupied countries, to work in Germany. Huge numbers of these died from the brutal treatment in the labor camps. National Archives (photo) and Evan Lattimer Collection (signature).

Sauckel, an insignificant, unattractive little man (fig.1) had started out as a labor leader and later was appointed by Hitler to his "manpower" staff. He was made Gauleiter of Thuringia in 1927 and advanced in rank in 1933. In March 1942 he was elevated to plenipotentiary-general for manpower. He was also made a Reich defense commissioner, in which capacity he was responsible for slave labor "recruitment" for Nazi Germany. Physically, he was the most insignificant of all the defendants at Nuremberg; intellectually he was below the group average, with an IQ of 118. He was extremely immature emotionally. He had attended grammar school for only five years and then went to sea as a cabin boy. The rest of his education was picked up in a score of forecastles and in virtually every port in the world.

Almost with the opening of the First World War, the merchant ship on which he was serving was captured and Sauckel became a prisoner of war in France for the next five years, returning home almost a year after the war ended. Thereafter he worked as a factory hand and in due time as a toolmaker. He became a labor leader during the twenties and was involved in the factional strife that raged among German Social Democrats, Communists, and other groups. He took part in many strikes and labor negotiations and in 1927 he was made district leader and eventually Gauleiter of Thuringia. In 1933, Hitler repaid his loyalty with an appointment as governor of Thuringia (fig. 2).

After the war began in 1939, he was appointed one of the general leaders of labor in Hitler's "four-year plan." His political credo was only that of a simple, uneducated individual who accepts what the party says as gospel and operates as if it were established truth. He was convinced that the Allied nations plus the "international Jews," of course, had done irrepara-

Der Führer und Reichskanzler   Berlin, den 1. Januar 1936.

An
den Reichsstatthalter in Thüringen
    Herrn S a u c k e l
        in
    Weimar.

        Ich unterstelle Ihnen das Thüringische Innen-
ministerium im Rahmen des Landeshaushalts als Abteilung
"Innere Verwaltung". Mit Ihrer Vertretung in der Leitung
dieser Abteilung habe ich den Staatsrat Ortlepp beauftragt,
in dessen bisheriger Dienststellung bei Ihnen eine Änderung
nicht eintritt.

        Mit der Leitung des Volksbildungsministeriums habe ich
den Ministerpräsidenten Marschler beauftragt; soweit der
Geschäftsbereich des Volksbildungsministeriums die Theater,
die Kunststätten und die Universität umfaßt, ist der Leiter
des Volksbildungsministeriums Ihnen unterstellt.

        Wegen der Frage der Entlassung des Ministers Wächtler
aus dem Landesdienst und der damit zusammenhängenden
Regelung seiner Versorgungsansprüche sowie wegen der Ernennung des Staatsrats Ortlepp zum Staatssekretär bleibt
Mitteilung vorbehalten.

Fig 2—Hitler gives Sauckel unusual authority, as governor of Thuringia
In this letter dated 1 Jan 1936, on Reich chancellery stationery, Hitler also puts Sauckel in charge of the Department of Interior Administration, including the museums, theaters, universities and the Department of Education in Thuringia. It is countersigned by Frick, as Minister of the Interior. No one could be more poorly qualified to hold these positions than Sauckel. Hitler made all his decisions for him. Evan Lattimer Collection.

ble damage to the German people. He said he felt that it was his mission to fight against these influences. His letters to Hitler were literally worshipful in tone. He had for Hitler the loyal fidelity of a dog to its master, according to Dr. Kelley.

During the revelations of corruption among the Nazis that Sauckel saw demonstrated at the Nuremberg trial, he came to feel that Himmler and Goebbels had corrupted Hitler, and he held them responsible for leading the Party into the crimes against humanity. He contended, however, that his own hands were clean of blood and he was really confident that he would not be executed. His main point was that he was merely employed to obtain labor for Germany. That so many of

the imported workers died in Germany was not his problem (fig. 3). He saw no connection between the deaths and his orders that Germany was to have first choice of all available labor forces in conquered countries. He admitted nothing wrong in the uprooting of hundreds of thousands of foreign nationals so that Germany might win the war. After all, he had been told and he believed that Germany had the absolute right, and even the duty, to mobilize all the labor in Europe. He honestly believed that Germany was the savior and defender of Europe, and he had convinced himself that the deportation of countless thousands for forced labor in Germany was for the good of all Europe.

Sauckel was one of the few individuals in the Nuremberg jail who had neither the breadth of vision nor the depth of conscience to realize his guilt. It was not surprising that Sauckel actually derived satisfaction from being on trial with these leaders of the Nazi movement. I suspect he even carried a shred of this glory with him to the gallows. Heretofore he had been accustomed to being (and being classed) as a second-rate Nazi. To be classed with the major Nazis—even as a war criminal on the scaffold—was, for Sauckel, definitely aggrandizement of the ego.

During the trial he was in a state of constant anxiety. Dr. Gilbert's impression of Sauckel was that he was an

Fig 3—Sauckel's slave-laborers
Endless columns on underfed slave laborers marching to work in bitter-cold weather, clad in the thin blue-and-white-striped "pajamas" of the Nazi concentration camps. These were the foreign "workers" provided by Sauckel, who denied any responsibility for their fates.

Der Reichsführer-SS

Nürnberg, 13. September 1936

SS-Gruppenführer

S a u c k e l Fritz , SS-Nr. 254 890

Ich verleihe Ihnen den Degen der SS

Ziehen Sie ihn niemals ohne Not!
Stecken Sie ihn niemals ein ohne Ehre!

Wahren Sie Ihre eigene Ehre ebenso bedingungslos, wie Sie die Ehre anderer zu achten und für Schutzlose ritterlich einzutreten haben!

Dieser Degen soll in Ihrer Sippe Besitz verbleiben, wenn Sie ihn ein Leben lang untadelig getragen haben. Scheiden Sie vorher aus der SS aus, so fällt er zurück an den Reichsführer-SS.

Vergessen Sie keinen Augenblick, welch großes Vertrauen die Schutzstaffel Adolf Hitlers Ihnen durch Verleihung dieser Waffe geschenkt hat.
Bleiben Sie in guten und schlechten Tagen immer der gleiche!

Führen Sie den Degen in Ehren!

Fig 4—Sauckel awarded SS Honor dagger by Himmler
In September, 1936, Himmler jumped on the bandwagon by awarding Sauckel the "Honor Dagger" of the SS organization. Nothing could have been more inappropiate, in view of Sauckel's physical and mental inadequacies. Evan Lattimer Collection.

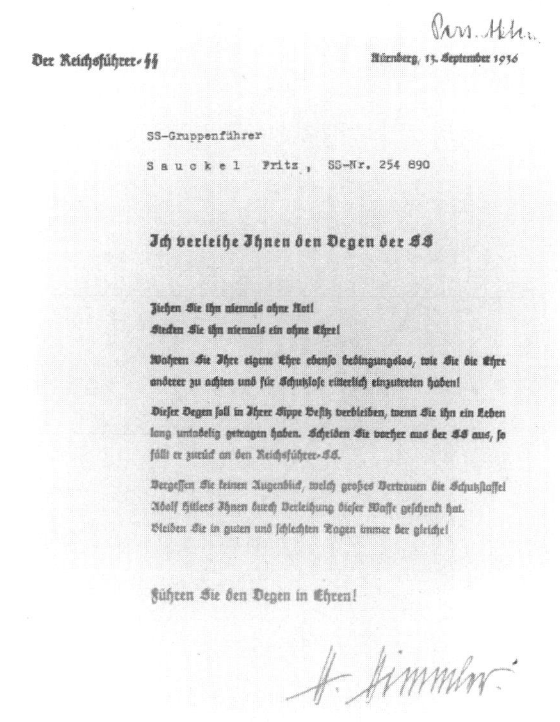

insignificant little man of 51 who was an unimpressive, naïve realist, whose conventional sense of values had been distorted by his blind faith in Hitler as the answer to unemployment. The "labor organizer" was now in a state of anxiety and depression over the revelation of atrocities which he swore he knew nothing about.

When the indictments were handed down, Dr. Gilbert went around to each man that night and asked him to write down his reaction to the indictments. Sauckel, even as chief of slave labor recruitment, found it hard to reconcile the indictment with his "love" for the workers. "The abyss between the ideal of a socialist community which I imagined and advocated as a former seaman and worker, and the terrible happenings in the concentration camps, has shaken me deeply," he said. When the prisoners were compelled to look at the concentration camp motion pictures, Sauckel was completely unnerved. His face twitched and he trembled from head to foot. He stretched out his fingers and cried wild-eyed, "I'd choke myself with these hands if I thought I had the slightest thing to do with those murders. It is a disgrace for us and our children and for our children's children."

As the evidence of Hitler's duplicity and evil policies built up, Dr. Gilbert found that Sauckel would react severely to these revelations. When he visited him in his cell, Sauckel trembled as if Gilbert had come to torture him. He would immediately begin to defend himself with trembling voice and wringing hands, "I want

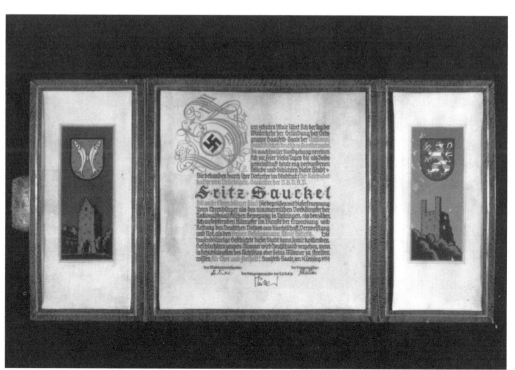

Fig 5—Sauckel's honorary citizenship document
Saucke was made an "Honorary Citizen" of Thuringia, when he became its Governor. This document extolls his good work in the labor ministry on behalf of the other officials of the province. Evan Lattimer Collection.

to tell you that I know absolutely nothing about these things and I certainly had absolutely nothing to do with them. It was just the opposite. I wanted to make conditions as good as possible for the foreign workers." And when Dr. Gilbert asked what he thought of Hitler now, after these revelations, he replied, "Well, it is hard to say. We are of different opinions whether Hitler knew about these things, I just don't know. But there is no doubt that Himmler did these things and they cannot possibly be justified. I just can't get it through my head how those things were possible. About the misuse of foreign workers, I am really not responsible for that. I

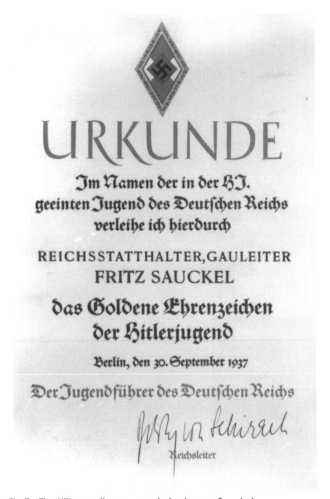

Fig 7—The Hitler youth movement also honors Sauckel
Baldur von Schirach, the Jugend Führer, bestows on Sauckel the Gold Medal of the Hitler youth organization. Hitler wanted all his appointees honored. Evan Lattimer Collection.

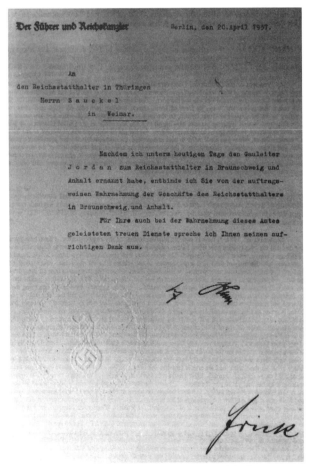

Fig 6—Sauckel now becomes Reichsstaatshalter of Thuringia, Brunswick and Anhalt
Here Hitler advances Sauckel as the Reichsstaatshalter of Brunswick and Anhalt as well as Thuringia, in 1937. Hitler praises Sauckel for his loyal service. It was in 1942 (5 years later) that he also made Sauckel the boss of all labor recruitment for Germany. In that post Sauckel organized the deportation of five or six million people from the occupied countries, into Germany, with a tremendous mortality. Frick also signed this order, as Secretary of the Interior. It is also interesting that Frick claimed he never saw Hitler after about this time. Evan Lattimer Collection.

was like a seamen's agency. If I supply deckhands for a ship I am not responsible for any cruelty that may be exercised aboard ship, without my knowledge. I just supplied workers to places like the Krupp Works, at Hitler's orders. I am not to blame if they were later mistreated. Don't you see my point of view? These things are terrible, I grant you, of course."

As the trial progressed and Göring became more and more antagonistic about talking to Dr. Gilbert, he also impressed upon Sauckel that anything he said to Dr. Gilbert might be used against him. The judgment of the court on Sauckel was: guilty on counts three and four; sentence: death by hanging.

Sauckel was perspiring and trembling all over when Dr. Gilbert came to interview him after the sentencing. He said, "I have been sentenced to death but I don't

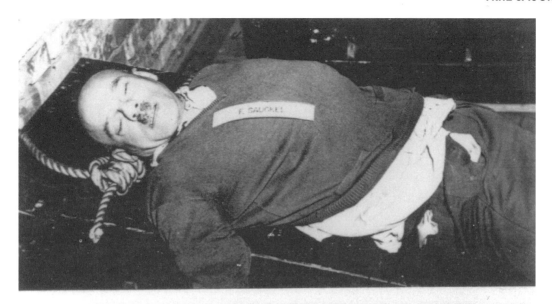

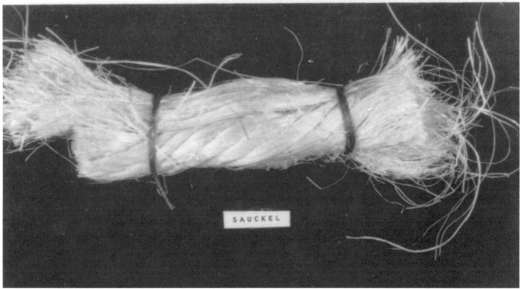

Fig 8—Sauckel in his coffin and Sauckel's hanging rope
A segment of the rope used to hang Sauckel, cut off ahead of time by the hangman, Sgt. Wood, as his souvenir. National Archives and Evan Lattimer Collection.

consider the sentence fair. I've never been cruel myself, I always wanted the best for my workers but I am a man and I can take it." Then he started to cry. He was the only prisoner who simply could not accept his sentence. He kept shouting, "My sentence is wrong." He began to go to pieces, with nightly episodes of shouting and screaming.

Even the cold intellectual Seyss-Inquart tried to console Sauckel, at Dr. Pflücker's urging, though he himself was facing the gallows. Both Frick and Göring were embarrassed by Sauckel's craven screams and said to Dr. Pflücker that they wished they could do something for him.

All his appeals were denied, and on October 16 he went to his death on the gallows, still protesting that he was an innocent man. To me he was the saddest sack of all (fig 8).

CHAPTER TWENTY-TWO

Hjalmar Schacht

Fig 1—Hjalmar Schacht, self styled economic wizard of Germany

His austere, cold and unfriendly expression would be relaxed if he wished to have a serious conversation with you. He was intelligent, was familiar with America, and had done remarkable things in reviving the German economy. Evan Lattimer Collection.

Schacht was the economic wizard who put Germany back on its feet after World War I (fig. 1). As director of the national bank and as currency commissioner, Schacht halted the disastrous inflation and stabilized the deutschmark. He was president of the Reichsbank twice: 1923-1930 and 1933-1939. He was the minister of economics, responsible for raising the money that enabled Hitler to rebuild and rearm Germany and he was the man who convinced Franklin Roosevelt to concede a moratorium on the onerous war reparations (fig. 2). But during the trial Schacht repeatedly made the point that he had *quit* Hitler as soon as he realized that Hitler was out of control and planning to wage war.

He had never joined the Nazi Party. He retired to his farm, but continued to say uncomplimentary things about Hitler's programs. He was finally thrown into Dachau (where Kaltenbrunner was his jailer, as he pointed out with disgust). He was discovered in the prison camp at the close of the war, presumably scheduled for death as a traitor to Hitler. There were others who thought that he was being spared only because Hitler might want to use him as a pawn in possible negotiations with the Allies.

By far the most intelligent of the group being tried, he was "outraged" that he had been brought into this trial with this "gang of criminals," as he called the other defendants. He was able to bend the language so as to explain everything that he did in a beneficial light, and in the long run was acquitted of all the charges against him. Since stabilizing the currency and putting the country on a sound economic footing was hardly a war crime, I was frankly amazed that they had brought him to trial in the first place. Being in the death camp at Dachau seemed to me an assurance that he was

Fig 2—Schacht with Franklin Roosevelt
One of Schacht's major accomplishments was to persuade Roosevelt to permit a moratorium on the reparation payments which Germany was supposed to pay after World War I. These were a crippling burden and Schacht's success in easing them was very important to Germany.

not on Hitler's side. Later, it became apparent that the Germans were not so sure about his innocence; they wanted to retry him.

Schacht (whose parents had admired American newspaperman Horace Greeley and had given their son his name—Hjalmar Horace Greeley Schacht) kept stating that he had done absolutely nothing wrong, that there was no sense in trying him, and that he was perfectly confident that he would be acquitted. In this he was correct, although not as surely as he thought. He was a tall, slender, aristocratic intellectual who had traveled all over the world. He had no physical complaints but was fed up with the trial. He was also fed up with the other defendants whom he openly referred to as "criminals," except for von Papen. Though Schacht was indeed acquitted, he could not leave the prison because he was told he would immediately be arrested by the German civilian authorities. The Germans did not like him, it seemed.

He adopted the role of the self-righteous, cranky old financial genius and expressed nothing but contempt for all the other defendants. In the lunchroom, one of the photographers aimed his camera at Schacht and the crusty old financier saw him. With a quick movement, he hurled his mug of steaming hot coffee over the photographer's camera and his uniform. The uniform was ruined. As a result, Colonel Andrus took Schacht's coffee ration away from him until Schacht came voluntarily to him and apologized for what he had done. Schacht in fact found it difficult to get along with any-

one. He was quite open in his criticism of Göring, Keitel, Rosenberg, and Ribbentrop. He was given to screaming with rage whenever things went against him. Göring reciprocated Schacht's loathing and ignored him.

All of our psychiatrists and psychologists rated him as highly stable, highly intelligent, and well able to handle the ordeal of the trial. He had been married twice, and his present wife was a much younger, very attractive woman. He spoke excellent English and French. After his forced retirement from government, he had continued to express and write about his dissatisfaction and condemnation of Hitler and Hitler's tactics, for which he was thrown into Dachau in 1944. He said he did not know about the concentration camps until he was in Dachau and heard people being marched to their deaths.

Fig 3—One of Schacht's books
The title of this book was "The End of the Reparations." This described his success in canceling this crippling debt. Evan Lattimer Collection.

He was relaxed when things were going his way, reading or playing solitaire much of the time. He was obviously contemptuous of Colonel Andrus, who in turn, thought Schacht was a person who had nothing but contempt for the rest of the world. Our psychiatrists, however, rated him quite differently. He reacted well: he was at peace with himself and at all times showed his confidence that he would be released. It was interesting to hear him rephrase every condemnation in words that softened every blow. He was quite gifted at this. He was of the opinion that the others should indeed be hanged, and was especially irritated that he was in the same dock with Kaltenbrunner. He was declared innocent and discharged by the court, but was immediately re-arrested by the German civil authorities, sentenced to eight years at hard labor, but was acquitted on appeal. He spent a total of four years in prison.

Dr. Gilbert found he had a brilliant mentality, capable of creative originality. Schacht told Gilbert he felt confident of acquittal because of his opposition to Hitler. Dr. Dunn said of him, "The defendant is an old man who is very alert and interested in my visit. He presents himself as being very much at ease and relaxed and maintains an air of affability and good humor. He professes to be very hopeful, with nothing burdening his conscience. There is no evidence of anxiety or depression except for the impression of strain which he is attempting to cover, fairly continuously. He professed amazement over being on trial now, after having been a prisoner of Hitler over so many months in the Dachau concentration camp. He talked freely about his fellow prisoners. His IQ was the highest of the group at 143. He brought out the fact, over and over, that he had withdrawn from public life following conflict with Hitler. Throughout the interview, he maintained his air of graciousness and affability. He professed to feel very sure of eventual release, in which he proved to be correct. A severe sentence would come as a great shock and might well throw him into an agitated state."

Even as the three men who were acquitted at the tribunal (Schacht, von Papen and Fritzsche) were celebrating their good fortune and giving interviews to the press with great enthusiasm, they received word that the German civil authorities were waiting for them outside the jail and had even formed a ring around the prison so they could not escape. At the invitation of Colonel Andrus, all three of them decided they would stay in the jail while deciding what to do.

After four days, Schacht and Fritzsche left the jail. Schacht went to the house in Nuremberg where his wife had lived at one time, but there the German civilian police arrested him. They took him to court where

he raised so much hell, as he put it, that they let him go back to his wife's old house for a good night's sleep, just as they did with Fritzsche, as it turned out. The next day, Schacht's carefully chosen lawyer, Dr. Rudolf Dix, who was very skillful and generally accepted as the spokesman for the entire group of German lawyers representing the defendants, came to his rescue. Dr. Dix persuaded the court to release Schacht on his own recognizance during any denazification proceedings. He was to "check in" personally during this time with the authorities. With typical arrogance, Schacht immediately rented a car and drove away with his wife, toward her home in the north. In doing this they had to go through Stuttgart where the decisions of the court at Nuremberg were no longer honored. He was promptly arrested and clapped in jail while denazification procedures were initiated. Schacht kept protesting that he had never joined the Nazi Party and had been repudiated by Hitler even as he had repudiated Hitler. Nevertheless, the court sentenced him to eight years at hard labor, as an "arch-criminal."

Schacht's lawyers persuaded the court on appeal to acquit him again, on September 2, 1948. He then got back in his car and drove to the British zone where his wife now lived. The local authorities *again* arrested him and insisted on further denazification proceedings in the town of Luneburg. He was finally acquitted in toto toward the end of 1950. He was outraged at the Germans because he had persuaded the entire international tribunal that he was innocent, yet his own countrymen insisted on retrying him—like a bunch of children and amateurs, as he said. The value of good legal counsel was again made very obvious in the manipulation of the facts which were very convincing in themselves, so far as I was concerned. I thought the German civil authorities were very obtuse.

Schacht was now penniless since all of his assets had been either lost or appropriated. His other properties had fallen into the hands of the Russians and he was heavily in debt to his high-grade lawyers. He was now 71 years old and had to support his wife and two children. He contracted to publish a book about his experiences titled *Account Settled*, which he had written during this time in jail. This book sold some 250,000 copies and got him back on his feet financially.

Surprisingly enough, several foreign governments recognized his cleverness in financing a destitute Germany and the Indonesian government paid him to come as their consultant on financial and economic matters. This he turned into a triumphal tour through Rome and Cairo (where the governments again treated him as a guest and used some of his professional services). He was also treated very handsomely in India.

These contacts were so successful and his work was so good that he was invited for a second tour to Egypt and Iran, and then finally in 1952 to Damascus for a plan for founding a central bank for Syria. He finally settled in, for Christmas, in 1952. He was now 75 years old but started a second book, titled *Confessions of the Old Wizard: The Autobiography of Hjalmar Horace Greeley Schacht.* He quieted down after that, but lived eighteen more years, running his own bank. He died in 1970 at the age of 92. This was in spite of having been in the concentration camp and having lived through the strictures and rigors of the German wartime food shortages. He had predicted at one point that he would live to be 90 years old, because he said all of his family died at that age.

Without Schacht's help early in the game, Hitler and his Nazis could never have rearmed as quickly and as overwhelmingly as they did. There were many who thought that he was such an important person in the build-up of the Nazi regime that he should have been punished more severely. It seemed to me, however, that it was Hitler himself who got Schacht acquitted when he threw him into the concentration camp at the end, as an enemy marked for death. Schacht played this for all it was worth and his performance was superb.

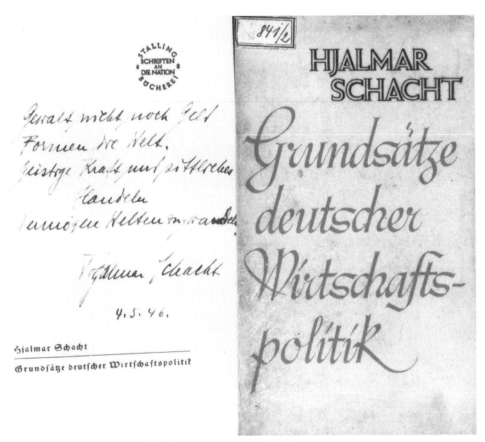

Fig 4—Schacht's poetic inscription in his book on Effective German Economic Policy
He writes in verse that "Neither power nor money form the world. Only Spiritual force and striving can change the world." Dated May 4, 1946. It is interesting that both he and Admiral Dönitz tended to write little poems to express their views. Both of them were so austere and cranky that this seemed surprising. They both used classical German terminology in their little poems. Evan Lattimer Collection.

CHAPTER TWENTY-THREE

Baldur von Schirach

Fig 1—Baldur von Schirach
The handsome, chubby, young (38-year-old) aristocrat was forced out of Hitler's inner circle even after he had formed the Hitler Jugend, and had instilled in them a personal, fanatic devotion to Hitler. His American mother gave him an almost American manner. Psychologist Gilbert thought that he had a strong homosexual leaning, and his wife divorced him while he was in prison. He had some handsome sons by her. He had been "Gauleiter" of Vienna, but his outspoken wife had offended Hitler by criticizing the deportation of the Jews from Vienna. After that he was strictly on the "outside." He had permitted the deportation of Jews in Vienna to Russia, and for that he got 20 years in prison. National Archives (photo) and Evan Lattimer Collection (signature card).

Baldur von Schirach was a large, rather plump, nice-looking man, who had been the leader of the German youth. Born in 1907 in Berlin, the son of a theatrical director and an American mother, he was the youngest of the group of defendants and was ever mindful of his descent from nobility. He considered himself an artist and a poet and had been the president of The Friends of the German Academy. He had attended Munich University where he heard Hitler speak in 1925 and, inspired by him, joined the Nazi Party.

He was appointed leader of the National Socialist Students' Union, and in 1932 was elevated to national leader of the German Youth and a member of the German Reichstag. In 1933, he was named overall leader of the Youth of the German Reich and wrote many poems, songs, and books for the Youth Movement. He was then made Gauleiter of Vienna and a member of the Reich Defense Commission. He was also named to the post of Reichsstadthalter of Vienna.

Many of the other prisoners disliked him because of his superior attitude and his habit of maneuvering behind their backs, complaining to the authorities without first speaking to them about the problem. On the other hand, many of them referred to the fact that von Schirach himself had been outmaneuvered by Martin Bormann, Hitler's private secretary who was very skillful at stabbing people in the back when he thought they were getting too close to Hitler. They indicated that Bormann had effectively ended von Schirach's career as an important factor in the government a few years earlier. During the trial he became a strong ally of the nationalistic Göring, tattling on the other prisoners and carrying back Göring's threats to them. After Göring was removed from the lunch rooms, he fell under the influence of a group headed by Speer and he began to divorce himself from Göring. As the evidence came out of Göring's complicity in the murders of the Jews, von Schirach became genuinely penitent.

Von Schirach claimed that he was only training the German youth to develop them as good citizens. His organization was very much like the Boy Scouts, he said: "I had no idea that this training would contribute to or later be used to develop blind obedience to such brutal demands."

It was quite a mystery to this intelligent man that the youth had gone on to become storm troopers with such sadistic traits. Dr. Gilbert characterized him as "a conscious aesthete with a narcissistic streak, whose early rise to power went to his romantic head. He is now disillusioned, by what he feels was the betrayal of the German Youth by the older leaders." His IQ was fairly high at 130. Dr. Dunn noted that he was a very poised man who greeted you very pleasantly in colloquial English. His manner was one of establishing each interview as a social occasion, rather than a professional one. He gave an account of how he fell under the influence of Hitler, and the importance of Henry Ford's writings in setting his anti-Semitic attitude. He presented his "Hitler Jugend" as a German Boy Scout movement that was set quite apart from the less desirable features of the Nazi movement, and he was quite derogatory in discussing Hess's peculiarities, and the technique of

Fig 3—A book by von Schirach
A book by von Schirach entitled Das Lied der Getreuen (The song of the Faithful). Evan Lattimer Collection.

manipulation used by Bormann to rise to power at the side of Hitler.

Dr. Kelley never worried about Schirach as a suicide risk because he thought he would be able to escape from the pressures by artistic activities or poetry. He thought he had to vindicate the role of Hitler Youth and had offered to conduct seminars with all of the Hitler Youth leaders at Birkenau or Dachau, to educate them on the terrible side of the Nazi movement. He offered to give himself as a hostage for any of these activities. All of these were turned down by the authorities. He recounted his remorse and said that he was resigned to death. He was grave and tremulous when interviewed, but also showed his poetic inclinations by writing a poem titled, "To Death."

Always mindful of his heritage in German nobility and culture, he told his lawyer that as long as he could keep his head he would hold it up high. When he was asked how he became anti-Semitic, he said that in his youth he had moved in aristocratic circles and never even came in contact with Jews. He had no reason to be anti-Semitic but he did notice a sort of underhanded quiet prejudice against the Jews, "even in the best circles." This did not impress him, however, until somebody made him read a book alleged to have been written by Henry Ford, *The International Jew*. He was at the impressionable age of 17 and believed every word of it, not knowing that authorship of the book and its sequel

Fig 2—Von Schirach's car pennant
As the leader of the "Hitler Jugend" von Schirach's automobile carried the pennant to denote his importance. Evan Lattimer Collection.

Fig 4—Von Schirach reviews his troops
The child-soldiers of Hitler Jugend, do a march-past as their leader (von Schirach) gives them the Nazi salute. Note Streicher, standing below von Schirach, and sharing in the glory.

Fig 5—Three cheers for Texas
A note from von Schirach to Texan Jack Wheelis, the guard officer in charge of the prisoners in the Nuremberg Prison. He adds his sentence (20 years) and adds his titles as Head of the Hitler Jugend and Gauleiter of Vienna. Evan Lattimer Collection.

denied by Henry Ford, and that both were used by the Nazis, especially Streicher, to persuade many people of the power of the Jews. Hitler's avid anti-Semitism was picked up by him. During his period as the Gauleiter of Vienna, he approved a mass evacuation of the Jews from Vienna to the east. It was his opinion that this trial's horrible disclosure of the criminal nature of the Nazi activities against the Jews would end anti-Semitism worldwide. He thought the German youth needed to be reeducated, however, and was willing to help with this if they would permit him to do so.

Justice Jackson characterized von Schirach as a poisoner of a generation. He said he initiated the Hitler Youth in Nazi doctrines, trained them in legions for service in the SS and the Wehrmacht, and delivered them up to the Party as fanatic unquestioning executors of its will.

After the sentencing, von Schirach's face was grave as he returned to his cell and marched in, head high. "Twenty," he said as the guard unlocked the handcuffs.

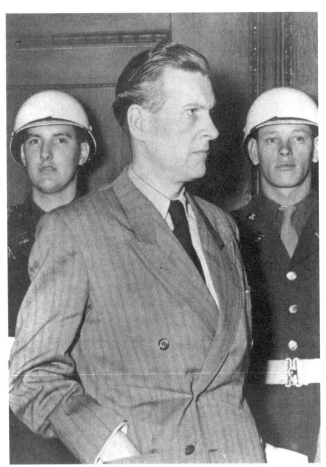

Fig 6—Von Schirach in the dock at Nuremberg
Always calm and self-possesed, von Schirach strolls to his seat in the dock as the trial is about to resume.

He had been sentenced to twenty years' imprisonment. Dr. Gilbert told him his wife would be relieved to know that he had not gotten the death penalty, which she had feared. "Better a quick death than a slow one," he answered. He asked what the other sentences were so far, and seemed to agree that each one was about what he had expected.

After the transfer to Spandau, Dr. Walther Funk brought in the word that Schirach's wife had divorced him in November of 1950. This may have had something to do with the fact that the wives of Hess, Funk, Göring, and Schirach were all held in Bavarian prison camps for some time after the trial began. Schirach reflected on the fact that the rules of their imprisonment did not permit them access to any lawyers to deal with civil matters such as divorce. In January of 1965, Schirach suffered a detached retina on one side, which was treated with conservative therapy and resulted in a severe loss of vision in that eye. He was kept in the hospital for three months. In July 1965, his other retina detached and damaged his vision severely. On this occasion he was taken to a German ophthalmologic hospital where a specialist in treating detached retinas operated on him. They apparently sclerosed various spots on the back of the eyeball and got the retina to reattach. After some weeks of observation he was declared as having an excellent result. He also suffered from phlebitis, with some clotting in his legs.

Upon his release from prison, after serving 20 years, Schirach adopted a quiet lifestyle and stayed out of the public eye, though he wrote a book titled, *I Believed in Hitler.* He died unnoticed in 1974, at age 67.

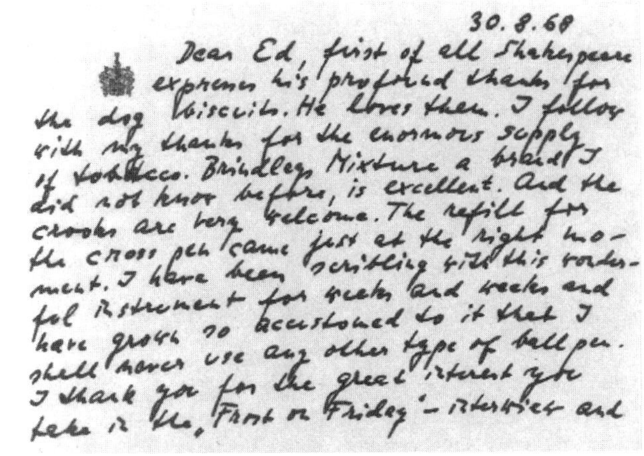

30. 8. 68

Dear Ed, first of all Shakespeare expresses his profound thanks for the dog biscuits. He loves them. I follow with my thanks for the enormous supply of tobacco. Brindley Mixture a brand I did not know before, is excellent. And the crooks are very welcome. The refill for the cross pen came just at the right moment. I have been scribbling with this wonderful instrument for weeks and weeks and have grown so accustomed to it that I shall never use any other type of ball pen. I thank you for the great interest you take in the, "First or Friday" - interview and

Fig 7—A note in contemporary "American"
Von Schirach writes to "Ed," a friend in California, thanking him for dog biscuits for his dog "Shakespeare." Also for the enormous supply of Brindley's tobacco and the "Cross" pen. Evan Lattimer Collection.

CHAPTER TWENTY-FOUR

Dr. Arthur Seyss-Inquart

Fig 1—Seyss-Inquart's portrait and signature

In this view, in his uniform, he is looking obliquely at the camera which was quite characteristic of him. His thick glasses with their thin frames, gave him a cold appearance, which Von Papen said was misleading since he found him to be a typical cheerful Viennese. He sat alongside Von Papen in the prisoner's box. The young-liberal, college-professor-type, who had first betrayed his fellow Viennese to Hitler, then helped Frank rule Poland, and was later placed in charge of the occupied Netherlands and Belgium. There he ruled with a murderous hand but with a certain "panache." Dr. Gilbert was suspicious that he had a homosexual tendency and certainly some of his letters to the other prisoners (like Sauckel) suggested that. This is his portrait as Reichstatthalter of Austria. National Archives (photo) and Evan Lattimer Collection (signature card).

Dr. Seyss-Inquart was a tall, slender, unattractive lawyer with thick wire-rimmed glasses and a habit of looking obliquely at you (fig 1). He had the highest uncorrected IQ of anyone in the group, at 141. He had a noticeable limp resulting from a mountain climbing accident in his youth and aggravated by his service in the Austrian Army.

He was born in the Province of Moravia, which was at that time part of Austria. He had been wounded during the First World War and relieved from army duty, whereupon he took his law degree and graduated in 1917, shortly before the independent Czechoslovakian state was formed. He then migrated to Austria and entered Austrian politics in 1930. From 1934 to 1938, he worked with the illegal Austrian Nazi Party even though he did not actually join it. The chancellor, Kurt von Schuschnigg, assuming that he was a loyal Austrian, appointed him minister of the interior and security. He thereupon double-crossed Schuschnigg and opened the border to the German troops. He was admitted to the German cabinet as minister-without-portfolio in 1939 and deputy governor of Occupied German Territory in Poland, 1939-1940, as Hans Frank's assistant. He was made high commissioner for the Netherlands, 1940-1945. It was under his direction that Holland was robbed and her manpower destroyed. He tried to lead the

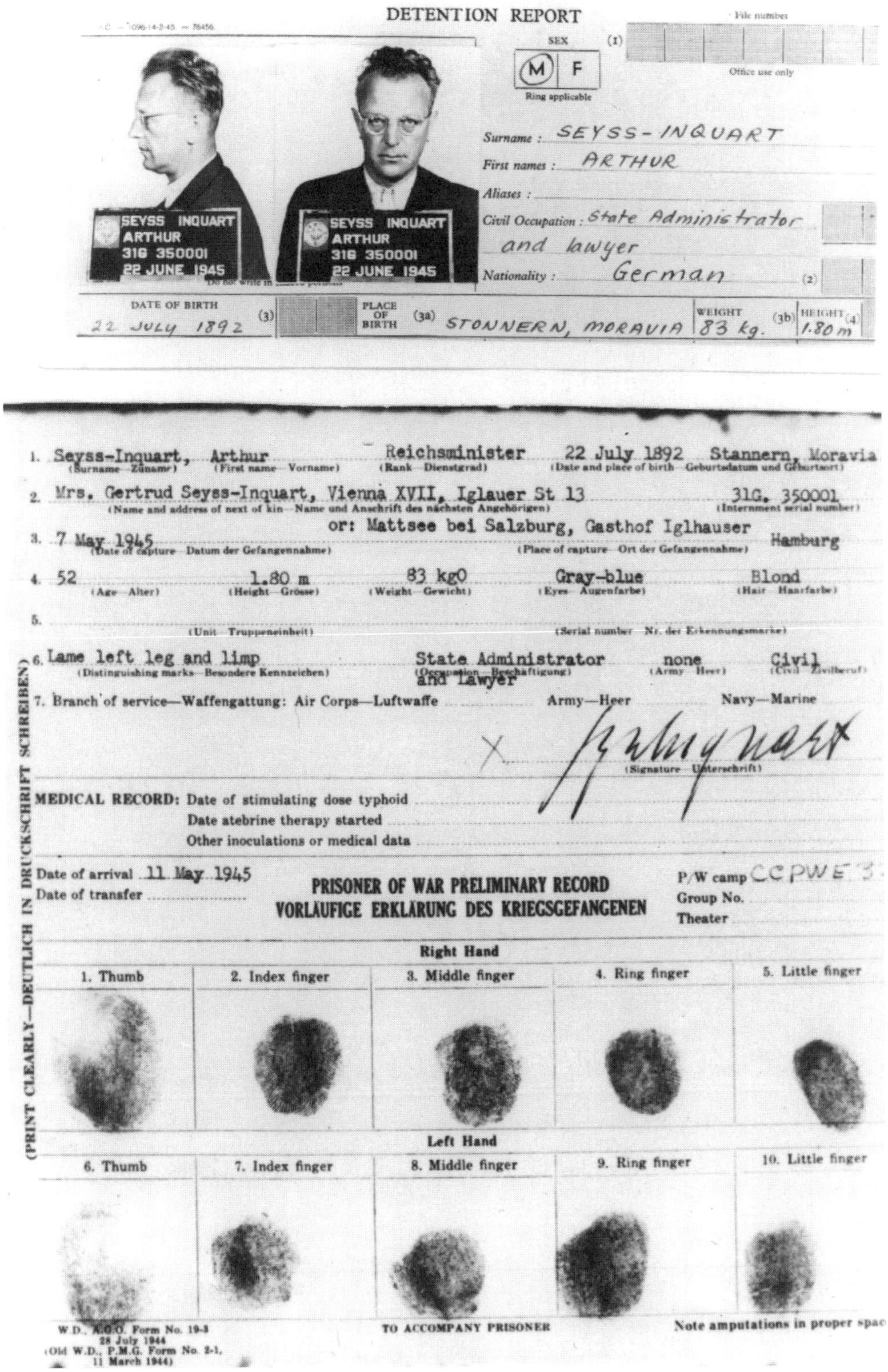

DETENTION REPORT

File number

SEX (1) M F — Ring applicable

Office use only

SEYSS INQUART
ARTHUR
316 350001
22 JUNE 1945

Surname: SEYSS-INQUART
First names: ARTHUR
Aliases:
Civil Occupation: State Administrator and lawyer
Nationality: German (2)

DATE OF BIRTH (3) 22 JULY 1892
PLACE OF BIRTH (3a) STONNERN, MORAVIA
WEIGHT (3b) 83 kg.
HEIGHT (4) 1.80 m

1. Seyss-Inquart, Arthur (Surname—Zuname) (First name—Vorname) — Reichsminister (Rank—Dienstgrad) — 22 July 1892 Stannern, Moravia (Date and place of birth—Geburtsdatum und Geburtsort)
2. Mrs. Gertrud Seyss-Inquart, Vienna XVII, Iglauer St 13 or: Mattsee bei Salzburg, Gasthof Iglhauser (Name and address of next of kin—Name und Anschrift des nächsten Angehörigen) — 31G. 350001 (Internment serial number)
3. 7 May 1945 (Date of capture—Datum der Gefangennahme) — Hamburg (Place of capture—Ort der Gefangennahme)
4. 52 (Age—Alter) — 1.80 m (Height—Grösse) — 83 kg0 (Weight—Gewicht) — Gray-blue (Eyes—Augenfarbe) — Blond (Hair—Haarfarbe)
5. (Unit—Truppeneinheit) (Serial number—Nr. der Erkennungsmarke)
6. Lame left leg and limp (Distinguishing marks—Besondere Kennzeichen) — State Administrator and lawyer (Occupation—Beschäftigung) — none (Army—Heer) — Civil (Civil—Zivilberuf)
7. Branch of service—Waffengattung: Air Corps—Luftwaffe — Army—Heer — Navy—Marine

(Signature—Unterschrift)

(PRINT CLEARLY—DEUTLICH IN DRUCKSCHRIFT SCHREIBEN)

MEDICAL RECORD: Date of stimulating dose typhoid
Date atebrine therapy started
Other inoculations or medical data

Date of arrival 11 May 1945
Date of transfer

PRISONER OF WAR PRELIMINARY RECORD
VORLÄUFIGE ERKLÄRUNG DES KRIEGSGEFANGENEN

P/W camp CCPWE 3
Group No.
Theater

Right Hand

1. Thumb	2. Index finger	3. Middle finger	4. Ring finger	5. Little finger

Left Hand

6. Thumb	7. Index finger	8. Middle finger	9. Ring finger	10. Little finger

W.D., A.G.O. Form No. 19-3
28 July 1944
(Old W.D., P.M.G. Form No. 2-1,
11 March 1944)

TO ACCOMPANY PRISONER

Note amputations in proper spac

Fig 2—Seyss-Inquart's Prisoner-of-War preliminary-record and detention report

This report, on which he lists himself as a lawyer and State Administrator, shows that he was born in Stannern, Moravia, that he is 5'11" tall and weighed 170 pounds. He was captured in Hamburg on May 7, 1945 at age 52. He says that his hair was blond and his eyes were gray-blue.

Dutch doctors into a policy under which their only function would be rehabilitation: any patients who could not be rehabilitated to "do the state's work" should be cast aside and abandoned; no resources should be wasted on them. The Dutch doctors saw through his ruse and refused to cooperate. They even turned in their licenses to practice medicine rather than accept this proposal for surrendering their right to cure everybody. Seyss-Inquart then sent 100 of these doctors to concentration camps in Germany.

He was captured May 7, 1945, in Hamburg. At the time of his capture he listed his occupation as "state administrator and lawyer." He was 52 years old, 5' 11" tall and weighed 170 pounds. He was cold and aloof toward us, and always of the opinion that what he had done had been best for Germany. In fact, his only concern was for the German people, with no sympathy whatsoever for the victims.

After the sentencings, Seyss-Inquart wrote a note to Colonel Andrus asking if he, Frank, and Sauckel would be permitted to have a cold shower each morning, as in the past, in order to keep up their physical and mental conditions. He petitioned that those sentenced to death should be able to meet during the daytime, as before the verdicts were announced. He mentioned that as the Reichscommissioner of the Netherlands, he himself had often given such permissions and had received many letters of thanks. "You may be convinced, Colonel, that I myself, as well as all my fellow sufferers, expect calmly the end of an inevitable, and in a certain sense necessary, event and will certainly do nothing which could render more difficult your task." He was allowed his cold shower, but no visiting.

Seyss-Inquart was completely reconciled to his fate of being hanged and refused to defend himself in court. He said again and again that if you sit in the front row in good times you must also sit there in bad. He used his last two weeks to convert to religious activity in what appeared to be a superficial and less-than-convincing manner. Many of the prosecutors had a secret admiration for this cold-hearted man.

When Hitler decided to commit suicide and organize a final testament with tentative government appointments to posts of responsibility, he appointed Seyss-Inquart as the new foreign minister. This was not surprising in view of Seyss-Inquart's skill as an administrator as the governor of Austria, as administrator in Poland, and as the top administrator for the Nazi-Occupied Netherlands. His highly efficient, emotionless conduct as a ruler of the Netherlands obviously appealed to Hitler and led him to replace von Ribbentrop whom Hitler regarded as a figurehead.

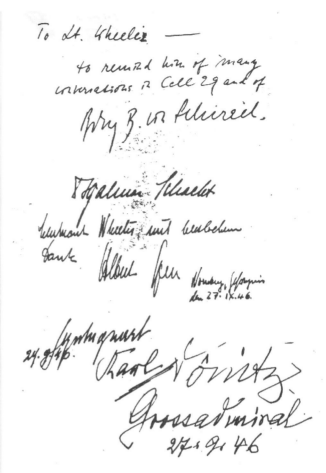

Fig 3—A note to Lt. Wheelis
This note was written by von Schirach to Wheelis "To remind him of many conversations in cell 29 and of baldy von Schirach. Speer added his "heartfelt thanks" but Seyss-Inquart merely signed it with no "embellishment" or "statement." Schacht and Dönitz merely signed it. Even on the gallows he had no "last words." He was so insistent on "going quietly" that I was surprised he would even sign a note like this. Evan Lattimer Collection.

After Hitler's death and the appointment of Admiral Doenitz as the new Führer, Seyss-Inquart made a very risky voyage by torpedo boat from his headquarters in the Netherlands to visit Dönitz in Hamburg during the admiral's one-week tenure as chief of state. Dönitz urged him to stay with him for the final surrender, but Seyss-Inquart refused, saying that he should return to the Netherlands to accept his fate at the head of the unit there.

I was surprised that von Papen, who sat next to him in the dock, described him as, "the complete Austrian, cheerful, relaxed, often telling Viennese stories." While he was an ardent Nazi, Seyss-Inquart, like Speer, resisted Hitler's order to reduce the countryside to "scorched earth." The determination with which he persecuted the Dutch, however, got him the death penalty with no dissensions. He accepted this coolly.

It was in keeping with his personality that he refused to defend himself in court and went to this death uncomplainingly just as he had indicated he would (fig. 4).

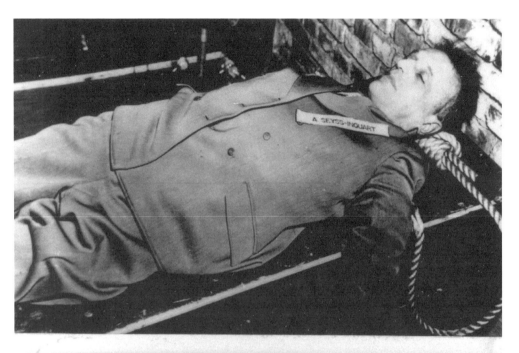

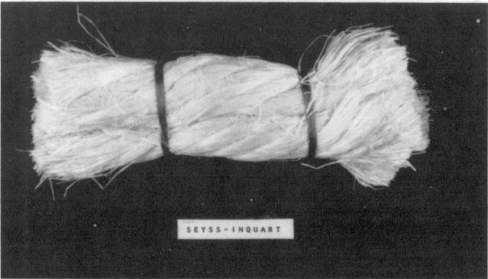

Fig 4—Seyss-Inquart dead on his coffin after the hanging, and a segment of the rope used
National Archives and Evan Lattimer Collection.

CHAPTER TWENTY-FIVE

Albert Speer

Fig 1—Albert Speer
Albert Speer, the quiet, reserved, shaggy-browed architect who became a production genius. He was 40 years old when the trial started. National Archives (photo) and Evan Lattimer Collection (signature card).

Albert Speer was the other very impressive person among our prisoners (along with Göring). He was certainly the most attractive of the group (fig. 1), and proved to be an extremely capable person. He was from a pleasant, upper-middle-class family, was well educated and very intelligent in a pragmatic way. His manner was quiet, boyish, almost shy, and he got along well with everybody, complying with all of the onerous regulations without difficulty and with unfailing politeness. Speer was fluent in several languages and often assisted the court interpreters when they stumbled over a word while trying to keep up with the difficult technical testimony. Leaning forward in his seat, he would look at the interpreters and shake his head "no" indicating an error, which they would then hasten to correct. If they still had trouble, he would inconspicuously pass them a note with the correction. He never objected to the sometimes overly restrictive actions of a new guard. The contrast between him and the rest of the loudly-complaining Nazis was noticeable.

I was astonished to learn that he was not only Hitler's personal architect, designing the monumental buildings that Hitler favored, but he had also been gradually placed in charge of *all* war production by the time the war ended. He had proved to be amazingly skillful as a manager when placed in total charge, and had greatly increased the production of arms, munitions, tanks, aviation gasoline, and finally, all warplanes. Freed from the conflicts of interest between competing departments, he doubled the production of fighter planes overnight and then kept the numbers increasing, even though the Allies bombed his factories every few days. He was a large-scale planner and an organizer of enormous ability, an example of the most competent type of German engineering mind, able to plan on a grand

Fig 2—Hitler and Speer at the Eiffel tower after the fall of Paris
Hitler believed that it was the massive monuments leaders left behind by which they are remembered. Hitler steadies his shaking left hand.

realizing the consequences. Psychologically, he was well-balanced and did not appear to be upset by anything that happened at the trial, ominous though things appeared at times. Speer said he had been attracted to Hitler, as were all the Germans, because of Hitler's potential to become a dynamic leader of a disorganized Germany. Hitler had discovered Speer, accidentally, through a good piece of work he had done in designing a building for the early Nazi Party. His cost overruns were far too high for the Party leaders, who fired him. Then Hitler discovered his grand designs. Hitler promptly "adopted" him and had him design numerous monumental buildings and memorials. From then on, cost was no problem.

Speer's ability to plan, design, and build on a grand scale was exactly what Hitler wanted, since he repeatedly stated that a man is remembered only by the monuments he leaves behind (fig. 2). It was Hitler's declared intention to leave grand monuments to his memory, and Speer was exactly the person to help him do it. As it turned out, the only really great monument that was ever finished was the enormous Zeppelin Stadium in Nuremberg (fig. 3). Encompassing an area equal to several football fields, it has a colonnade of the most beautiful Italian marble along one side, about one quarter-mile long. Speer had been given the job of designing the German Pavilion for a World's Fair in

scale, and to revise in order to execute the monumental job of war production. He was highly intelligent, belying the modest IQ score of 128 assigned to him by the modified type of routine psychological testing done by Dr. Gilbert. There was a rumor that he had deliberately sought to "spoof" the intelligence tests, resulting in a score that did not truly represent his high degree of capability.

Speer had been by far the most productive of any of the men being tried, and was quite obviously better than any of the other German industrialists in the same work. He had benefited, of course, by inheriting the established organization of his predecessor, Professor Todt, who very skillfully had built the autobahns, the "West Wall" forts, and the submarine pens, but who was killed in an airplane crash in 1942, thus elevating Speer to his position at once. The stories of Speer's capability were truly amazing. Dr. Kelley compared him to a young racehorse of great capability who was wearing blinders. He could see only straight ahead and all he did was to run at his greatest capacity without

Fig 3—The enormous Zeppelin Stadium at Nuremberg built by Speer
There were marble grandstands arranged round the periphery of this field which was large enough to encompass several football fields, Across one end was this colonnade one quarter mile long, made of Italian marble. It had a podium on the front and a large swastika in marble, on top. At the far end was another colonnade with a memorial to the Nazi heroes. This turned out to be the only one of Speer's gigantic monuments which was ever completed. Had the war not ended, Germany would have been dotted with similar impressive monuments by Speer, with Hitler's backing. Patton dynamited the swastika off the podium you see here. Evan Lattimer Collection.

Fig 4—Speer's own house in Berchtesgaden
This handsome pagoda-like but modest house was in the "secured" inner area, but out of sight of the huge houses built by the rest of Hitler's group. The American Army used it as a rest and rehabilitation home and enjoyed staying in it.

Paris and made it outstanding by using searchlights to illuminate the tall structure as it soared into the sky. This gave it an ethereal quality that impressed everyone, including Speer. He therefore went on to augment the Nuremberg Zeppelin Stadium by surrounding the entire periphery with 150 military antiaircraft searchlights, each pointing straight up, for the great nighttime Party rallies. This created an enormous colonnade of light around the structure, which was most impressive. Later Speer reflected that his greatest accomplishments had not had too much substance, but were largely made up of light.

Speer admitted that he had been flattered by Hitler's attentions and enjoyed the unlimited access to methods, materials, and fine automobiles that his position carried. He was allowed to build for himself a beautiful little house, in the well-protected compound at Berchtesgaden. It resembled a modernized Japanese pagoda more than anything else (fig. 4). We used it as a rest camp after the surrender. It was around a corner and out of sight, so that the rest of the Nazi buildings (including Hitler's house) were not visible from it. He commented that Hitler was very kind to him and would never be rude or overbearing with him or the other architects. This was quite in contrast to Hitler's brutal demeanor with the politicians.

Hitler made little sketches of grandiose buildings in the evenings, and turned them over to Speer to develop further (figs. 5-8). Speer saved all these sketches and had one of his men, Apel, keep them at his main architectural office, assembling them into a catalogue (fig. 9). A note by Speer verified each one and identified it.

As the war continued, Speer gradually began to realize that Hitler was a tyrant and was destroying the country. He tried to reason with him but to no avail. He finally joined (though privately) in the thinking that Hitler had to be killed, but was frustrated in his plans to do so. In his testimony at the trial in a persuasive, straightforward, honest manner, he confessed his shock and repugnance at discovering the atrocities of the Nazi regime and recanted his attachment to Hitler and the Nazi government. Everyone who heard him, believed him, and there was a feeling among practically all of us who heard him speak that he would have been acquitted had it not been for one thing.

Running the country's wartime economy on the tremendous scale that he did, demanded some fourteen million laborers for Speer's work. One source for this labor force was the concentration camps. Speer maintained, and could prove, that he consistently asked for German civilian laborers and did not want displaced persons or concentration camp laborers, because the Germans were so much better as workers. He admitted, however, that he sometimes had to accept whatever

Fig 5—Speer watching Hitler make architectural sketches
Hitler greatly enjoyed dashing off small sketches of his ideas for monumental buildings. Speer was impressed at how accurate they were despite the haste with which they were usually made.

Fig 6—Hitler's sketch for huge opera house in Linz
This was #35 on Apel's catalogue-list. It was to be an opera house, as well as a theater, according to Speer. Evan Lattimer Collection.

Fig 7—Hitler's sketch for a liberation monument and stadium
This was for the hills overlooking the town of Linz. Speer stated that this was drawn in his presence on 21 November 1941 at the Berghof. Evan Lattimer Collection.

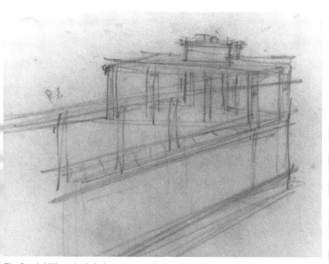

Fig 8—A Hitler sketch for a pergola for Goebbels

A bower for Goebbels' garden. Speer attested that the sketch was made in his presence but never built. This was #16 on Apel's catalogue-list of Hitler's sketches. Evan Lattimer Collection.

1. Verlängerung der Siegessäule	Berlin	Nov. 1937
2. Märzfeld	O.S.	22.X.1936
3. Balkon an der Reichskanzlei	Berlin	1935
4. Profil "Neue Strasse" München	Berlin	14.III.1937
5. Vorhalle für Weltausstellung Brüssel		1934
6. Kuppelbau Berlin	O.S.	5.XI.1936
7. Skizze zu einem Glockenturm am Bückeberg (nach eine Fahrt durch Ostpreussen)		Nov. 1935
8. Linzer Theater	O.S.	Juli 1940
9. Linzer Bibliotheksbau	O.S.	Frühjahr 39
10.		
11. Querschnitt München Halle	Berlin	Dez. 1937
12. Gebäude des Zentralparteiverlages München	Berlin	Dez. 1937
13. Linzer Theater	O.S.	Juli 1940
14. Augsburger Turm und Halle	O.S.	Dez. 1937
15. Bibliothek Linz		1940
16. Hallenbau Wohnung Dr. G.		1933
17. Märzfeld	O.S.	22.X.1936
18. Stadttheater Linz Nürnberg Deutscher Hof		Mai 1938
19. Führerbau Theater	O.S.	März 1940
20. Ausstellung Rom	Nürnberg	Febr. 1939
21. Versammlungshalle München 120/240 m	O.S.	28.III.1937
22. Kamin Wohnung F.	Berlin	1934
23. Kamin Wohnung Dr. G.		1933
24. Vorderseite Haus Wach.		1935
25. Bayreuth Theaterplatz		26.VI.1936
26. Der Deutsche Platz	O.S.	22.X.1936
27. Theater Bayreuth		26.VI.1936
28. Säule der Bewegung für München	R.K.	7.II.1937
29. Linz Befreiungsdenkmal		21.XI.1941
30. Flakturm	Berlin	Sept. 1940
31. Flakturm	Berlin	Sept. 1940
32. Opernplatz in Königsberg	Berlin	Sept. 1940
33. Waffenmuseum Linz		13.V.1942
34. Linzer Theater		Juli 1940
35. Linzer Theater		Juli 1940
36. Holbundes Theater		1940

Fig 9—Speer's list of Hitler's sketches

Speer had Otto Apel, one of the men in his architectual office, keep all of these sketches drawn by Hitler and made a catalogue-list of them, part of which is here.

was offered to him. These included a small number of displaced people and a very small number of concentration camp victims. During the trial, a damaging photograph was introduced, showing him visiting one of the concentration camps with Gauleiter Eingruber (fig. 10). The prosecution insisted that they must have been talking about the use of inmates from that camp for his labor battalions. It was his only visit to such a camp and he was given the VIP tour of the good sections only. Speer could easily have denied that they were discussing laborers, but he made no effort to suggest that this was not the subject of their conversation. Against this background, he was sentenced to 20 years of imprisonment.

He was inclined to self-flagellation at that point, and permitted the discussion to be led in such a way that it sounded as if he were soliciting more concentration-camp labor. We all listened to the slippery diplomats, von Papen and Schacht, manipulate the language to avoid negative implications and were amazed when Speer refused to do the same thing.

In his memoirs, Speer admitted that when he saw both von Papen and Schacht go free, he realized that he could have done the same. It was the opinion of all of the personnel at the trial who listened to Speer that, in his idealism, he had condemned himself in a way that was not entirely justified, certainly by comparison with the others. His own attorney was very upset at Speer's insistence on accepting responsibility for things outside his own ministry, but he was adamant on the matter of "collective guilt" of the entire group.

Speer Spoke of Hitler's Preoccupation with Premature Death

On several occasions Speer mentioned to me Hitler's preoccupation with a possible premature death. Speer was the only one of our prisoners who shared any truly private moments with Hitler. Sometimes these occurred when they stopped for a picnic lunch during one of their motor trips. As he relaxed, Hitler would sometimes drop into what Speer referred to as his "personal" attitude. Hitler was fond of saying that if he attained his "Grand Plan" of world domination, he would be regarded as the greatest military conqueror of all time. On the other hand, if he failed he would be vilified and condemned as history's greatest villain. This was so obvious that it did not impress me at that time as being significant. However, with the new data about Hitler's relentlessly advancing, untreatable Parkinson's disease, his preoccupation with an early death assumes much greater significance.

Fig 10—The nearly fatal photograph
This picture got Speer 20 years in prison as I saw it. (It nearly got him hanged.) It is the only record of his ever even visiting a concentration camp (Mauthausen) where he was invited to accompany Gauleiter Eingruber on a "VIP" tour, where they were shown nothing bad. There was no proof that he was requesting slave-labor, but the prosecutors tried to say so.

Back then, I thought it merely reflected Hitler's well-founded concerns and his successful techniques for foiling assassins: he changed his schedules abruptly and kept his routes secret.

The second matter that Speer brought out was Hitler's preoccupation with establishing heroic monuments to himself. Hitler's many comments that great men were remembered by the great structures they created were reasonable enough. Hitler began to give Speer sketches not only for enormous monuments in Berlin and Munich but even in his hometown of Linz. As it worked out, the only one of these giant monuments that was completed was the great Zeppelin Stadium at Nuremberg. While this tendency to megalomania was not surprising, the rapidity with which Hitler wanted all this done reflected more than the usual need for memorials during a man's lifetime.

The third reason I was not surprised at Hitler's worries about an early death was the obviously deteriorating military situation with the loss of entire armies at Stalingrad and in North Africa, and then our successful invasions of Italy and Normandy. Thus, I did not think Hitler's worries unreasonable. Speer would shake his head and indicate that, toward the end, Hitler's disintegration was more than one would expect when finally discovered. In this he turned out to be entirely correct as noted (in Chapter Two), Hitler's gross, diagnostic tremor lent itself to a new diagnosis. His unrecognized or unlabeled Parkinson's disease was moving very rapidly ahead during his last years, and I believe his realization of this was the major factor in his mental and tactical disintegration. Speer observed all of this happening and recognized it as a terminal course, without being able to put a diagnostic label on it. Now that we know Hitler's diagnosis everything falls into place bearing out Speer's observations very satisfactorily. *Someone had told Hitler he only had a few more years to live.*

At the end of the war, Speer cooperated with American strategic bombing committees in a very helpful way. He advised them on what to do to Japan to cripple its industry in the most efficacious way, based on his own experience with American precision bombing. For example, he said that if we had only returned a second time to bomb the ball-bearing factory at Schweinfurt, Germany, as we had done on August 17, 1943, the Nazi war machine would have ground to a halt. Unfortunately for us, we did not realize this, and the damage we had caused was repairable.

Conflict with Hitler's Secretary, Martin Bormann, and SS Chief Heinrich Himmler

Martin Bormann clung continually to Hitler's side and endeavored to force Speer (along with everyone else) out of any position of influence with Hitler. He got his first opportunity to eliminate Speer when Speer came down with phlebitis after a knee operation related to a ski injury. He then had two large blood clots

Fig 11—The jet fighter; Speer's frustration

The awesome Messerschmidt 262 was the world's first jet fighter. It could have decimated our bomber fleets, but Hitler could not let it continue to be used as a fighter. He insisted it be converted to a light bomber, for which it was useless. He refused to let Speer mass produce it, until it was too late.

break off and damage his lungs in January 1944, while convalescing from the operation.

While he knew his doctor (Gephardt) was a famous knee specialist, he did not know that the SS doctor was one of Heinrich Himmler's and Martin Bormann's very few intimate friends, and had been conducting outrageous experiments on victims in the concentration camps. Gephardt tried to sequester Speer and restrict his activities. In the in-fighting among Bormann, Himmler, and Göring, one of the techniques of the Third Reich to get rid of a powerful rival, was to declare that person sick and then eliminate him, implying that his condition had worsened. Speer was sure that this strategy was being used against him, so he had telephones set up in his sick room and ran his organization from there.

Gephardt had operated on his leg and had it in a plaster cast for three weeks. When finally allowed to stand, Speer had a violent pain in his chest and back and spat up blood. This was obviously from a pulmonary embolism (a blood clot to the lung). Gephardt purposefully ignored this and *again* got Speer up. Two days later, Speer had a second pulmonary embolism and nearly died.

Speer's wife then went to Dr. Karl Brandt, Hitler's doctor, who immediately sent Dr. Friedrich Koch, an internist at Berlin University, to examine Speer. Dr. Brandt specifically ordered Dr. Koch to be the *only* one in charge of Speer, and Koch stayed in a room near him night and day until he was better. It came out that Gephardt, Himmler and Bormann had decided that

Speer was dangerous and getting too powerful and would have to "disappear." If Speer had died from the embolism, it would have been a convenient way for Bormann and Himmler to get rid of him, as I saw it. Himmler was trying to build up an industrial organization for his SS Group for postwar control of the country. When the American bombers began to bomb his hospital, Dr. Gephardt was convinced that Speer was the target and permitted him to be moved.

At this time Speer learned that the American Eighth and Fifteenth Air Forces were concentrating on bombing the German aircraft industry out of existence. Once again Speer's production skills brought him back into the limelight and into Hitler's favor. At this time Speer asked for total mobilization of all the labor in Germany, including women, but in spite of this, Hitler still held back.

The American precision bombing was now destroying Germany's production in a well-organized plan, concentrating on certain essential industries. This was paralyzing Germany very effectively. About this time, addressing the German leaders, Hitler concluded by saying that there was no doubt that if they lost the war German private business would not survive, since destruction of the entire German people would accomplish a total destruction of business. He said if the war was to be lost they would not have to worry about shifting to a peacetime economy. Everyone would have to decide whether he preferred to starve in Germany or labor in Siberia.

Fig 12—Dönitz and Speer had been good friends, as you can see in this photograph
It was only after Dönitz had been sentenced to prison that he decided Speer had recommended him to Hitler to be the next Chancellor. This got him the 10 years in prison, as he saw it, and he never forgave Speer.

Hitler's Disastrous Meddling in Aircraft Usage

The Messerschmitt and Heinkel companies had developed jet fighter aircraft that were much faster and much more deadly than anything the Allies had. Speer was getting these into mass production when Hitler suddenly canceled the plans and insisted that the ME 262 (the superior jet fighter plane) be converted into a high-speed light bomber (fig. 11). He ordered all the weapons on board removed so the aircraft could carry a greater weight of bombs, which was still very small. As a fighter plane, this craft would have been able to shoot down several four-engined bombers in each flight. Now, as a bomber, it would be practically useless, but Hitler was insistent. The remote-controlled flying bomb, known as the V-1, had come into production, but in spite of its novelty, it was relatively ineffective. Next came the development of the V-2 rocket, 46 feet long and weighing 13 tons. Despite all of this, the total load of randomly delivered explosives was only equal to twelve flying fortresses from the American air force. Another very promising development, the ground-to-air defensive rocket, was set aside on Hitler's orders

and never developed. This type of mental rigidity may well have been aggravated by his Parkinson's disease.

Falling Out with Hitler

By September 1944, it had become even more obvious to Speer that the war was lost and there was no possible way to save it. Hitler again reminded him that defeatist talk could be seen as treason. Speer again tried to persuade Hitler that the war was lost, on the basis of the production of armaments being completely destroyed by the bombing. He began to beg Hitler not to order the destruction of the electrical, fuel, bridge, communications, and railroad facilities in Germany, so the populace would be able to take care of themselves after the war was over. Speer knew that there was a passage in *Mein Kampf* where Hitler, himself, had written that "The task of diplomacy is to ensure that a nation does not go heroically to its destruction and that failure to follow this concept must be called criminal neglect of duty."

Now that Speer realized that Hitler was mentally impaired and intent on the destruction of Germany, he resolved to kill him. He located the air intake to Hitler's bunker in the garden in Berlin and set about trying to procure a supply of poison gas of the type used in the concentration camps. By the time he was finally able to do this, he found that Hitler (who had been gassed in WWI) had anticipated an artillery gas attack by the Russians and had had the air intake extended to a much higher level and guarded by armed sentries. Speer then spent the last several months of the war trying to devise ways to stop Hitler's orders to destroy Germany's infrastructure. Time and again he risked his life to countermand orders. Finally he had an arrangement made where all orders for destruction would be given only by his organization. He implied to Hitler that he would destroy things when the right moment came, but he never did. He even sent out messages to stop any anticipated "Werewolf" activity as being counterproductive, in that it would enrage the occupying powers who would then be even harder on the surviving German populace. Speer was able to stop the navy from destroying the port facilities by this stratagem.

The Surrender and Trial

After the surrender on May 8, Speer joined the new German Führer, Admiral Dönitz, (his old friend) in the British zone. The British turned him over to the Americans, who interrogated him first for several days in the castle of Glücksburg, near Flensburg, near where Dönitz had his headquarters on the ship *Patria*. This was about May 24. Speer was then flown to our center at Mondorf and afterward taken to meet with the bombing experts of the American Air Force at the Trianon Palace Hotel at Versailles, and at the small palace at Chesenay nearby. Ironically, Speer had stayed there while he designed the spectacular German pavilion for the Paris World's Fair in 1937. The Trianon was now Eisenhower's headquarters.

Speer contributed huge amounts of information about the success of various types of bombings and advised the Americans on how to attack the Japanese economy in the most effective way. At the end of this relaxed interlude, Speer was moved to Kransberg Castle (which Speer had rebuilt) for a few more days of interrogation and then, via another prison, to Nuremberg in late September.

The trial began officially on November 20, 1945. The prisoners' suits were taken out of mothballs and the black cotton gabardine fatigues worn in the cells were set aside during the courtroom hours. The defendants were allowed to choose which of their clothes should be cleaned and pressed for the trial. Every detail was discussed with the commandant, Colonel Andrus, even down to the matter of sleeve buttons. Seats were assigned in what was thought to be the order of importance of each defendant, with Göring at the lower right. Hess and then Ribbentrop sat beside him. Speer was third from the last on the second row of benches, in the company of Seyss-Inquart and von Neurath. Streicher and Funk sat just in front of him.

The trial began with a devastating grand opening address by the chief American prosecutor Justice Robert H. Jackson. Speer took comfort from one sentence in which Jackson accused the defendants, but not the German people, of guilt for the regime's crimes. This thesis corresponded precisely with what Speer had hoped would be a subsidiary result of the trial, namely, that the hate directed against the German people, which had been fanned by the propaganda of the war years and had reached an extreme after the revelation of their crimes, would now be focused upon them, the defendants.

Dr. Gilbert was unfamiliar with Speer at the beginning of the trial and referred to him as the "Tall, shaggy-browed armaments minister, who attracted very little attention at first. He appeared to have a much more sincere and less demonstrative conception of the Nazi guilt than anyone else, however." He seemed to Gilbert to be the most realistic of all the prisoners; he told him that he had no illusions about his fate and that the indictments were no particular shock to him. He realized that history demanded such a trial in view of the enormity of the crimes committed, and considered it a good thing, in general. When Dr. Gilbert went from cell to cell asking each man to write a comment about his indictment, Speer quickly wrote, "The trials are necessary and is a shared responsibility for such horrible crimes, even in an authoritarian state." It was Gilbert's conclusion that Speer's repenting was not an expedient (as was Frank's), but rather, he did indeed perceive that he had been on the wrong track in a disastrous way.

Speer pointed out that he had been made war production chief in 1942, without any previous experience. That he had told Hitler repeatedly that the war was lost and that they should save Germany from utter destruction, regardless of personal consequences. When Hitler had answered that if Germany couldn't win the war, it did not deserve to survive, it upset Speer greatly, shattering his illusions. It was then that he came to the conclusion that the whole Nazi system was rotten to the core and that he had made a terrible mistake in subscribing to Nazism and supporting Hitler as effectively as he had done.

It impressed everyone that Speer was much more sincere in his recanting of the crimes of the Nazi group. It was also notable that he did not try to evade the responsibility of his contribution to the war production effort. He agreed that he had something like fifteen million people in his organization, producing armaments of all sorts and that some of these people were from other countries and that a tiny number had indeed been concentration camp inmates. He repeatedly had to fend off the efforts of the SS to take over his production facilities for their own purposes, in order to improve their incomes. He had appealed to Hitler on various occasions to countermand the orders of Göring and Himmler, and whoever else was undermining his effort. He did this with outstanding success, getting Hitler to reverse himself several times in his favor. His rivals in the Nazi hierarchy repeatedly tried to do away with him, but failed, partly due to his very great competence and his sincerity in his work, all of which Hitler recognized and appreciated.

Speer recognized that in opposing the other members of the hierarchy, he was exposing not only himself but his family to assassination, but proceeded anyway. If it had not been for his efforts to preserve the bridges, the railroads, and the power plants of Germany from the destruction Hitler had ordered, the country would have been in a much worse state of chaos after the surrender.

It was clear to me that he was prepared to use his fantastic talents to help rebuild his shattered country. He knew where the few factories were that had been spared and how they operated and would have been a great asset to the rebuilding of the country.

Dr. Pflücker had given Speer a tranquilizing pill to take just before he started his statement of his defense in court. Speer said that this was a godsend, because he became afflicted with stage fright and found this pill to be a great help. Dr. Pflücker told Speer many things to reassure and please him, including the fact that his verbal attacks on Göring were giving Göring some bad days.

By far the greatest strain on each prisoner, including Speer, came during the time each man spent on the stand, explaining his actions. This was followed by one or more sessions of penetrating cross-examination. Speer's frank condemnation of several of his codefendants sparked growls of hatred from them, especially Göring. These periods of interrogation were a severe emotional strain and for the first time Speer said he was totally exhausted and complained of stomach pains. No ulcer symptoms followed, however, in spite of the hatred now focused upon him by the men whom he had pointed out and condemned by his testimony.

Göring was the worst, threatening that if they ever came out of this trial alive an old German tradition of trying traitors by a secret community court would see to it that Speer and all of his family were killed. It was

the kind of thing you expected from Göring. This threat to Speer's family caused him great anguish, but luckily no one answered Göring's call for violence. As a means of moral support, Sunday church services, with their lusty singing of hymns, turned out to be a comfort to Speer, even though at first he had disdained them. Our Chaplain Gerecke was a great support for him.

Shortly after his arrival at Nuremberg, Speer had been interrogated by one of the deputy prosecutors, Thomas Dodd, with devastating results. Speer said that the questions were sharp and aggressive and that they clashed frequently. Speer felt that he did not want to be cowed and he answered candidly and without evasion, giving no thought to his future defense. He said he deliberately omitted many details that might have pointed out extenuating aspects of his actions. Back in his cell, he realized he had made a mistake, and felt that he was trapped. In fact, these same indiscreet statements constituted the essential part of the charge against him.

The court's final statement on Speer pointed out that he did not enter the Nazi government in a war capacity until 1942, so his indictments on charges one and two were dismissed. However, the evidence against Speer under counts three and four related entirely to his participation in the slave-labor program. In mitigation, it must be recognized that he was one of the few men who had the courage to tell Hitler the war was lost and to take steps to prevent the senseless destruction of production facilities both in the occupied territories and in Germany. He carried out his opposition to Hitler's scorched earth program in some of the Western countries and in Germany by deliberately sabotaging it, at considerable personal risk. The fact that he had actively participated in plans to kill Hitler could have been a powerful argument in his favor, judging from the success of that ploy used by other defendants, but he did not pursue it.

In the end, Speer stoically accepted his sentence, looking the judge right in the eye, despite his realization that he might have done much better by very slight adjustments in what he said. It seemed to me that he made the mistake of talking too much, rather than just answering questions, as all good lawyers advise.

It occurred to many of us that his talents should have been put to work to alleviate the extreme hardship suffered by the German populace as a result of our devastating bombing. Thus his own tendency to self-punishment denied his people his services in the reconstruction period after the war. It was almost as if he demanded to be punished, and it got him 20 years in Spandau prison, so well described in his book, *Spandau Diary*.

Speer's most frequent medical complaint at Nuremberg was tachycardia (rapid pulse) with extra systoles (abnormal extra heartbeats), obviously brought on by the psychological stress of the trial. These attacks occurred several times. All were transitory and required no medication, other than a little sedation. The cardiac irregularities that came during some of these attacks caused him great worry, but actually were not of a serious type.

He was to suffer a severe attack in October 1946 and another in February of 1947, at which times he became dizzy. The second attack was at a time when he was called upon to testify for General Milch. We know that he had had a pulmonary effusion (fluid around the lung) in 1944 which had resolved spontaneously and then again later, in December 1954, when he was in Spandau prison. At that time he spat up blood, but again it resolved spontaneously without evidence of tuberculosis. He was experienced at using heat, rest, and elevation to treat his recurring phlebitis. X-ray examinations were apparently negative at that time as well. He may have thrown a small pulmonary embolus (blood clot) from his legs, as he had suffered in 1944 after the knee operation.

Speer admitted to being overcome by waves of depression at Nuremberg and at Spandau, but was able to control himself, and with his strong will, to come to terms with his situation. His depressions were short-lived and responded to exercise and absorption in drawing sketches of buildings.

Speer went out of his way to be helpful, in a dignified manner, to everyone with whom he came in contact. For Eva Braun, for example, he had designed a personal monogram made of her two initials back-to-back in the form of a butterfly, or four-leafed clover, which she adopted with delight (fig. 13). He charmed the guards at the Nuremberg prison, who were sometimes crude, unfeeling, and even cruel in their treatment of the prisoners. The prisoners were trying desperately to get some sleep and had problems with the lights shining in their eyes throughout the night. This greatly irritated some of the older prisoners but did not appear to bother Speer in the slightest, so far as one could tell from his attitude. (Eventually they were permitted to sleep with the backs of their heads toward the light, so it did not shine in their eyes.) He commented at various times about the great patriotism of most of the young American soldiers who were guarding the prisoners. He said he was very much surprised at this attitude among these youngsters who were basically civilians brought in to do this very boring work. They were in a faraway country and had to stand all day long listening to talk in a language they could not understand. This was typical of Speer's perception of things around him.

He also commented that one became actually grateful for some harassment by the guards, since it indicated that some attention was being paid to the person. Dr. Goldensohn spoke to me about the fact that they even appreciated being asked to sign things, since it drew attention to them. This was a surprise to me, since it seemed to me to be a kind of annoying harassment, but not only the psychiatrist but later Speer pointed out to me that it was a welcome diversion.

As it happened, Speer knew a good deal about Charles Lindbergh and admired him greatly. We discussed him at length. They were both technological wizards but very quiet, very pleasant people.

Göring and perhaps Speer were the only two defendants at Nuremberg who had devised ingenious plans in advance to smuggle a suicide capsule into the prison and keep it hidden in case they wanted to use it. As noted earlier, Göring had concealed one and probably two of the cyanide ampoules in their protective containers in his jars of opaque skin cream. Biographer Leonard Mosely, in his book, *The Reichs Marshal*, alleged that Speer had a cyanide capsule hidden in his tube of toothpaste. Mosely said he kept it all during the trial and all during his twenty-year imprisonment in Spandau, and that Speer took it home with him unused. Speer later denied having done this. In any case, the planting of a "reserve" capsule in an innocent-appearing repository had to have been done well before they were all captured.

Speer did a modest amount of sketching while in prison and wrote a secret diary on toilet paper while in Spandau, and had the pages smuggled out by sympathetic guards. After he was permitted to have books from the prison library, he realized that architecture had changed a great deal during his time in prison and was worried about whether he could get back into the swing of practicing architecture after being away from it for so long.

During his time at Spandau, he laid out an exercise program of walking so many kilometers each day around the prison yard. He even designed an imaginary itinerary that would take him entirely around the world during the twenty years he would be in prison. He stuck to this so religiously that it was not too surprising that he developed a swelling of the knee (the same one the Germans had operated on) in his thirteenth year in prison, which limited his activity for many days and weeks. It seemed likely that his knee cartilage was the source of his problems, since with rest, they subsided each time. His varicose veins had to be pampered occasionally by rest, hot towels and elevation. By the end of his 20 years in prison, he had nearly "walked around the world."

In the final analysis, Speer turned out to be by far the most likable and capable of the prisoners. He was always helpful, always amiable, and had shown tremendous capability as a manager of German war productions.

Following his release from prison, Speer received a great deal of sympathetic correspondence from American aircraft industry people. I have several letters which he wrote to them, asking for material for a book on the air war in Europe. He was curious to know the exact numbers of fighter planes produced, both with one and two engines, in the U.S. and in Great Britain in September 1944. He also wondered how many were produced in Japan that same month and how many one-engine and two-engine fighters were produced in the U.S., Great Britain, and Canada combined, in June and July 1944. He obviously wanted to point out that in spite of his superb efforts at home, the numbers in the combined Allied arsenal were far greater.

He also mentioned a four-engine jet bomber for bombing New York in January 1945. He was curious to know what the American Air Force considered the distance from Hamburg, Germany, to New York and how long it took the Americans to develop a jet bomber with a range of 14,000 kilometers with a bomb load of four tons. With these same correspondents, Speer exchanged Christmas greetings and said that he had gotten greetings from General Ira Eaker and Air Marshal Harris of the RAF, who had bombed Germany roundly all during the war.

In still another letter, he wondered if they could procure for him the testimony of Production Minister Saur, whom Hitler had put in Speer's place when Speer became too pessimistic. Speer wondered what Saur said in his postwar interrogations at Chesenay (near Versailles) and at Cransberg. He had heard it rumored that Saur's interrogation reports were still restricted material in 1977. He also said that knowing Saur's testimony would be a great help to him in his own studies, obviously for his own book on the matter. He said that Saur had become his rival during the last year of the war, so that he was never able to have access to records of his activities.

After his release, Speer did well as an author and lecturer. He died quietly while on a trip to England, at age 76.

Fig 13—Eva Braun with Speer and her famous monogram he designed
He used her initials to make a butterfly, or a four-leafed clover effect, as shown in the composite of her linens. Speer was very helpful to everybody. Evan Lattimer Collection and Staatsbibliothek Collection.

CHAPTER TWENTY-SIX

Julius Streicher

Fig 1—Julius Streicher
The loud-talking vicious Jew-hater, editor of the Nazi newspaper "Der Stürmer." National Archives and Evan Lattimer Collection.

Julius Streicher was a revolting, little newspaper editor who was obsessed with anti-Semitism (fig. 1). His lurid newspaper, *Der Stürmer*, had issue after issue with the grossest caricatures of Jews in the most horrible poses (fig. 2). Streicher's denigration of the Jews was the only thing that made Hitler keep him on as the editor, even when all the rest of the top Nazis had come to scorn him and, in the case of Göring, to hate him. He was an effective rabble-rouser with a very loud voice. He claimed that what had impressed him about Hitler in the beginning was the fact that he could speak longer than Streicher himself. Most of the German populace appeared to detest him. Certainly almost all of the other Nazi prisoners would have nothing to do with him. The only other prisoner who would speak to him at all was Ley, a fellow rabble-rouser whose greetings Streicher would reward by calling him "that Jew-bastard" as soon as Ley turned away. Ley committed suicide so early that Streicher was again alone very quickly. He characterized himself as a school teacher but showed very little evidence of ability in this area.

Streicher drew sketches of the prison yard (fig. 3), and in fact had been masquerading as an artist when he was pointed out to our search teams from the 101st Airborne Division (fig. 4). He had let his hair and beard grow, and in contrast to his usual "cue ball" haircut, it came in white and luxurious, so he had no resemblance to the photos of him which we had been given. If the locals had not turned him in, he would never have been recognized (fig. 5).

Physically, he was a little "dynamo." He amazed the G.I. guards by rising very early, pouring cold water over himself, and then exercising violently for an hour in his cell. He bragged about his sexual prowess and boasted

that if we would bring him a woman he would show us a thing or two. He even bragged that he had already been in the Nuremberg Prison on a "sex charge." With all of his braggadocio, I was surprised to find that his wife was a very quiet, modest little woman, who was taken in by Dr. Pflücker and his wife to stay with them when she came to visit Streicher.

What frightened us the most about Streicher was his very low IQ and his aggressive instincts. Hitler had placed him in a position of authority as Gauleiter of Franconia and had made him a member of the Reichstag, as well as the editor of his newspaper and an honorary officer of the SA.

What forced Streicher out of the Nazi Party was that he had cast aspersions upon Göring's paternity of his daughter Edda. Göring had threatened to kill him and it was only the intercession of Hitler that saved Streicher. Thereafter, Hitler limited his activities to publishing his newspaper and made him live on his farm, without access to the Nazi hierarchy.

Streicher had one episode of tachycardia in mid-summer, but refused to go to the local hospital for an electrocardiogram. Dr. Goldensohn had a famous psychia-

Fig 2—Julius Streicher's art
Streicher was a disgusting "bully-boy" of the most repulsive type. Even his fellow Nazis shunned him. The crude anti-Semitic articles which he published in his newspaper "Der Stürmer" were so gross as to disgust even his colleagues. He enjoyed being included in this group of "top" Nazis. It was his own aggressive unrepentant performance which won the noose for him. Evan Lattimer Collection.

Fig 4—Streicher's capture by my own 101st Airborne Division
He had let his "cue-ball" haircut with a black stubble, grow out. His hair and beard came in white, which changed his appearance completely, so that he was unrecognizable. The local Germans turned him in. Even they hated him, as did all the other defendants.

(Left) Fig 3—A Streicher drawing
This shows a corner of the detention center at Mondorf, Luxemburg, where the prisoners were detained and interrogated before the transfer to Nuremberg. The high fence and a guard tower can be made out. Raymond Zyla Collection.

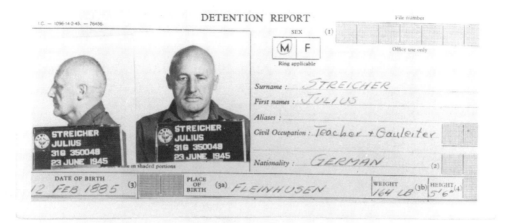

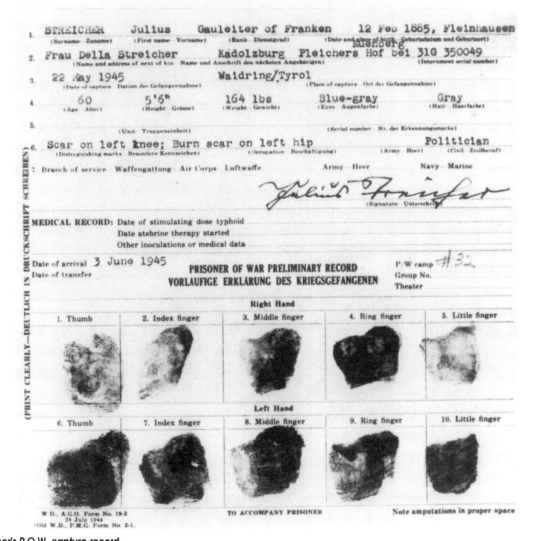

Fig 5—Streicher's P.O.W. capture record

Streicher's P.O.W. preliminary record indicated that he was captured at Wailbring, in the Tyrol. He was captured on May 22, 1945, indicating that he avoided capture for about 2 weeks by posing as an itinerant landscape painter with white hair. He was listed as 5'6" which I suspect was at least 2" taller than he really was. He is listed at 164 pounds with a scar on his left knee and a burn scar on his left hip. It was interesting that he listed himself as a politician rather than as an editor, possibly trying to disassociate himself from his radical newspaper, "Der Stürmer."

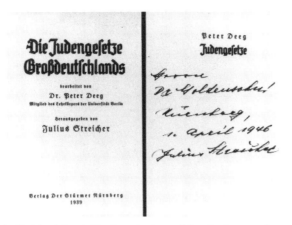

Fig 6—Streicher's book "The Laws for Jews of Greater Germany"
He dedicated the title page with an extravagant greeting to our Jewish psychiatrist, Dr. Goldensohn, who he admired. Evan Lattimer Collection.

Fig 8—Streicher's Bible
He kept this in his cell, annotating passages that he claimed proved that the Bible is pornographic and anti-Semitic. Evan Lattimer Collection.

Fig 7—Julius Streicher in court, at age 60
Streicher was a disgusting "bully-boy" of the most repulsive type. Even his fellow Nazis shunned him. The anti-Semitic articles which he published in his newspaper "Der Stürmer" were so gross as to disgust even his colleagues. His role as a newspaper editor, at Hitler's insistence, did not appear to merit a death penalty, according to several of our prosecutors. It was his own provocative, unrepentant performance which won the noose for him.

Fig 9—The title page of Streicher's Bible
He had been working at this since he acquired it in 1931. He wrote on the front page (barely visible) as follows: "Herr Julius Streicher, for his daily communication with God." Evan Lattimer Collection.

trist, Dr. Braceland, as a visitor and the two of them examined Streicher. They decided to let him go back to the trial, but the psychiatrists were worried that he might topple over in court. Streicher realized that Goldensohn was trying to help him and took a strong liking to him, much to Goldensohn's embarrassment. When Goldensohn brought books from the local libraries for each of the prisoners to autograph, Streicher wrote affectionate greetings of embarrassing length to Goldensohn, which got him some ribbing from his medical colleagues (fig. 6).

Streicher could be not only loud but also comical. After he had been condemned to be hanged, he continued to study English in his cell. Dr. Pflücker asked him

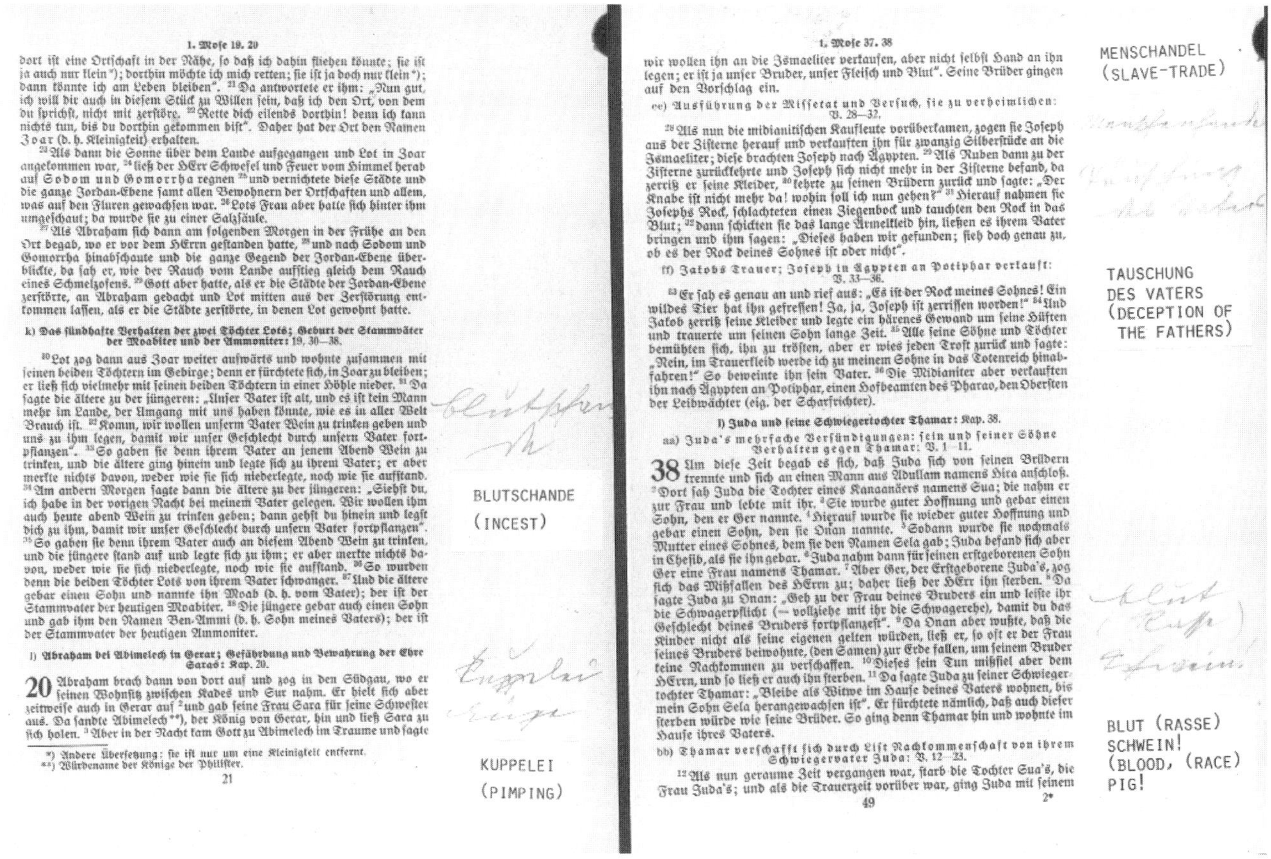

1. Mose 19. 20
dort ist eine Ortschaft in der Nähe, so daß ich dahin fliehen könnte; sie ist
ja auch nur klein*); dorthin möchte ich mich retten; sie ist ja doch nur klein*);
dann könnte ich am Leben bleiben". 21 Da antwortete er ihm: „Nun gut,
ich will dir auch in diesem Stück zu Willen sein, daß ich den Ort, von dem
du sprichst, nicht mit zerstöre. 22 Rette dich eilends dorthin! denn ich kann
nichts tun, bis du dorthin gekommen bist". Daher hat der Ort den Namen
Zoar (d. h. Kleinigkeit) erhalten.
23 Als dann die Sonne über dem Lande aufgegangen und Lot in Zoar
angekommen war, 24 ließ der HErr Schwefel und Feuer vom Himmel herab
auf Sodom und Gomorrha regnen 25 und vernichtete diese Städte und
die ganze Jordan-Ebene samt allen Bewohnern der Ortschaften und allem,
was auf den Fluren gewachsen war. 26 Lots Frau aber hatte sich hinter ihm
umgeschaut; da wurde sie zu einer Salzsäule.
27 Als Abraham sich dann am folgenden Morgen in der Frühe an den
Ort begab, wo er vor dem HErrn gestanden hatte, 28 und nach Sodom und
Gomorrha hinabschaute und die ganze Gegend der Jordan-Ebene über-
blickte, da sah er, wie der Rauch vom Lande aufstieg gleich dem Rauch
eines Schmelzofens. 29 Gott aber hatte, als er die Städte der Jordan-Ebene
zerstörte, an Abraham gedacht und Lot mitten aus der Zerstörung ent-
kommen lassen, als er die Städte zerstörte, in denen Lot gewohnt hatte.

k) Das sündhafte Verhalten der zwei Töchter Lots; Geburt der Stammväter der Moabiter und der Ammoniter: 19, 30–38.

30 Lot zog dann aus Zoar weiter aufwärts und wohnte zusammen mit
seinen beiden Töchtern im Gebirge; denn er fürchtete sich, in Zoar zu bleiben;
er ließ sich vielmehr mit seinen beiden Töchtern in einer Höhle nieder. 31 Da
sagte die ältere zu der jüngeren: „Unser Vater ist alt, und es ist kein Mann
mehr im Lande, der Umgang mit uns haben könnte, wie es in aller Welt
Brauch ist. 32 Komm, wir wollen unserm Vater Wein zu trinken geben und
uns zu ihm legen, damit wir unser Geschlecht durch unsern Vater fortpflanzen". 33 So gaben sie denn ihrem Vater an jenem Abend Wein zu
trinken, und die ältere ging hinein und legte sich zu ihrem Vater; er aber
merkte nichts davon, weder wie sie sich niederlegte, noch wie sie aufstand.
34 Am andern Morgen sagte dann die ältere zu der jüngeren: „Siehst du,
ich habe in der vorigen Nacht bei meinem Vater gelegen. Wir wollen ihm
auch heute abend Wein zu trinken geben; dann gehst du hinein und legst
dich zu ihm, damit wir unser Geschlecht durch unsern Vater fortpflanzen".
35 So gaben sie denn ihrem Vater auch an diesem Abend Wein zu trinken,
und die jüngere stand auf und legte sich zu ihm; er aber merkte nichts davon, weder wie sie sich niederlegte, noch wie sie aufstand. 36 So wurden
denn die beiden Töchter Lots von ihrem Vater schwanger. 37 Und die ältere
gebar einen Sohn und nannte ihn Moab (d. h. vom Vater); der ist der
Stammvater der heutigen Moabiter. 38 Die jüngere gebar auch einen Sohn
und gab ihm den Namen Ben-Ammi (d. h. Sohn meines Vaters); der ist
der Stammvater der heutigen Ammoniter.

l) Abraham bei Abimelech in Gerar; Gefährdung und Bewahrung der Ehre Saras: Kap. 20.

20 Abraham brach dann von dort auf und zog in den Südgau, wo er
seinen Wohnsitz zwischen Kades und Sur nahm. Er hielt sich aber
zeitweise auch in Gerar auf 2 und gab seine Frau Sara für seine Schwester
aus. Da sandte Abimelech**), der König von Gerar, hin und ließ Sara zu
sich holen. 3 Aber in der Nacht kam Gott zu Abimelech im Traume und sagte

*) Andere Übersetzung: sie ist nur um eine Kleinigkeit entfernt.
**) Würdename der Könige der Philister.

21

1. Mose 37. 38
wir wollen ihn an die Ismaeliter verkaufen, aber nicht selbst Hand an ihn
legen; er ist ja unser Bruder, unser Fleisch und Blut". Seine Brüder gingen
auf den Vorschlag ein.

ee) Ausführung der Missetat und Versuch, sie zu verheimlichen: V. 28–32.

28 Als nun die midianitischen Kaufleute vorüberkamen, zogen sie Joseph
aus der Zisterne herauf und verkauften ihn für zwanzig Silberstücke an die
Ismaeliter; diese brachten Joseph nach Ägypten. 29 Als Ruben dann zu der
Zisterne zurückkehrte und Joseph sich nicht mehr in der Zisterne befand, da
zerriß er seine Kleider, 30 kehrte zu seinen Brüdern zurück und sagte: „Der
Knabe ist nicht mehr da! wohin soll ich nun gehen?" 31 Hierauf nahmen sie
Josephs Rock, schlachteten einen Ziegenbock und tauchten den Rock in das
Blut; 32 dann schickten sie das lange Ärmelkleid hin, ließen es ihrem Vater
bringen und ihm sagen: „Dieses haben wir gefunden; sieh doch genau zu,
ob es der Rock deines Sohnes ist oder nicht".

ff) Jakobs Trauer; Joseph in Ägypten an Potiphar verkauft: V. 33–36.

33 Er sah es genau an und rief aus: „Es ist der Rock meines Sohnes! Ein
wildes Tier hat ihn gefressen! Ja, ja, Joseph ist zerrissen worden!" 34 Und
Jakob zerriß seine Kleider und legte ein härenes Gewand um seine Hüften
und trauerte um seinen Sohn lange Zeit. 35 Alle seine Söhne und Töchter
bemühten sich, ihn zu trösten, aber er wies jeden Trost zurück und sagte:
„Nein, im Trauerkleid werde ich zu meinem Sohne in das Totenreich hinab-
fahren!" So beweinte ihn sein Vater. 36 Die Midianiter aber verkauften
ihn nach Ägypten an Potiphar, einen Hofbeamten des Pharao, den Obersten
der Leibwächter (eig. der Scharfrichter).

l) Juda und seine Schwiegertochter Thamar: Kap. 38.

aa) Juda's mehrfache Versündigungen: sein und seiner Söhne Verhalten gegen Thamar: V. 1–11.

38 Um diese Zeit begab es sich, daß Juda sich von seinen Brüdern
trennte und sich an einen Mann aus Adullam namens Hira anschloß.
2 Dort sah Juda die Tochter eines Kanaanäers namens Sua; die nahm er
zur Frau und lebte mit ihr. 3 Sie wurde guter Hoffnung und gebar einen
Sohn, den er Ger nannte. 4 Hierauf wurde sie wieder guter Hoffnung und
gebar einen Sohn, den sie Onan nannte. 5 Sodann wurde sie nochmals
Mutter eines Sohnes, dem sie den Namen Sela gab; Juda befand sich aber
in Chesib, als sie ihn gebar. 6 Juda nahm dann für seinen erstgeborenen Sohn
Ger eine Frau namens Thamar. 7 Aber Ger, der Erstgeborene Juda's, zog
sich das Mißfallen des HErrn zu; daher ließ der HErr ihn sterben. 8 Da
sagte Juda zu Onan: „Geh zu der Frau deines Bruders ein und leiste ihr
die Schwagerpflicht (— vollziehe mit ihr die Schwagerehe), damit du das
Geschlecht deines Bruders fortpflanzest". 9 Da Onan aber wußte, daß die
Kinder nicht als seine eigenen gelten würden, ließ er, so oft er der Frau
seines Bruders beiwohnte, (den Samen) zur Erde fallen, um seinem Bruder
keine Nachkommen zu verschaffen. 10 Dieses sein Tun mißfiel aber dem
HErrn, und so ließ er auch ihn sterben. 11 Da sagte Juda zu seiner Schwiegertochter Thamar: „Bleibe als Witwe im Hause deines Vaters wohnen, bis
mein Sohn Sela herangewachsen ist". Er fürchtete nämlich, daß auch dieser
sterben würde wie seine Brüder. So ging denn Thamar hin und wohnte im
Hause ihres Vaters.

bb) Thamar verschafft sich durch List Nachkommenschaft von ihrem Schwiegervater Juda: V. 12–23.

12 Als nun geraume Zeit vergangen war, starb die Tochter Sua's, die
Frau Juda's; und als die Trauerzeit vorüber war, ging Juda mit seinem

49 2*

Fig 10—Pages marked by Streicher in his Bible
These show his marginal notes with the words "incest" and "pimping" and "mass murderer." The entire Bible was marked by him, in this manner. Evan Lattimer Collection.

why he was continuing his study of English if he would be unable to utilize it after he was hanged in two weeks. Streicher said, "Oh, didn't you know English is the language spoken in heaven?" Dr. Pflücker thought about this a moment and then said to him, "But Streicher, suppose you don't go to heaven? Suppose you go the other way?" "Oh," replied Streicher, "that's all right, I already speak French." He had brought his Bible (fig. 8) in which he was marking passages that he claimed were clearly anti-Semitic (figs. 9 & 10). He later gave it to Third Army, CIC agent Gunther O. Sadel who had rescued him from a beating at the hands of a group who had read what he had said in his anti-Semitic, anti-Black newspaper.

Streicher went to his death on the gallows with a shout of bravado, refusing to give his name to the officers at the hanging and shouting the words, "Purim 1946," referring to a long ago threat to the Jewish people under Queen Esther, when the villain, Haman, was hanged on the gallows he had built for the Jews (fig. 11).

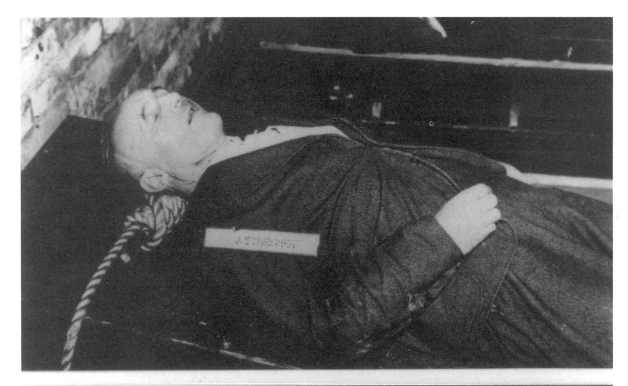

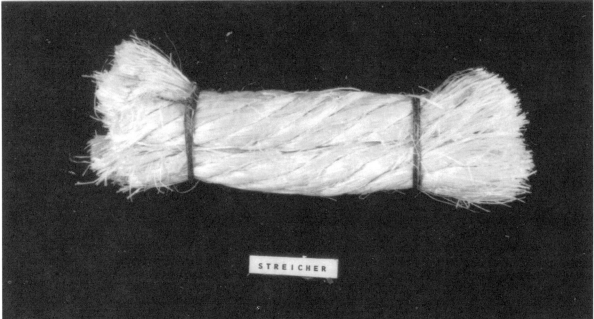

Fig 11—Streicher dead on his coffin
He went to his death, screaming at the hangman, "The Communists will hang you" and calling this "Purim 1946" after the famous Biblical hanging. Also a segment of the rope used to hang him. National Archives and Evan Lattimer Collection.

Lindbergh Inspects German Air & Missile Technology After the War

I was amazed to learn that on May 11, 1945, only three days after the surrender of the German armies, Colonel Charles A. Lindbergh had been flown to Paris as part of a U.S. Navy technical research mission, jointly with the United Aircraft Company, to analyze the unique new jet and missile technology advances that Germany had developed during the war. Lindbergh had the great advantage of having known most of the German aircraft builders personally. He knew where they had lived and where they could be found. He had been shown where their aircraft manufacturing facilities were, as well as their engine development and research facilities. He had acquired this information systematically when he was sent to Germany by our army on three different intelligence gathering missions, just before the war. Our army was delighted at all the information he had amassed. The Nazis had gone out of their way to show him everything (except their jets and missiles) in an effort to impress him with the power of their rearmament. He brought back an accurate and alarming analysis of their capability. It was easy to see that his analysis was correct. Only Hitler's stupidity had kept him from winning the war, as it seemed to me. He had possessed the power to do it, but he wasted it.

I had known Lindbergh since just after his famous flight over the Atlantic, when he was a fighter pilot at the Selfridge Field army air base, the home of our "First Pursuit Group" (actually our only pursuit group). This was in Michigan where I was born and spent every summer. On one occasion, Lindbergh, the hero of the day, gave my fellow Boy Scout and me a lift down the long, hot concrete road to the air base. He had become a "weekend warrior" and stayed with his mother who was a school teacher in Detroit, where he was born. I had watched him perfect the technique of

Fig 1—Messerschmitt shows Lindbergh around

Here we see Messerschmitt (left) pointing out the details of his latest fighter planes that Lindbergh was sent by our Army to inspect and evaluate, which he did with great thoroughness.

Fig 2—The Messerschmitt ME109

Thi was the hot fighter plane about which the Allies had heard and which Lindbergh was able to inspect and to actually fly. He made a very detailed report about its performance, which was then better than anything else in the world. Our production man with him was able to inspect the factory and thus estimate how many fighter planes per month could be produced by the Germans.

skip-bombing which he had developed there. He had bomb racks installed under the wings of his fighter and came in low, dropping the bombs so they skipped like stones on the surface of the water, hitting the target ship broadside at the water line. This technique was used very effectively by us against Japanese shipping during World War II.

When the Nazis began their illegal development of an air force, our Army Air Force intelligence officers asked Lindbergh if he would be willing to use his personal acquaintance with the old German WWI fighter aces, particularly Ernst Udet, to see if he could find out some accurate facts about the much-rumored, high-speed, German fighter plane, the ME 109. This had been developed by Messerschmitt, another friend of Lindbergh (fig. 1). The German fighter pilots had been seen to be extremely effective with it during the Spanish Civil War. We had very little factual data about it, and no idea how many the Germans would be able to manufacture per month or per day.

Lindbergh agreed to visit Germany as a guest of Colonel Smith, of our Air Force, who was the air attaché at our embassy in Berlin. Lindbergh was able to talk Udet into showing him the airplane. Udet was very proud of it and asked him if he would like to sit in the cockpit and judge how well it fitted him. Lindbergh was glad to do this. Udet then delighted him by asking if he would like to fly it! Lindbergh immediately said yes. The crew chief explained all the controls to Lindbergh, with Udet translating.

I once asked Lindbergh how he had dared to fly this multimillion-dollar, near "prototype" airplane with notoriously weak landing gear (fig. 2). He said that he had been practicing with a similar plane, just in case the Germans would let him fly it. He reminded me that he had been well educated in fighter planes at Selfridge.

Lindbergh put the ME 109 through its paces with great dexterity, learning a great deal about its performance. He said it was superior to any other fighter aircraft in production anywhere in the world at that time. He and Colonel Smith also had with them an aircraft production man from the U.S. Army, who saw the factory and was able to estimate how many airplanes per week the Germans were producing. The total numbers and the data were alarming. Lindbergh made a very detailed report of his findings for our Air Force, indicating that the German Air Force was much more of a menace than anybody had realized. Lindbergh was extremely good at writing out detailed accounts of his analytical observations, supported with measurements and figures.

This trip was so successful that our Army immediately proposed that he visit Germany again and ask

Udet about the 300-mile-an-hour midwing bomber, the JU 88, the Germans were beginning to brag about. Lindbergh visited again, was entertained by Göring (fig. 3), saw the airplane, and came back with a further detailed, startling report, once again supported by the production figures our Air Force production man deduced. This indicated that Germany had a superb new bomber, better by far than anything else in the world, to add to its Heinkel 111 standard bomber which was already being mass produced. They also learned that the old "Stuka" dive-bomber, the JU 87, was being phased out. It was used for "close support" of troops and there was a sufficient supply of these. The Germans were obviously focusing now on bombers that could be used outside Germany and for strategic bombing, as against England.

Lindbergh made yet a third trip, again at the earnest request of our Air Force, and learned still more about the German production and performance of its military aircraft. His reports were long and detailed. The French then asked him to make an additional two trips to Germany to try and buy aircraft engines for France, with which the Germans said they were willing to help. This would have made the French Air Force dependent on Germany for their engines, and the French were surprisingly eager to do this.

Thus Lindbergh had learned still more about the German production facilities and where they were located. During his third trip, the American ambassador hosted a reception for the German Air Force officers at our embassy. Our Army was anxious to keep Göring on good terms with Lindbergh so we could continue the intelligence-gathering Lindbergh had done so well. When Göring arrived, he came down the receiving line and when he got to Lindbergh he handed him a box

Fig 3—Lindbergh and his wife were entertained by Göring at his home
Note the huge hammered silver frame around Hitler's portrait. This can be seen in Chapter 3 on Göring.

with a medal in it. He said it was in honor of Lindbergh's 1927 flight from New York to Paris. Lindbergh glanced at it, stuck it in his pocket after thanking him, and thought very little about it. When he got back to his hotel room and opened the box, he discovered it was the Order of the German Eagle (fig. 4), a civilian honor the Germans had given to many other prominent people, such as the president of France. There was no way Lindbergh could have refused the medal under the circumstances, where Göring was a guest of the American ambassador. Furthermore, we were courting Göring so he would permit Lindbergh to see more of his new airplanes, It was no moment to "kick sand in his face" by offending him. Lindbergh's wife, Anne, commented as soon as she saw it that it would be an "albatross" around his neck. This it certainly proved to be. The day after it was given to him, the headlines of every newspaper in the world blared the news that Lindbergh had "accepted" this high Nazi honor. It was never mentioned that many other civilians had received the same medal without comment from the press.

The liberal press was hysterical in condemning Lindbergh for accepting this honor. Actually, the purpose of the event was to make those officers more receptive to inviting Lindbergh back again. Certainly there were no grounds for irritating them by refusing a medal given for his New York to Paris flight. Every country in the world had given him medals for this accomplishment. Many people thought that when Hitler declared war on us, Lindbergh should have sent the medal back. In refusing to do this, it was said that

Fig 4—The order of the German eagle
This is the type of medal which Göring gave to Lindbergh at a reception at the American Embassy when we were endeavoring to induce Göring to permit Lindbergh to see more and more of his fighter aircraft. There was no way that Lindbergh could have refused it or returned it without offending Göring.

he revealed his "stubborn Swedish" heritage, declaring the medal had nothing to do with the war, but was for his pioneering transatlantic flight. This was, of course, true.

Armed with accurate and alarming information about the potential effectiveness of the German Air Force, Lindbergh preached vigorously that we should not attack Germany because we were not ready. The Spitfire was barely off the drawing board and was being produced in very small numbers. The Americans had no fighter plane anywhere near as well developed as any of the German planes he had seen. Franklin Roosevelt was furious with Lindbergh, while the British, the Jewish communities, and the liberal press all lit into him with vigor because of his opposition to our getting into the war at that time. Most of the American populace was on Lindbergh's side in this debate, as it appeared to me. The crowds attending his speeches were enormous. Actually, England had already been "saved" by Hitler's (then inexplicable) decision not to attack it, but to attack Russia instead.

After the Japanese attack on Pearl Harbor, Lindbergh immediately abandoned the very popular "America First" peace movement and asked to reactivate his commission as a fighter pilot. President Franklin Roosevelt, who had been furious with Lindbergh for arguing against our getting into the war, was advised by his confidante, Harold Ickes, to keep Lindbergh in a position where Roosevelt could control him. Ickes pointed out that Lindbergh was very popular and that governments had sometimes been overthrown by military heroes who were very popular but had a different philosophy from that of the current government. Ickes knew that Lindbergh's views had been popular among a majority of the American people. Ickes made it abundantly clear that he feared Lindbergh. For those of us that knew Lindbergh, this was patently ridiculous since he had no political aspirations and would never have accepted a political office. Ickes had Roosevelt offer Lindbergh an administrative post where he could be kept under tight control.

Lindbergh thereupon resigned his Army commission but volunteered as a civilian to go to the Pacific to troubleshoot some of the difficulties we were having with our new military airplanes. For example, the Vought "Corsair," our most modern Navy fighter plane, was having great difficulty with vibration when it was power-dived beyond 500 miles an hour. The regular test pilots would come back saying, "Yes, it vibrates at exactly 500 miles an hour." Lindbergh took it up and power-dived it, then wrote a report that pointed to the source of the trouble in the propeller design. He took his findings back to the factory in New England and had the defect corrected. After that, the plane was highly effective. Lindbergh then recognized that it would pick up more than twice the bomb load the young pilots had been carrying on it. He informed them of this and they said, "Oh no! You'll get us killed." He said, "I'll show you." He then proceeded to pick up progressively heavier bomb loads until he had more than doubled the bomb load of that airplane, making it immeasurably more effective as a weapon. MacArthur was delighted with his contribution.

Next he discovered that young flyers in our Lockheed "Lightning" P-38 fighter planes were having trouble getting the two heavy, in-line engines started in the mornings, and once they got them started they did not want to disturb the ratio of air and gasoline being used, leaving it on a "gasoline-rich" mixture. He said that once they got the engines started and in the air, they could lean their mixture, adjust their manifold pressures and then fly much farther on the same load of gasoline. But once again he was disbelieved and so, to prove his point, he accompanied a flight of B-29 bombers all the way to Tokyo and back.

After that, Lindbergh flew as a fighter pilot with one of the Marine aircraft wings, shot down at least one Japanese plane (a type called a "Sonia"), and was nearly shot down himself. He loved to fly the P-38 even though he kept dislocating his shoulder raising the heavy canopy that covered the cockpit. He originally had injured the shoulder in one of his several lifesaving parachute jumps as an airmail pilot. I saw this dislocation reoccur when I knew him later on: he was reaching for a kitten under a sofa at the home of his father-in-law, Ambassador Morrow, who lived in my town.

Lindbergh recounted one episode to me, of coming home from a mission with some ammunition left and looking for "targets of opportunity" on the way home. He was flying along the beach of a Japanese-held island and surprised a lone Japanese soldier out at the edge of the water washing his clothing in the low surf. Lindbergh said that he swung around and had the man in the sights of his eight machine guns but could not bring himself to mow down this solitary man. The soldier realizing his total vulnerability, merely stood up and waited for the hail of death. It never came.

I then told Lindbergh that I had been in that exact same position as the Japanese soldier, myself, when a German fighter plane surprised me. He lined up on me when I was out away from a hedgerow, relieving myself. I was the obvious target on which the nose and tail of this German ME 109 lined up and I thought I was a goner, but the pilot, like Lindbergh, spared me. Probably, one soldier was not worth the mass of ammunition those guns would pour out in one burst.

When Roosevelt learned of Lindbergh's work as a civilian consultant, he demanded that he be returned at once, and threatened any company that permitted him to fly their planes with a loss of all government contracts. If Roosevelt had permitted Lindbergh to help pinpoint all the Nazi aircraft factories for our bombers, it would have shortened the war.

After Lindbergh returned to the States, he was requested by Henry Ford to help straighten out the troubles in Ford's production lines for B-24 bombers. Ford thought he could produce huge four-engine bombers the way he mass-produced cars, but discovered there were many new and peculiar problems. Lindbergh was quick to help him in overcoming these difficulties, thus making Ford's production line for B-24 bombers a phenomenon of the war.

When the war ended, Lindbergh, because of his superior knowledge and contacts, was immediately approached to participate in the race to recover the German aircraft and rocket experts before the Russians could sweep them all up. After his arrival at our Navy headquarters near the Arc de Triomphe in Paris, he was assigned a C-47 transport plane with a jeep and trailer, which took him first to Munich. He knew exactly where the BMW engine factory was and his group was immediately able to procure various advanced samples from the engine builders who knew Lindbergh and were glad to cooperate with him. From there the group went to the Luftwaffe headquarters in Bavaria, at Zell-am-Zee.

Lindbergh quickly found General Martini, the German officer who was in charge of all Luftwaffe communications and electronic data research, and interrogated him at length. By May 19, he had located, visited, and procured samples from all the important Luftwaffe factories, headquarters, and research facilities. A day earlier he had toured Berchtesgaden, meeting my friend, the redoubtable Colonel Robert F. Sink, commander of the 506th Parachute Infantry Regiment of the 101st Airborne Division, also known as the Five-O-Sink. Colonel Sink's way of achieving his objectives was to tell practically everybody that he would punch them in the nose if they didn't do what he wanted, immediately. This was remarkably effective because he might indeed do it.

After touring the wreckage of Hitler's, Göring's, and Bormann's houses, Lindbergh was assigned to a villa that was full of wounded Germans, but he refused to kick them out. Colonel Sink agreed, which appealed to Lindbergh's sense of propriety. Lindbergh always carried a sleeping bag and could live out of his briefcase with no trouble, as he often said. By May 19, Lindbergh had interviewed all of the Messerschmitt officials and had them deliver their data on all of their latest airplanes to him, complete with samples. Dr. Heinkel likewise complied. (The Heinkel 162 jet airplane had one huge jet engine mounted separately, above the fuselage. It had "droopy" wing tips which seemed cumbersome at the time but have since been revived in some of the latest jet airplanes.) Lindbergh was able to examine the Arado 234 airplane, which was finally being converted to a four-jet craft for longer range bombing, possibly of New York.

Lindbergh was told that Hitler had ordered that drawings of the jet-powered ME 262 and JU 163 be sent to Japan, but they were not sure whether they ever got there because the submarine carrying them apparently had trouble. Lindbergh then visited the Junkers factory in Leipzig which had been ordered by Hitler to build the JU 163 rocket planes. They had to stop building JU 88 bombers, which had been highly successful, to accommodate this foolish demand. He had also had them mount a fighter plane on top of a bomber and fly the piggyback combination to a target where the pilot released the bomber, loaded with huge amounts of explosives, and guided it directly into the target. The pilot cut away in his fighter plane and returned for another bomber, like a flying bomb. This had turned out to be very wasteful of their diminishing resources, but the drama of it appealed to Hitler.

The countryside was covered with small airplane storage revetments off the concrete highways where fighter planes had been concealed in the trees along the roads. They had used the highways as runways. American infantrymen had shot up most of these airplanes and sometimes would sit in them as they were towed around the field by trucks. Despite the destruction, Lindbergh was able to salvage various unique navigating instruments and some high-altitude flying equipment that had not been appreciated before. He went next to Oberammergau to find the cranky but brilliant Willy Messerschmitt who was reduced to living in a tiny shack. After the surrender, Messerschmitt had been taken to Great Britain as a POW, but was quickly released. The British were pleased with his 262 turbojet plane with rocket assistance for rapid acceleration and climb. It could climb a mile and a half in three minutes. Messerschmitt knew they were working on a similar jet (which I had seen in England), but it was not operational. He told Lindbergh that his Messerschmitt 262 jet fighter had been ready in 1938 but Hitler was not interested in it. Udet recognized what a valuable treasure it was and kept pushing for them to mass-produce it, but Hitler and the production man, Erhard Milch, refused. The ME 262 was so superior to anything we had that it would have decimated our bomber fleets. Only Hitler's stupidity kept it from fruition. Messerschmitt said he realized that the war was lost in 1941 when he saw the U.S. aircraft production estimates. He and Speer were the only ones who believed them, however. Hitler derided them, even though Messerschmitt knew better.

Lindbergh also rounded up Dr. Helmut Schelp, the head of jet and rocket research development, whom the Russians were trying hard to kidnap. Many of his most advanced drawings and plans had been buried to protect them from discovery by the Russians, but he was glad to dig them up and turn them over to Lindbergh. Lindbergh then went on to the BMW factory in Ulm, the staff of which indicated that they would build any missing engine parts for any BMW engines that Lindbergh wanted. He had the same good reception at Heidelberg and Stuttgart and at all the Messerschmitt factories. They all knew him and respected him. He took one ME 262 jet and dismantled it completely, taking the parts back to Paris for reshipment home. He did the same with one of their rocket planes. These strange cargoes frightened the Paris hoteliers greatly, I remember.

He then went to an experimental aeronautical institute in Munich and was able to recover large numbers of documents and designs from their research center. Herr Prene, the rocket expert, and their ramjet experts were all glad to cooperate with Lindbergh. He also saw experimental Junkers and Messerschmitt rocket airplanes being built in a tunnel factory and recovered some samples of the rocket airplane, the ME 163. He found eight Junkers research men and got them to the U.S. zone, to protect them from kidnapping by the Russians.

Lindbergh found Focke-Wulf 190 aircraft placed on top of JU 88 bombers for piggyback exploitation as flying bombs and had samples taken back to the U.S. He then visited the Hermann Göring Institute for Research and inspected the deep mountain tunnels used for supersonic rocket research and armament development. He also visited the Rocket Engine Institute at Nordhausen where there was a huge underground factory for V-2 missiles. It was full of partly completed rockets.

It was here that Lindbergh saw his first concentration camp. In Camp "Nora" there were 25,000 walking skeletons who had been part of the workforce manufacturing the V-2 rockets. Lindbergh, like the rest of us, had had no idea that this kind of thing was going on. He was just as horrified as we were. He said he was "appalled at seeing how one group of human beings could behave towards their fellow creatures."

Lindbergh was extremely analytical and understood all of the details and implications of what he saw. I marveled at his ability to do that. He asked penetrating questions of all the aircraft people. He then sat down and wrote out detailed reports of everything that he had seen and made sure that the samples of the various types of high-speed airplanes and rockets were dismantled and carried back to Paris where he had them shipped to the United States. He was very good at this, and far better than most test pilots or strictly military personnel, because he felt he had no limitations placed upon him in his investigations.

He had covered 1700 miles in the four weeks he was there, and had quickly led our people to the most desirable and knowledgeable German aviation and rocket scientists and their data. They gladly surrendered their research to him, even digging it up from their secret hiding places. He was a very effective and likable representative for our country, a "straight-arrow" to everyone who knew him. He made a remarkable contribution to the speed with which we were able to recover and analyze the German wartime accomplishments in aviation and rocketry. Without Lindbergh, we would have lost a massive amount of information, material, and personnel to the Russians. He served us well at the war's end, just as he had gathered accurate and disturbing data for us before the war.

Eisenhower Promotes Him to Brigadier General

In recognition of his contributions, President Eisenhower promoted Lindbergh to brigadier general in the Air Force Reserve. Lindbergh was very proud of this recognition. On one occasion when I forgot myself and called him "Colonel," at the dinner table at my home, he corrected me, with a big grin, "It's General now." At the fiftieth anniversary of Lindbergh's famous flight to Paris, Neil Armstrong was the guest speaker. I congratulated Armstrong on knowing that Lindbergh would have been pleased that he had referred to him as General, exactly as Armstrong did in his speech.

In addition to his own military contributions, Lindbergh knew that high altitude aerial combat was now possible, using the tremendous engines in our most modern fighter planes, like the P 47 "Thunderbolt." He therefore subjected himself to low-oxygen experiments in aircraft simulators, to determine what oxygen concentrations had to be maintained if the pilots were to remain conscious at these very high altitudes and operate these complicated fighting machines. He volunteered to do this, and was particularly valuable because of his knowledge of what skills were needed, and how quickly they were impaired by the falling oxygen levels.

Another engineering accomplishment of his had been to build for Dr. Alexis Carrel an artificial heart pump

with which chicken hearts and other organs could be maintained, long after they had been taken out of the body. This was so successful that the Navy then asked him to develop a similar artificial heart pump made out of plastic (the Carrel prototype had been glass), for use in their cardiac surgical services. Lindbergh undertook to do this job, even though plastic is much more difficult than glass to work with. Very few people know of his contributions in these fields.

Lindbergh also had access to donors such as the Guggenheim Foundation, who supported legitimate advanced research work. He was able to get backing for our first rocket scientist, Dr. Robert Goddard, so that we were not totally without any research basis when the war came along and the Germans developed their devastating high-altitude intercontinental ballistic rockets, such as the V-2. Another person for whom he

Fig 5—Lindbergh inscribes title page of his book about his wartime adventures to the author Evan Lattimer Collection.

got funding when it was not otherwise available was Igor Sikorsky, who had developed a helicopter in competition with the Germans. Sikorsky could get very little help with this project, because the autogiro, whose overhead rotor looked similar to a helicopter, had been such a failure. Sikorsky's actual helicopter was *far more* valuable.

Lindbergh was very interested in any scientific apparatus, and I can remember taking him to microbiology laboratories at Columbia University when we had our first practical electron microscopes for studying cancer cells. I was bragging about the fact that we could magnify up to five million diameters, between the electron microscope and our projection apparatus. He was delighted to sit down and "fiddle" with all of this machinery. Our technicians at the Columbia Medical School, knowing of his aversion to publicity, were always studiously occupied with their work, whenever he came into the laboratory. He would then go up to a person at that piece of equipment in which he was interested, would stick out his hand, and say, "I'm Charles Lindbergh, please show me how your apparatus works."

He was an extremely pleasant, very sensible and thoughtful person, who was interested in everything. I knew that his family had been pioneers in early America, so I once brought him a suitcase full of engraved powder horns, on which the frontiersmen had engraved their maps. He had never heard of this map-carrying capability and was very interested, going over my "map-horns" in great detail and appreciating this new dimension to his knowledge. He was especially interested in everything to do with the environment and wildlife preservation, to which he devoted his entire last several decades. Everyone who really knew him recognized him as amiable, capable and earnest. He was a valuable world-class contributor who was much maligned, unjustifiably.

How The Collection Started

Fig 1—The author firing his luger pistol
Evan Lattimer Collection.

The items in this collection were acquired by a large number of American military personnel. Very few items were taken directly from the prisoners by me during the trial. I regarded demands for souvenirs from my patients as inappropriate harassment. This view proved to be naive, as we shall see.

During the trial, I observed that various prison personnel did acquire a number of personal items such as photographs, books, and fountain pens. I thus had some idea as to what might be genuine, in future trading of souvenirs.

After the Normandy invasion, as we had thrust deeper and deeper into France and then Germany, our armies had begun to overrun large German army units. Their weapons were collected in huge piles and we Americans selected fine examples of each type. Their rapid firing, sub-machine guns, called "burp" guns because they fired an entire twenty-round clip in one "burp," and their nicely made Luger pistols were favorite collectibles. They provided a currency with which one could trade for other items later. I had one particularly fine, long-barreled Luger pistol with which I became fairly adept (fig. 1). Its firing pin had been damaged, but a gunsmith in a large German army compound fashioned a new one.

When I took over Field Marshal von Rundstedt's "throne room" for my urology clinic, in Kassel, Germany, I found the desk drawers full of elegant, parchmentlike documents announcing the death of some German soldier, with blanks to fill in his name and a signature place at the bottom. I used these fine fragments of "parchment" as stationery for many weeks. Occasionally you would find a personal item that belonged to some famous German officer. These were useful in bartering with our own CIC (Counter Intelligence Corps) officers who ranged ahead with our advancing troops and thus found opportunities to loot the desks of the more famous Germans, including Hitler. Since it was their job to find these notables, it made it much easier for them to acquire valuable souvenirs. I traded many items with them.

On the rare occasion when we operated upon a civilian child who was in distress, the parents might present us with some memento of souvenir value. As we over-ran the death camps, I had no stomach for the macabre souvenirs which one might have collected, such as book covers or lamp shades made of human skin bearing ornate tattoo designs.

Once the top Nazis had been selected for the possibility of being tried, I was surprised to find that a market in their autographs was building up. This was partly their own doing. I thought it would be regarded as a form of harassment to ask them for autographs but on one occasion when they discovered someone had asked for an autograph, they all volunteered autograph specimens thereafter, in an effort to curry favor. Even Göring, who was the imperious "Top Dog," offered to sign dollar bills for the G.I. guard whenever a new man appeared, in order to get on his good side. Our psychiatrists, particularly Dr. Goldensohn, pointed out to me that actually they appreciated being asked to sign something, especially one of their own books. He went to the local library and found books authored by practically all of the defendants. He brought them to the prison without any trouble since the libraries had been instructed to divest their collections of all Nazi books. The prisoners were eager to write extravagant dedications to the doctor in the books which he brought to them for their signatures. It was through Dr. Goldensohn (after his death) that I acquired several of his autographed books, written by the defendants.

At least one officer, who had been in charge of the prison baggage room, acquired a number of valuable souvenirs which appeared to me to have been given to him by the owners—off the record—as a method of ensuring his cooperation in acquiring some of the small comforts of prison life. Another source of souvenirs from the baggage room were the items taken out and used as exhibits in the investigations of some of the three suicides that occurred during the trial. Some of these relics were retained among the possessions of the investigators after the trial was over. Ben Swearingen tracked down many of these.

In the last week before the hangings, the laundry went out as usual. When the items were returned, half the owners were now dead and gone. These leftover laundry items found their way into the souvenir market.

After the trial ended, the Bavarian government confiscated the possessions of the dead men and had them sold by Weinmueller's auction house in 1974. By then, a culture of Nazi artifact collectors and dealers had developed all over the world, particularly in the United States. These men went to auctions and purchased large numbers of often elegant souvenirs for moderately high prices, knowing that there were collectors in both the United States and England who would pay well for them. There was often an interval of several years before they were offered, during which time some of us had begun to earn a little money and could afford to purchase some of these items. A group of very knowledgeable researchers and scholars became collectors and dealers. Some of these people, particularly Ben Swearingen, returned to Germany periodically to rent rooms in homes adjacent to Hitler's old Berghof, near Berchtesgaden. They sought out people like the family of Eva Braun and the household help who had worked in the Berghof. They paid them well for their services in finding memorabilia.

The small group of educated dealers in Nazi artifacts continued to grow in the United States and in Britain, and their catalogues were carefully perused by those interested in collecting. Books were written about the several types of available items (such as silverware) connected with Hitler, Eva, and the other leaders. Experienced authors began to write about the top Nazis and were anxious to see any of the personal treasures that had been owned by them. The dealers who specialized in these items were well aware of the special interests of each collector and kept them very well informed about their new offerings. Mr. Swearingen

Fig 2—The author firing the German sub-machine gun (Schmeisser) called a Burp Gun because the whole 20 round clip was fired in one big "burp." Evan Lattimer Collection.

advertised in military journals and collectors' newspapers for any artifacts of the Nazi regime and collected a surprising number of very important items. He did some excellent detective work in verifying the items, even adding more information about them. Many of the soldiers who had personally liberated valuable items, treasured them greatly and would never give them up. If they died however, or became insolvent, their wives were quick to dispose of "the old man's junk." I acquired several items by this route. Dr. Goldensohn's autographed books came to me in this way. I had also operated on his father.

Macabre souvenirs such as the segments of the ropes used to hang each of the Nazis were collected in defiance of the strict instructions of the Nuremberg prison commander, Colonel Andrus, who had gone to great lengths to try to be sure there would be *no* souvenirs left. The cynical army hangman, Sgt. Wood, circumvented the colonel very skillfully by cutting off pieces of each noose, as souvenirs, *before* the hangings. These items in the collection reached the market only after Sgt. Wood had died and his wife sold them.

The dealers and collectors quickly learned who the people were who were interested in their products and would offer things either privately or at the moment a catalogue appeared. It was also not difficult to locate the collectors if you had something to sell in which they might be interested.

During the 50 years since the trial, I was offered many of the artifacts I now possess, plus many more which were priced so high that I felt I could not afford them or was doubtful about their provenance. Since I was interested only in memorabilia related to the men I had met at Nuremberg, this limited the number of items I bought. Then, as my interest in Hitler's medical history began to grow, I acquired more items that had belonged to Hitler, and Eva as well, often through Ben Swearingen.

During the years after the trial, I had put the entire matter on the back burner, and had concentrated on the business of developing a career in the academic and surgical worlds which consumed practically all of my time. Another factor, of course, was the necessity to earn enough money to be able to afford the more expensive and exotic memorabilia whose value was very well known to the collecting fraternity. I have always felt especially indebted to Mr. Swearingen whom I consider the most diligent and capable of all of the collectors and students in this field. My own knowledge of the personalities of each of the Nazi defendants and of their medical problems influenced my interest in such things as Göring's drug-laden suitcase, his cyanide-containing suicide capsule, and related items.

Hitler's Chauffeur Was a Source

One of my military friends became a Marine Corps guard at our Berlin embassy after the war. He discovered that the German Army veterans had alumni associations similar to our American Legion. They welcomed him to their meetings and he met Erich Kempka, Hitler's chauffeur, who drove the big black Mercedes touring cars Hitler favored. Each car had its own fitted black leather suitcase (fig. 26 in Chapter 2). It was Kempka's job to keep several changes of clothing at the ready because Hitler perspired profusely (very possibly due to his Parkinson's disease) and would come out soaking with sweat after making a speech. Shirts, pants, socks, neckties, and a rain cape always had to be ready. Fresh uniform jackets and black trousers were kept at each of his several headquarters at the various fronts where Hitler might need them in case of unanticipated visits. One jacket was missed in the move to destroy all his clothing because it was at an out-of-the-way camp.

Kempka hid all his items at his home, and even though the Russians kept him in prison for several years, his memorabilia remained safely concealed.

After his release, he, along with most of his colleagues, was having difficulty making a living, so he went looking for a discreet buyer for his Hitler items. My friend met him and they made an instant arrangement for Kempka to sell him one of the Hitler suitcases with its contents, with affidavits for their authenticity (fig. 26 in Chapter 2).

When my friend's family began to grow, he sold several of the Hitler items to me when I was visiting my home state of Michigan, where I learned of this collection of historical artifacts related to Hitler.

In addition, New York is the auction capital of the world and important collections are often assigned to major galleries such as Zyla's, Christie's, Sotheby's, Hamilton's, Smythe's and many others. Their World War II experts know of my interest in certain Nazis and alert me well in advance of any upcoming sale. There is generally a spirit of pleasant mutual cooperation among collectors of historical memorabilia which is gratifying to see.

Thus did the collection grow.

Fig 3—This Belgian Fort, crushed by the Germans, yielding bayonets and helmets used for trading other relics. Evan Lattimer Collection.

Andrus, Col. Burton C. *I Was the Nuremberg Jailer*. New York: Tower, Publications, 1969.

Anon, *German Occupied Britain*. Scott-David, 1971.

Ansel, W. *Hitler Confronts England*. Duke University Press, 1960.

Bewley, Charles. *Hermann Göring and the Third Reich*. New York: Devin-Adair Co., 1962.

Bezymenski, Lev A. *The Death of Adolf Hitler*. New York: Harcourt, Brace & World, 1968.

Boldt, Gerhard. *Hitler: The Last Ten Days: An Eyewitnesses Account*. Translated by Sandra Bance. New York: Coward, McCann and Georghegan, 1973.

Bullock, Allan. *Hitler: A Study in Tyranny*. New York: Harper & Row, 1962.

Conot, Robert E. *Justice at Nuremberg*. New York: Harper and Rowe, 1947.

Dolibois, John E. *Pattern of Circles*. Kent, Ohio: Kent State University Press, 1989.

Fest, Joachim C. *Hitler*. New York: Harcourt Brace Jovanovich. 1973.

Fleming, P. *Operation Sea-Lion*. Hart-Davis, 1957.

Frank, Bernhard. *Hitler, Göring and the Obersalzberg*. FRG: Anton Plenk Berchtesgaden, 1989.

Frischauer, Willi. *The Rise and Fall of Hermann Göring*. Cambridge, Mass: The Riverside Press, 1951.

Gaskin, Hilary. *Eyewitnesses at Nuremberg*. London: Arms and Armour Press, 1990.

Gibbels, Ellen. "Hitler's Parkinson's Disease: A videotape illustration," *Movement Disorders*, Vol. 7, No. 4, 383-384, 1988.

Gilbert, Gustav M. *Nuremberg Diary*. New York: Farrar Straus and Co., 1947.

Giziowski, Richard. *The Enigma of General Blaskowitz*. New York: Hippocrene Books, 1997.

Haaglund, Jarl V. "Hitler's Parkinson's Disease: A Videotape demonstration." Eskilstuna, Sweden: *Movement Disorders*, Vol. 7 No. 4, p. 383, 1992.

Harris, Whitney. *Tyranny on Trial*. Dallas: Southern Methodist University Press, 1954.

Hess, Wolf Rudiger. *Mord an Rudolf Hess?* ULM: Druffel Verlag, 1989.

Heston, Leonard L., and Heston Renate. *The Medical Casebook of Adolf Hitler: His Illnesses, Doctors and Drugs*. Introduction by A. Speer. New York: Stein & Day, 1980.

Hitler, Adolf. *Mein Kampf*. Boston: Houghton-Mifflin, 1991.

Hoehn, Margaret M., Yahr, Melvin D. "Parkinsonianism: Onset, Progression and Mortality." *Neurology* 17:427-442, 1967.

Kelley, Douglas M. *22 Cells in Nuremberg*. New York: Greenberg, 1947.

Kelley, Ellsworth K. "Adolf Hitler, his dentist and his dental problems." *Journal of the American Dental Association*, Oct: 424-425, 1965.

Lieberman, Abraham. "Adolf Hitler, His Diaries and Parkinson's Disease." *New England Journal of Medicine*, 309: 385-376, 1983.

Lieberman, Abraham. "Hitler, Parkinson's Disease and History." Phoenix, Arizona: *Barrow Neurological Institute Quarterly*, Vol 11, No. 3, 1995.

Lindbergh, Charles. *The Wartime Diaries of Charles A. Lindbergh.* New York: Harcourt Brace Jovanovich, 1979.

Macksey, K.J. *The German Invasion of England, July, 1940.* Macmillan, New York, 1980.

Minott, Rodney. *The Fortress That Never Was.* New York: Holt, Rinehart and Winston, 1964.

Mosely, Leonard. *The Reichmarshal.* New York: Doubleday and Co. Inc., 1974.

Musmanno, Michael. *Ten Days to Die.* Garden City: Doubleday and Co., 1951.

National Archives, Washington, D.C. Records of the International Military Tribunal, including Photographic Archive, 1946.

Office of the U.S. Chief Council for the Prosecution of Axis Criminality, *Nazi Conspiracy and Aggression.* Washington: U.S. Government Printing Office, 1947.

Payne, Robert. *The Life and Death of Adolf Hitler.* New York: Praeger, 1973.

Ribbentrop, Anneliese. *Joachim von Ribbentrop: Zwischen London und Moskau.* Druffel-Verlag, 1953.

Russel, Lord. *The Scourge of the Swastika.* New York: Ballantine Books, 1954.

Schenck, Ernst G. "Hitler's Final Days." *A.M.A. News*, 1:34-43, Oct. 11, 1985.

Schwarz, Paul. *This Man Ribbentrop.* New York: Julian Messner, Inc., 1943.

Sereny, Gitta. *Albert Speer: His Battle With the Truth.* New York: Alfred A. Knopf, 1995.

Speer, Albert. *Inside the Third Reich.* New York: Macmillan, 1970.

Speer, Albert. *Spandau: The Secret Diaries.* New York: Pocket Books, 1977.

Swearingen, Ben. *The Mystery of Hermann Göring's Suicide.* New York: Harcourt Brace Jovanovich, 1985.

Taylor, Telford. *The Anatomy of the Nuremberg Trials.* New York: Alfred A. Knopf, 1992.

Thomas, Hugh. *The Murder of Adolf Hitler.* New York: St. Martin's Press, 1995.

Toland, John. *Adolf Hitler.* New York: Doubleday and Co., 1976.

Weitz, John. *Hitler's Diplomat.* New York: Tickner and Fields, 1992.

PHOTO CREDITS

National Archives
Ch. 1, Fig. 2, 5-7, 9, 12, 17-21, 24-27, 30; Ch.2, Fig. 3, 5, 7, 23, 32-34, 36-38, 48-49, 53-55, 59-61; Ch.3, Fig. 4, 22, 33-35, 37, 39, 63, 65, 73, 83, 84, 90; Ch.4, Fig. 2, 6, 7-8, 14; Ch. 5, Fig. 1-2 ,8 ,10 ,13 ,15 ,18 ,24 ,27; Ch. 6, Fig. 1; Ch.8, Fig. 1-2, 5; Ch. 9, Fig. 1-2, 6; Ch. 10, Fig. 1; Ch. 11, Fig. 1-2; Ch. 12, Fig. 1-4; Ch. 13, Fig. 1, 4, 5, 7; Ch. 14, Fig. 1-2, 4; Ch. 15, Fig. 2-3; Ch. 16, Fig. 1, 4; Ch. 17, Fig. 1-3, 5; Ch.18, Fig. 1; Ch. 19, Fig. 1-3, 5, 7, 9-11, 13, 17-18; Ch. 20, Fig. 1-2; Ch. 21, Fig. 1, 3; Ch. 23, Fig. 4; Ch. 24,Fig. 1, 4; Ch. 25, Fig. 1, 2, 5, 9-13; Ch. 26, Fig. 1, 4, 5; Ch. 27, Fig. 3.

C.W. Alexander
Ch. 1, Fig. 32; Ch. 3, Fig. 20-21, 63, 91; Ch. 4, Fig. 10, 12-13, 15-16; Ch.5, Fig. 19-22; Ch.13, Fig. 6; Ch. 17, Fig. 4; Ch. 23, Fig. 6; Ch. 26, Fig. 7.

Abraham Lieberman
Ch. 2, Fig. 4.

Raymond Zyla
Ch. 3, Fig. 3; Ch. 9, Fig. 4; Ch. 19, Fig. 14; Ch. 26, Fig. 3.

Col. Bernhardt Frank and Anton Plenk
Ch. 2, Fig. 6, Hitler, Goring and The Obersalzberg

L. Bezymenski
Ch. 2, Fig. 7, 55, 58, 71-72

After-the-Battle Magazine
Ch. 2, Fig. 28, 31, 56-57. Ch. 4, Fig. 20, 22

Univ. Texas History Center at Austin
Ch. 3, Fig. 79, 89

Wolf Rudiger Hess
Ch. 4, Fig. 17, 21

Robert Matteson Collection
Ch.5, Fig. 11, Ch. 13, Fig. 5

Lloyd M. Roach Collection
Ch. 5, Fig. 12, 14

Thomas Von Kantzow Collection
Ch. 3, Fig. 15, 23-24

Keith Wilson Collection
Ch. 3, Fig. 68

Steven L. Carson Collection
Ch. 3, Fig. 36)

Imperial War Museum
Ch. 3, Fig. 14,

Gerd Heidemann
Ch. 3, Fig. 19

Douglas Kelley Collection
Ch. 5, Fig. 29

Gustav Gilbert Collection
Ch. 5, Fig. 30

Richard Worthington Collection
Ch. 5, Fig. 31

Leon Goldensohn Collection
Ch. 5, Fig. 32

Roy A. Martin Collection
Ch. 5, Fig. 33, Ch. 7, Fig. 9

New York Hospital Alumni Association
Ch. 5, Fig. 34

David Smith Collection
Ch. 5, Fig. 35

Braceland Collection
Ch. 5, Fig. 36

Manley Ford Collection
Ch. 5, Fig. 37

Whisenand Collection
Ch. 5, Fig. 39 Ch. 11, Fig. 8

John Patton Collection
Ch. 5, Fig. 40

K.F. Merten Collection
Ch. 7, Fig. 7

H.P. Frentz
Ch. 2, Fig. 7

Mrs. Genelle Salles
Ch. 3, Fig. 79

Corbis Photo Archive
Ch. 22, Fig. 2

Don Honeyman
Ch. 23, Fig. 4

Distelhorst Collection
Ch. 7, Fig. 2

The Air Museum in England
Ch. 1, Fig. 2

Associated Press
Ch. 15, Fig. 5